PENGUIN BOOKS

ME AGAINST THE MUMBAI UNDERWORLD

Isaque Ibrahim Bagwan retired as an assistant commissioner of police in May 2009 after serving in the Mumbai Police for over thirty-five years. He was awarded the prestigious police medal for gallantry thrice. According to Mumbai Police records, he is the first officer from the force to have killed a criminal in an encounter. He is also the first police officer to have shot at and apprehended a criminal during proceedings in a sessions court in Mumbai.

Bagwan was also praised for his quick thinking and valour, which saved hundreds of lives, by the Pradhan Committee Report that was sanctioned to look into the 26/11 terror attack. He had taken charge of Nariman House during the deadly assault and restricted the terrorists for over sixteen hours with just twelve men. He also assisted in ensuring the safety of the people in the buildings around Nariman House until the NSG commandos arrived.

ME *against the* Mumbai Underworld

ISAQUE BAGWAN

BLUE
SALT

PENGUIN BOOKS

An imprint of Penguin Random House

PENGUIN BOOKS

USA | Canada | UK | Ireland | Australia
New Zealand | India | South Africa | China

Penguin Books is part of the Penguin Random House group of companies
whose addresses can be found at global.penguinrandomhouse.com

Published by Penguin Random House India Pvt. Ltd
7th Floor, Infinity Tower C, DLF Cyber City,
Gurgaon 122 002, Haryana, India

First published in Penguin Books by Penguin Random House India and
Blue Salt Media 2018

ISBN 9780143443148

Typeset in Aldine401 BT by Manipal Digital Systems, Manipal
Printed at Thomson Press India Ltd, New Delhi

www.penguin.co.in

In memory of my parents, and for my elder brother,
who taught me the importance of honesty,
fearlessness and integrity

CONTENTS

Santacruz Police Station

Detection Crime Branch, CID

Detection Crime Branch: Other Cases

The Crime Branch: Drug Control

Posted to Colaba Police Station Again

Cuffe Parade Police Station

Marine Drive Police Station

Malabar Hill Police Station

Assistant Commissioner of Police

FOREWORD

The word 'heroic' is attached with a few names, and Isaque Bagwan is one such name in the history of the Mumbai Police. This book outlines the journey of a gutsy police officer whose experience throws light on the world of crime in Mumbai, bringing to life scenarios and situations that he came face-to-face with during his career. This book begins like a flashback in a movie. Right from his inspiration to joining the force to his method of solving cases, the book documents some unique and interesting incidents based on actual police records. The narrative will undoubtedly make the reader respect the Mumbai Police more. The book covers most of the crimes that took place during Bagwan's tenure, making the collection an encyclopedia of sorts. Bagwan's adventures can be a reference for readers looking to understand the Mumbai crime world and will act as a guide and inspiration for budding officers.

Vishwas Nangare Patil
Special Inspector General of Police

ACKNOWLEDGEMENTS

'सद्रक्षणायखलनिग्रहणाय'

—Mumbai Police motto

I spent thirty-five years in service by following this mantra. The philosophy still resonates. The journey from being an SI to becoming an ACP has been full of challenges that I overcame with sheer guts and devotion to duty. My responsibilities always outweighed excuses, and I always chose action over words as my weapon for vindication. I was fortunate to have worked under the tutelage of one of the stalwarts of the Mumbai Police, former ACP Madhukar B. Zende, who guided and moulded me from my very first day.

I would also like to express sincere thanks and appreciation for my senior officers and colleagues who encouraged and supported me, and to the constables and *hawaldars* who form the backbone of the Mumbai Police.

LIST OF ABBREVIATIONS

ACB: Anti Corruption Bureau

ACP: Assistant Commissioner of Police

Addl CP: Additional Commissioner of Police

API: Assistant Police Inspector

ASI: Assistant Sub-Inspector

ATS: Anti-Terrorism Squad

BCCI: Board of Control for Cricket in India

BJP: Bharatiya Janata Party

CID: Crime Investigation Department

CRPF: Central Reserve Police Force

DCP: Deputy Commissioner of Police

DIG: Deputy Inspector General

DRI: Directorate of Revenue Intelligence

FIR: First Information Report

GRP: Government Railway Police

IPS: Indian Police Service

ISI: Inter-Services Intelligence

JCP: Joint Commissioner of Police

MLA: Member of Legislative Assembly

MP: Member of Parliament

LeT: Lashkar-e-Taiba

MOB: Modus Operandi Bureau

NCC: National Cadet Corps

NSA: National Security Act

NSG: National Security Guard

PI: Police Inspector

RTO: Regional Transport Officer

Sr PI: Senior Police Inspector

SBI: State Bank of India

SI: Sub-Inspector

SLR: Self-Loading Rifle

SRPF: State Reserve Police Force

ULFA: United Liberation Front of Assam

VT: Victoria Terminus

1

FIRING MY LAST SHOT

It is well established that a policeman's job is thankless. He is criticized if he fails to meet expectations, and he is forgotten after he has done his duty. By God's grace, my work was applauded by both citizens and the media throughout my career. The police department, too, acknowledged my work in the line of duty. I am overwhelmed and honoured at being awarded the prestigious police medal for gallantry thrice. I am proud to have been a part of the Mumbai Police and having served my city and nation.

I have devoted my life to protecting the innocent and curtailing crime in the ever-changing and ever-surprising city of Mumbai, formerly known as Bombay. Entrusted with enforcing the law, I have stood up against injustice, fought hard to bring criminals to book and moved mountains to uncover crucial evidence. My case reports and investigations have been recorded in tightly bound files that lie buried under heaps of folders at various police stations and courtrooms. The uniform that used to be my second skin is neatly tucked away in a corner of my closet. Often, past events flash before my eyes, almost as if I were living them again. I often discuss a few of my cases with family and friends as the memories demand to be recalled. I must, however, clarify that sharing my experience with you is not the primary purpose of this book.

I have come across people from different walks of life and backgrounds, including officers from various departments of the government, ministers, businessmen, civilians, informers, criminals and many others who have been accurately described as part of my investigations. Other than being part of records, the events involving these people form an important and inseparable part of the history of Mumbai. And like other records, history too must be assimilated with facts, validated with proof and preserved for generations to come.

I have been witness to the planned manipulation of this history which is integral to the city. It has been painful to see the truth being tampered with to suit personal agendas. I cannot do much about the incidents which have already been misconstrued, but I can build a bastion around the events that I have been a part of and cement them with facts. A few of the important cases that I dealt with have been compiled in this book as proof of the events that took place during my career as a police officer in Mumbai.

There is one particular incident that compelled me to write about my experience. In 2006, when I was posted at Malabar Hill police station, a well-known journalist came to me with a reference from ACP Madhukar Zende, whom he had earlier approached for information about the Mumbai underworld. He wanted more details about the gangs and case records as he was writing a book on it. ACP Zende had asked me to help the gentleman. Over the next few months, I shared with him my experience with the Mumbai underworld. I also told him about the first-ever encounter in the history of the Mumbai Police: the encounter involving Manya Surve whom I and another officer had shot dead. Time passed by and, in May 2009, I retired as ACP, Mumbai. Then, in 2011, I read in a newspaper that a movie was being made on the Manya Surve encounter. According to the article, the movie was to be based on the case. I gave my 'no objection' to the makers without accepting any monetary benefits, but only after they assured me that they would showcase absolute facts and only exercise minor cinematic liberties for the purpose of entertainment.

A few days later, ACP Zende and I were invited to the launch of the book based on the gangs of Mumbai by the same journalist to whom I had narrated details of the underworld. ACP Zende, a voracious reader, went through the book. He found glaring factual errors in the murder case of Sabir Kaskar, Dawood Ibrahim's brother. ACP Zende, who had investigated this case, pointed out that Manya Surve had played no role in Sabir's murder as per police records. However, the role of another criminal, Jaffer Jamal Siddique, who was one of the main accused in the case, had been eliminated from the book while other unknown and unrelated names had been included. Since the movie on Manya Surve's encounter was adapted from this book, the characters had initially been named as per the actual identities. After I saw the trailer for the movie, I realized that the screenplay had been modified further and the facts been twisted and fictionalized to grab eyeballs. I was very upset with the contorted depiction. After consulting the then Commissioner of Police (Mumbai) Satyapal Singh, and as advised by him, I informed the print media about the false portrayal in the movie. I asked for my name, along with my family members' names, to be withdrawn from the movie. After an exchange of notices and pressure from the press, the names of the characters were changed and the tagline of 'a true story' was withdrawn. Truth had emerged triumphant, but I was aggrieved and felt let down by the misrepresentation of events that I had been a part of.

This episode shook me up so much that I started jotting down my own experience. It is my humble request to fellow officers in the police that they preserve a copy of all case papers for their personal record. I am thankful to Deepak Rao, author of *Mumbai Police: 150 Years,* and my son, Sohail Bagwan, for helping me translate the Marathi edition of my book, *Isak Bagwan*, into English.

With this, I fire my last round, my last shot.

2

1 JUNE 2009: DOWN MEMORY LANE

The alarm rang at 5.45 a.m. After completing my daily exercise routine, I sat down at the dining table. My wife served breakfast as usual. Halfway through, I noticed my wife and elder son, Sohail, looking at me strangely. I wondered if I had forgotten someone's birthday. I glanced at my wristwatch and realized that it was past 8.45 a.m. I turned to Sohail and asked, 'Why is my Qualis not here yet? Give me my mobile phone. I must check with my driver, Jadhav, and the wireless operator, Amale.'

My wife and son exchanged glances and placed my gallantry medals before me. These three medals adorned my uniform every day. That was when I realized that they were no longer on my uniform. It was as if I had been struck by lightning. I had retired the previous day, 31 May 2009, after thirty-five years of distinguished service. I sat there smiling, contemplating the events and the passage of time. Every now and then, I continue to take a trip down memory lane.

3

MY ROOTS

The day started early in Baramati village, even before dawn broke through the sky. You could hear the farmers as they got ready to head out. Life in a small farming village kept us on our toes. I would accompany my father to the bazaar where he would conduct his business of selling fruits and vegetables. On the days that he went out to the farms or to purchase goods, I managed the business by myself and handled the staff and the customers with ease. Whenever I was able to make a few annas for myself, I would hand them over to my mother, Zehra *Bi*. I still remember how her eyes would fill with tears of joy as she kissed my forehead and blessed me for doing my bit for the family at just ten years of age. I managed time well between school and my father's business. It was more than a 2 km walk to M.E.S. High School, which took strict action against students who did not attend. I made sure I was not one of them. Whenever I had time to spare, I would run to the open fields with my friends. We played, we fought, we giggled, we bonded, and we shared our dreams. I wanted to join the armed forces. India had recently gained independence and, like everyone, my heart was brimming with patriotism. I could already picture myself as a soldier for my motherland, fighting away enemies.

My father, Ibrahim Manik Bagwan, was a noble and respected man. He was the municipal corporator of Baramati at one point and an ardent social worker. Also, he was a man of principles who believed in discipline. My brothers and I were often at the receiving end of his rage for our shenanigans. Tall and broad-shouldered, his presence alone was intimidating. He wrestled at the local grounds before going about his work at the bazaar and the farms. Though we were a big family, my father took good care of his five sons and four daughters, stressing our education. After a long day's work, we would sit by the *chulha* (an earthern stove) for a sumptuous meal which usually comprised *aamti* (a Maharashtrian-style dal), *besan* sabzi, jowar rotis and rice. We would be left licking our fingers by the end, all our worries forgotten. I still reminisce about my mother's cooking.

My mother, a strong-willed woman and a hard worker, taught my siblings and me many life lessons through her bedtime stories. 'If you work hard, you can reach for the stars,' she would say. Apart from giving us immense love, she also sculpted our habits and personalities. I was extremely attached to her. I am who I am today because of my parents' guidance.

Growing up, I was in awe of police officer J.R. Sawant who had been instrumental in bringing down the crime rate in Baramati. Thugs and criminals were terrified of him. He was the talk of the town. I was attracted to the aura of the khaki uniform. I concentrated on building a strong physique and participated in many sports events and wrestling competitions. I also enrolled as a NCC cadet and soon mastered the parade and drill. In 1973, I graduated from T.C. College with a first division and was eager to join either the army or the police force.

My father had other plans for me. In those days, an advocate was regarded as an esteemed individual, especially in a small village like Baramati, and my father wanted the best for me. He impelled me to become a lawyer by enrolling in a college in Pune. His coaxing persuaded me to take up law. However, I was sceptical about venturing into the uncertain future alone. I remember how

I ran to my childhood friend Ramesh Jadhav's house. He had been my batchmate in school. It didn't take me long to convince him to come to Pune. Ramesh's parents agreed with his decision, but his uncle was against it. He refused to let go of Ramesh. I was disheartened at first, but I didn't give up hope. I was determined not to leave for Pune without Ramesh. Having developed good communication skills while working with my father, I eventually managed to convince Ramesh's uncle.

The next morning, Ramesh was my co-passenger on the state transport bus headed for Pune. We were excited as we were all set to enter a new phase of our lives. I had left home with my mother's blessings. My father had given me Rs 3000 to pay the tuition fee for the law course and to keep the rest as pocket money.

In Pune, we boarded a crowded local bus from Deccan Gymkhana to the college. After fifteen minutes, we got down and made our way towards the admissions office. We happily gazed at the college premises and reached the cash counter. My happiness evaporated in a jiffy as I reached for the money in my pocket. My fingers wriggled through a well-cut hole. I had been pickpocketed. Tears streamed down my face. I could only imagine my father's anger. His hard-earned money was gone because of my carelessness. Not only did I feel miserable but I was petrified at the thought of facing him. Ramesh tried his best to console me. He even said that he would not go ahead with his own admission. I asked him to complete his admission process, which he did.

I returned to Baramati that very night and narrated the ordeal to my mother. I was shivering with fear. Fortunately, she calmed my father down and I was spared his wrath. Within a week, my father again gave me the college fee and some pocket money, telling me to join the law college immediately and to be more careful. However, the very next day, I stumbled upon a notice in the Marathi newspaper *Sakaal* for recruitment to the post of SIs in Maharashtra Police. My eyes lit up and I felt a surge of emotions as I was passionate about joining the police force. So, I gathered the courage and talked to my father, but he was reluctant about me taking up any other career. Later, my elder brother, Razzak, convinced him to let me join the police. There was no looking back. I cleared all the pre-admission exams and joined the Maharashtra Police Academy in Nashik, while Ramesh Jadhav went on to become a renowned government prosecutor.

4

TRAINING VIGNETTES

3 July 1974

The sound of the bugle charged through the air as I entered the Police Training College, now known as Maharashtra Police Academy in Nashik. It was established in 1908 by the British and had produced officers of all ranks. I was instilled with a sense of pride and purpose from the day I stepped in. I joined as a cadet SI with several others from across Maharashtra. I still recall some of my batchmates—Mehdi, Chache, Chate, Himmat Ghadge, Vikas Gaikwad, Subash Chutke and Sudhakar Datar. All of us were brimming with optimism and wanted to make it big. G.W. Shiveshwarkar, IPS, was the principal of the training college. He was assisted by Sr PI Patki, a strict disciplinarian whose thundering voice struck fear in the hearts of all cadets. Amar Singh, the drill instructor, was in charge of parade and physical training. Any slacking on the parade ground was met with a resounding smack on the bottom with a stick. After he retired, Mohideen Shaikh, a six-foot-tall man took his place.

I was a passionate sportsman who participated in various events at the training college. However, I took special interest in the judo and karate classes. These martial arts reminded me of the days when I used to wrestle with my friends in the mud by the Karha river. My skills in unarmed combat were amplified with the training. My physique and fitness were held up as examples for other trainees by the instructors. I still remember being lifted and cheered by my batchmates after I won the judo and karate championship at the training college. It is one of my most memorable moments which I am still very proud of.

After completing our training in Nashik, we were posted to Marol Police Training Centre in Mumbai where we were taught about the laws, procedures for recording cases, the police manual and office procedures. My dream of being posted to a police station was about to come true.

COLABA POLICE STATION

5

FIRST POSTING, FIRST DAY

After graduating from the training college in July 1976, I was posted to Bombay's Colaba police station as an SI. Since no one in my family lived in Bombay, except one aunt, my mother was concerned. However, my father and brother convinced her not to worry about my accommodation. My brother gifted me a brand new JAWA motorcycle. On the first day of reporting, I entered the police station with great enthusiasm and smartly saluted Sr PI D.P. Shringarpure. He rang the bell for his orderly. 'From today, this officer is attached to this police station. Explain the procedures to him.'

I left the cabin with another smart salute. The orderly introduced me to my seniors: SIs Vinod Bhatt, Anil Borade, Suresh Kandale, Avinash Gadre, Anil Talpade, D.S. Sawant, Usman Gani Maner, Ashok Desai and Raja Tambat. All of them were eager to know about the village I was from. They called me *bablya*, a term used for a child in Marathi, which annoyed me. I replied, 'My name is Isaque Bagwan, not Bablya.' All of them burst out laughing, leaving me confused. Finally, Raja Tambat called me aside and explained. 'Isaque, every SI who passes out of training college and is posted to a police station is called bablya. You will get used to it.'

My colleagues helped me with the procedures to be followed, which involved preparing case papers and maintaining the station house diary. I was hesitant initially as all the work was done in English, but I soon got used to it. The training had taught us all this but that was theoretical, this was reality. There was a vast difference.

When PI (Crime) Madhukar Zende entered the police station, everybody got up to salute him. As per protocol, I reported to him. In a stern voice, he asked, 'Which part of Maharashtra are you from?'

'I am from Baramati in Pune district.'

'I also studied in Baramati and lived there with my uncle.'

I was delighted to meet a person who hailed from my village. PI Zende placed his hand on my shoulder and said, 'You are afraid because it is your first day. Don't worry. We were all in your shoes once. All of us have been through this stage. You will gain confidence after some time. Do your work sincerely and honestly.' I was touched by his encouraging words.

'While performing your duties at the police station, remember one important thing. A person who comes here has some grievance and wants justice. It is paramount that you hear him out and restore his confidence. That is the first duty of the police. Try to solve his problem in the shortest possible time so that he leaves the station satisfied. If you do this, it will go a long way in increasing love, faith and respect for the police. The common man will praise your good conduct, thereby improving the image of the force.'

Taking a sip of water, he continued, 'While performing your duties, check each and every document carefully, and preserve them with utmost care. Most important are the articles seized at the time of recovery. Remember, we are not the owners but merely guardians. This must be kept in mind at all times. These are some of the principles you must follow from the first day of service. Only then will you be able to do justice to your uniform.'

On the very first day, PI Zende had reminded me how a police officer should behave and the good qualities he must strive to achieve. He focused on how being a policeman was about social welfare and not a service for personal and economic gains. Thus began my journey as a policeman at Colaba police station. From that day, I abided by his words. Even today, I can say with great pride that he has been like a beacon of light in my life.

I was provided government accommodation at Dina Lodge on Garden Road, off Colaba Causeway. I was still a bachelor and preferred to spend a lot of time at the police station, learning how to go about things and even eating there. The police station became my second home. My senior officers noticed this and knew that I was available 24/7. Recording FIRs, preparing *panchnama*s (descriptions of the crime scene with every minute detail about the person, object and environment at that time noted in the presence of two independent witnesses) and completing routine paperwork were all part of my job.

At that time, it was usual for a new recruit to be attached with a senior officer so that he could learn the ropes. Having PI Zende at the helm was an advantage as I could learn all the intricacies of police work. His profound knowledge about the history and geography of Bombay was an added asset. Suffice to say that I was eagerly awaiting an opportunity to be given charge of challenging cases like the ones he handled.

6

BAHRAINI FOOTBALLER'S
MURDER CASE

It was December 1977. I was at the police station. The Sr PI had left for the day after assigning duties to the staff on night duty. The duty officer's charge was with SI Anil Borade and the night relief officer's charge was with the detection officer, SI Subhash Jadhav. SIs Vinod Bhatt and Ashok Desai were also in the police station and were engrossed in discussing the various crimes under investigation. The phone rang. SI Borade lifted the receiver. 'Good evening, Colaba police station, Duty Officer Borade speaking.'

After listening to the caller, he exclaimed, 'What? Where? We will be there immediately.'

Putting the receiver down, he said, 'Somebody has been stabbed in front of the Air India building and is lying on the road in a critical condition. I should inform the most senior officer at the station.'

Borade informed SI Jadhav who was sitting in an adjoining room. He immediately ordered Borade to rush to the spot and start investigating. When we reached the Air India building, we saw the body of a fair-skinned youth lying on the footpath in a pool of blood. His body had multiple stab wounds. SIs Borade, Bhatt and Desai searched his pockets for identification documents and realized that he was a foreign tourist. Senior officers were informed and messages were flashed to the embassy of the country concerned. It was extremely serious as the murder of a foreign national reflected badly on India's image as a tourist destination.

In the darkness of the night, illuminated only by street lights, our constables started waking people sleeping on the footpath. A crowd had started gathering at the crime scene. One foreigner emerged from the crowd, speaking in English and a smattering of Hindi. 'Sir, both of us are from Bahrain. He is a football player. We had gone to Hotel Bombay International and were returning to Oberoi Hotel when we were attacked.'

The name of the hotel rang a bell. PI Zende had showed me the hotel during one of the night rounds. Hotel Bombay International had a posh disco called Studio 29 which would stay open till the wee hours. It was owned by Sabira Merchant, a well-known journalist and an anchor with Doordarshan. It was frequented by actors, children who boasted rich parents and those associated with the Bombay underworld. The two Bahrainis had gone to Studio 29 to enjoy the city's night life.

The murdered footballer's friend said that they had left the disco and were on their way to Oberoi Hotel when they were attacked by three to four men. Unfortunately, he was unable to describe any of them. The panchnama was being prepared. Borade and some senior officers had arrived and were questioning the football player's friend. His answers revealed that a customer at Studio 29 had got into a tussle with a foreigner and been beaten up in return. He had been thrown out of the bar. A thought struck me and I left for the hotel with a constable. By the time we reached, the bar had just closed. The manager and the staff were dividing the hefty tips they had received. They were stunned to see the police. The manager stepped forward and said, 'Sir, the bar has closed, but if you want I can get you something hot or cold.'

I declined the offer and came straight to the point. I asked him about the disturbance earlier in the evening. 'Sir, such incidents happen often at a bar. Some people are not able to handle alcohol and get involved in fisticuffs.' I suspected that the manager was hiding information. I raised my voice and asked him to describe the incident.

'Sir, a fair-skinned young customer got into a scuffle with Hamid Bhai.'

'What was the cause of the trouble?'

'Sir, they got into an altercation while dancing.'

'What happened after that?'

'Sir, the foreigner beat Hamid Bhai mercilessly. Had our staff not intervened, Hamid would have been grievously injured. He beat a hasty retreat and left the bar.' I decided to ask the manager a final question.

'This Hamid Bhai, which area is he from?'

There was disbelief all around. The manager and the staff were wondering how this young officer had never heard of Hamid Bhai. There was silence. Finally, the manager spoke. 'Sir, Hamid Bhai is the son of Aziz Dilip.'

The constable accompanying me said, 'Sir, Aziz Dilip stays in Bachuwali building in Dongri. He is the man behind *matka* gambling dens and sells illicit liquor.'

'Let's go to Bachuwali building.'

Everyone was astonished again. Since I was new to the city, the constable guided me to the address in Dongri and, on the way, briefed me about Aziz Dilip, mentioning that he was Karim Lala's sworn enemy. It was 6 a.m. when we showed up at Aziz Dilip's residence. He was surprised to see a policeman at his door.

'What is the matter? You have come really early in the morning.'

'Your son Hamid got into a fight at Hotel Bombay International. I have come to take him for inquiries.'

Familiar with his son's nature, he produced Hamid before us. 'Sir, you may take him, but do not harm him in any way. I am coming to the police station, but don't do anything to my son.'

I slapped Hamid hard once he was inside the jeep. 'Hamid, tell me who else was with you last night?'

'Sir, I was alone last night.'

'Don't lie to me, Hamid!'

'Sir, I swear in the name of god, I had gone to the bar alone. I have not done anything. On the contrary that fair-skinned person beat me black and blue. Ask him.'

'Hamid *miyan*, there is no way to ask him. You have already sent him to another world.'

'Sir, you are accusing me of something I haven't done.'

Hamid continued to stare at me. I hit him again, pointing to the bloodstains on his T-shirt. Hamid panicked. Under the influence of alcohol, he had forgotten to get rid of the bloodstained shirt. I had strong evidence against him.

'Hamid, you are the murderer. Now tell me who else was with you?'

Hamid was left with no choice but to tell the truth. He opened up about what had happened. 'Sir, yesterday night, that foreigner beat me up badly. I was angry. I went to Dongri and told Ibrahim what had happened. He was enraged too. We took Kamya and Tanya along and headed straight for Hotel Bombay International. Once there, we found that the foreigner had already left. We went looking for him and soon found him near the Air India building where we attacked him.'

'Where can I find Ibrahim, Kamya and Tanya?'

'Dongri, Sir.'

I rushed to Dongri and arrested Ibrahim. I also picked up Kamya, aka Kamlakar Patil, and Tanya, aka Tanya Koli, from Mazgaon. I brought them all to Colaba police station. The scene at the station was different. The murder had caused a sensation. PI Zende was quite annoyed with me. 'Bagwan, where were you? This murder case kept us awake all night. And who are these people? Why have you brought them here?'

I showed him the bloodstained T-shirt. 'Sir, these are the people who murdered the football player.'

'What?'

Everyone in the police station was stunned. I narrated the entire sequence of events after an FIR was filed.

PI Zende patted me on the back. 'This bablya has solved the case in less than twenty-four hours!'

Taking a cue from him, the rest of the staff also congratulated me. Just then, the police photographer came in with photos of the crime scene and the victim. When Hamid saw the photos, he exclaimed, 'Sir, the area is correct. That is where we attacked him, but this is not the foreigner who beat me. We killed the wrong person.' Hearing this, we were all shocked.

The fact was that the person who had attacked Hamid at Hotel Bombay International was not the person he had killed. In an inebriated state, Hamid had found someone he thought was his attacker and stabbed him. The victim's friend had managed to escape. Later, PI Zende skilfully presented all the witnesses and evidence before the honourable court, particularly Hamid's bloodstained T-shirt, and strongly objected to him being granted bail. Hamid's father, Aziz Dilip, approached the Supreme Court too but could not secure bail. The case dragged for about eight years. Later, the footballer's friend, the most important eyewitness in the case, could not appear before the court from Bahrain. The case was closed.

I was happy that my police career had started with such an interesting case. Thanks to my contribution to this case, I was mostly assigned intricate and baffling cases instead of routine paperwork.

7

'HOW CAN ONE OFFICER ARREST
FOUR CRIMINALS ALONE?'

During my tenure from 1976–79, Colaba police station remained sensitive for a number of reasons. One of them was the large number of foreigners, of all nationalities, who frequented Colaba and resided in small, cheap and seedy hotels, guest houses and lodges. It was the era of the hippy culture. Many robberies, even murders, were being reported from these hotels. This floating population attracted the drug trade and clandestine prostitution. The area also housed many commercial establishments and offices. Most buildings in Colaba had been constructed during the British era and were a mix of offices, shops and residences. After dusk, when the offices and shops would close, silence would descend on the whole area. A new world would awaken. It was this silence and darkness that precipitated criminal activity.

One night, as I was parking my motorcycle near the quarters at Dina Lodge, I heard a man with a Nepali accent shouting. I recognized him as the watchman of Hotel Godwin which was nearby.

'Sir, a woman on Walton Road is shouting "*Chor!*"' I was tired after a long day at work, but all excuses are brushed aside when duty calls. I kick-started my motorcycle and sped towards Walton Road. I spotted a woman at a window on the second floor of Dubash building, flashing a torch and screaming, 'Chor!' The poor lady must have thought that someone would come to her rescue. However, at that late hour, only the silence was punctuated by her call for help.

One has to walk down the lonely street behind the Taj Mahal Hotel at night to realize the eerie setting. I shouted out to the woman that I was a police officer. She pointed her torch towards me but was not convinced since I was in *mufti* (a casual shirt over the khaki pants). I tried convincing her. 'Madam, I am Isaque Bagwan. I am an officer at Colaba police station. Please point your torch towards the entrance.' It was so dark that I did not have the faintest idea about where the entrance was. Finally, the woman directed me to the door. I followed the torchlight and started climbing the spiral staircase that ran up the building. Many old buildings in Bombay had winding staircases at the back or on the side for use by the domestic help.

Suddenly, I spotted three to four people descending the staircase. One of them had a parcel in his hand. I shouted, 'Halt! I am a policeman. The building has been surrounded by the police.' For a moment, the men were confused. Taking advantage, I raced up menacingly, making them retreat. When I got closer, one of them lunged at me with a kitchen knife which slashed my arm, but I managed to deflect the blow. This frightened the gang. Their hesitance proved to my advantage. I placed a hand on my empty holster (carrying a weapon was not in vogue in those days) and said, 'Climb up or I will shoot you!'

They had no option but to retreat. I seized one of them with my bloodied hand and pushed them to the second floor. 'Madam, please open the door to your servant's room.'

Some tense moments passed. Finally, the frightened woman appeared but refused to open the door. It was a tricky situation. There was every chance that the four criminals would attack me. Every second was precious. I once again implored the woman to open the door. Ultimately, she gathered enough courage and opened it. I then locked the four men in the servant's room and showed the woman my identity card. She regained her composure and I called the police station. SIs Suresh Kandale and Vinod Bhatt rushed to the spot and took the criminals into custody. I handed over the bag containing the loot to my colleagues. It contained jewellery and Rs 65,000 cash. On realizing that there were policemen in the house, the woman's two daughters, son and mother-in-law also stepped out of their rooms. We were puzzled at how the criminals had managed to enter the house despite so many people being there. While we were questioning the criminals, our team picked up a suspicious person from the vicinity. The family recognized him.

'Bahadur. You?'

Bahadur was an employee of the Balani family in whose house the robbery had been attempted. We had to pressurize him a little before he spilt the beans. Sheela Balani, the woman who had called out for help, had a four bedroom-hall-kitchen apartment on the second floor of Dubash building. Her husband had a flourishing business abroad. Mrs Balani, along with her daughters and son, regularly went for the afternoon shows at cinema halls. Bahadur knew that the cupboard keys were with Mrs Balani's mother-in-law. Among Bahadur's friends was Thapa, a fellow Nepali from his village who had come to eke out a living in Bombay. He was employed at Kailash Parbat Hotel on Colaba Causeway. Thapa got along well with Nishikant and Gopi who worked at the same hotel. He was also friends with one Ramesh Shettigar. Now, Bahadur had been gossiping about the wealthy Balanis. Ramesh and Thapa, seasoned criminals with a police record, drew up an elaborate plan to loot the family. They put it into action when Sheela Balani and her family left for the 3 p.m. show at a nearby cinema hall. Bahadur called Thapa. When Thapa, accompanied by Ramesh, Gopi and Nishikant, arrived, Bahadur opened the door to the servant's room to allow them to enter. The four men then hid under beds in different rooms.

They smoked bidis under the beds and even used the toilets. They had come prepared. In the evening, after the Balanis returned, Bahadur went about his chores as usual. After winding up, he went from room to room to announce that he was leaving for the day. This was a signal. It was 11.50 p.m. Soon, it was midnight. The gang was waiting for the family to be in deep sleep before they emerged from their hiding places. They entered Mrs Balani's mother-in-law's bedroom, threatened her with dire consequences, and took away the cupboard keys from her. Sheela Balani woke up on hearing some strange sounds. She went to her mother-in-law's bedroom. The criminals attacked and wounded her. But even though she was bleeding profusely, she showed great courage in pushing away her attackers and closing the main door of the house. She then shouted for help and flashed a torch from the window. The four criminals, having accomplished their mission, started moving down the spiral staircase. However, they met their nemesis on the stairs. I had blocked their escape route.

All the criminals in this case were booked. The loot was recovered from the spot.

'Bablya has hit a bullseye!' Everyone at the station praised my work. The then Commissioner of Police (Greater Bombay) M.S. Kasbekar called me to his office and awarded me a commendatory note and Rs 500.

My joy knew no bounds. In due course, the accused were chargesheeted. Their advocate argued, 'How can one officer alone arrest four criminals?'

Additional Sessions Judge Makhijani said, 'Let us go to the scene of the crime and see for ourselves.'

The judge himself came to Dubash building where I demonstrated how I had managed to arrest the four criminals. The court was convinced. The judge awarded all the five accused four years' rigorous imprisonment and made a special mention in his judgment: 'Without any arm, officer shows excellent talent to arrest the accused with stolen property.'

The judge also ordered that this remark be included in my annual confidential report.

8

FIVE CRITICAL MINUTES

It was around 10 a.m. SIs Anil Borade, Raja Tambat, Vinod Bhatt and I were on duty when we heard a message crackling on the police wireless system. A man had attacked a person with a chopper at the INS quarters in Colaba.

I reached the INS quarters in less than five minutes. I saw a man rushing down the stairs, arousing my suspicion. When I stopped him, he appeared nervous.

'Open the bag!' I told him. He knew it was over. The bag contained blood-soaked clothes and a bloodstained chopper. Thirty-four-year-old Devi Singh Thakur was a cook in the Navy. He had quarrelled with an assistant named Priti Singh. In a fit of rage, Devi Singh attacked him with a chopper and killed him. Realizing what had happened, he packed the bloodstained clothes and chopper into a bag and decided to flee. However, one person had witnessed the murder and called the police who broadcast the information on the wireless system.

I reached the crime scene in no time and arrested the murderer on the spot. The case was handled by PI Anil Tambakhu. Devi Singh was awarded a life sentence. This case taught me the importance of quick action. Even five minutes can be very crucial when it comes to fighting crime.

9

RACECOURSE ROMANCE TURNS SOUR

One day, around 4.30 p.m. a well-dressed woman entered the police station. She appeared to be upset. I was the relief officer on duty.

'Yes, Madam. What is the matter?' She did not know what to say. I knew that she was in trouble. Her appearance suggested that she was an educated woman who came from a well-to-do family. I offered her a glass of water.

'Now tell me what happened? I know something is wrong.'

My reassuring words seemed to have a calming effect on her. 'Sir, I am from Bangalore. My name is Amruta Ranjan.' After introducing herself, she spoke to me for nearly an hour. She had undergone a terrible experience. She was highly educated, belonged to a wealthy family and had married an army officer. She also had two children. She was living with her parents since her husband was posted along the border. Her father was a big businessman. She had grown up in the lap of luxury and frequented clubs and parties. She also had a passion for horse racing, which is considered to be 'the sport of kings'. Her husband and father were aware of her love for racing. Life was going well for Amruta.

It was the season of the Bangalore Derby. How could Amruta miss it? She reached the racecourse and went straight to the paddock where the thoroughbreds were being paraded. She started studying the horses. It was here that Amruta met a well-dressed gentleman. The meeting was brief, but it was enough to change her life forever.

The derby had attracted huge crowds, and the racecourse was brimming with people. Amruta had lost that day, but she was not disheartened. Once the last race was over, Amruta sat at the bar, sipping a soft drink and wondering if her choice of horses was judicious.

'Excuse me. May I join you?'

This broke her reverie. Standing in front of her was the same neatly dressed person she had met in the paddock. Since the bar was crowded, he wanted to join her.

'Sure, have a seat.'

'Thanks.'

He introduced himself. 'I am Sriniwas Rao. I am from the States. What about you?'

Amruta introduced herself and the conversation flowed. Sriniwas was a successful businessman from the US who was fond of horse racing. They promised to meet again at the racecourse the next day. The friendship blossomed and they started attending all race meetings. One evening, while lounging at the Garden Restaurant, Sriniwas proposed to Amruta. She was annoyed. 'Sriniwas, what are you saying? I should marry you? How could you even think like that? Are you out of your mind?'

Unperturbed, Sriniwas said, 'Amruta, don't be offended. I know you are married. But you are beautiful and talented too. This talent will pay rich dividends in the US, not in India. Tomorrow, your husband will retire from the army. What is there for you in life after that? What returns will you get from his military service? A meagre pension? What after that? Your education and talent are being wasted here. Today, if you were in America, do you know where you would have reached? The sky is the limit. This is why you should accept my offer. As soon as we land in America, we will get married. You can look after my affairs there. I will get you a green card. Life will be as you had always wanted it to be. The choice is yours.'

Amruta walked away that evening, but Sriniwas's words resonated in her mind. There was some truth in them. On one hand, she had two children and on the other a prosperous career beckoned. The one person who could do it was Sriniwas, with whom she felt she was in love. After much thought, she decided to abandon her husband. The next day, she agreed to marry Sriniwas who asked her to collect her belongings, including gold ornaments and Rs 2 lakh in cash, and meet him at Bangalore airport. When Amruta arrived, he showed her their tickets to Bombay. In Bombay, he took her to a deluxe suite he had booked in Colaba's Hotel Crystal. Sriniwas told Amruta that they should go around the city for a couple of days before flying off to the US. He suggested that she must have the latest hairstyle before leaving, and that he knew a fashionable hair stylist opposite Jaslok Hospital on Peddar Road. He took her to the salon where a lot of women were already waiting their turn. He turned to Amruta and said, 'It is going to take a while. I am going out for a walk. You must wait here.'

After she got her hair styled, Amruta waited anxiously for Sriniwas for over two hours. She was worried. She hailed a taxi and headed to Hotel Crystal. The receptionist handed the keys to the suite to her. She raced up the stairs and opened the door. A shock awaited her. Her bag containing the jewels and gold ornaments was gone! She knew that she had been taken for a ride. She started screaming. The hotel staff came running and realized what had transpired. Regaining her composure, she asked the hotel staff to guide her to the nearest police station.

In view of the seriousness of the case, I informed my superiors: PI K.D. Pagare and Detection Officer Suresh Kandale. We flashed a wireless message based on Sriniwas's description provided by

Amruta. Since the starting point was horse racing, we decided to concentrate on Mahalaxmi racecourse. The Bombay racing season was about to begin. We took Amruta there, covered in a burqa, to see if she could spot Sriniwas. Amruta scanned the crowd but didn't see him. We did the same thing when the Pune racing season began. We returned disappointed and handed Amruta over to her father. An entire year went by. When the Bangalore racing season began, we accompanied Amruta to the racecourse. This time, fortune smiled on us. Amruta pointed out Sriniwas. We arrested him with help from the Bangalore Police and called for an armed police escort from Bombay. Sriniwas was kept in Bangalore Police's custody till the escort arrived. Sriniwas and the armed escort boarded a train to Bombay which halted at Miraj railway station. The armed escort stepped out of the compartment to stretch. Sriniwas requested for the handcuffs to be removed on the pretext of going to the toilet. This was a grave error. Finally, the Miraj railway police registered a case of a man escaping from custody.

All of us in Bombay were unhappy to learn of his escape. Another year and a half went by. Amruta spotted him again at the Bangalore races and informed the police. He was arrested and handed over to the Bombay Police. By then, I had been transferred to Santacruz police station. My connection with this case had ended, but I was still interested in knowing how it was going.

What happened later was strange. Sriniwas was a serial con artist who had cheated several women in a similar fashion. Cases had been registered against him in New Delhi, Calcutta and several other cities. He had been arrested and denied bail. When Amruta's case came up for trial in the Esplanade Court after three or four years, she did not appear. The reason for her absence is known only to her. The police's hard work in several cities had come to naught.

10

MURDER OF AN ARAB NATIONAL
AT SHELLEY'S HOTEL

Information reached Colaba police station that an Arab national had been found murdered at Shelley's Hotel near the Radio Club. SI Suresh Kandale and I went to the crime scene. The victim lay dead on the bed in a room on the ground floor. There were two pillows next to the bed. We concluded that he had been suffocated using these. The motive was theft. The hotel register revealed his identity. There was no record of any visitors for him. It was possible that one of the hotel employees had murdered him while trying to rob him. This was our initial line of inquiry as no one would entertain a stranger in their room. We questioned all the staff, but none of them aroused our suspicion. What emerged was that the Arab was a homosexual. I questioned the watchman since nobody could have entered the hotel without him knowing. Initially, he stayed silent. He opened up only after intense questioning.

'Sir, two boys had gone to his room. One of them was wearing a yellow T-shirt. He must have been between twenty and twenty-five years of age and had brown eyes and curly hair.'

I planned on scouring Crawford Market, Musafir Khana, Khadak Dongri, Pydhonie and Bhendi Bazaar, where *dalal*s and pimps supplied boys who went to hammams—communal bathing centres where the poor and needy are provided water for bathing—to satisfy the sexual desires of men. I decided to visit the hammams. We had received information of the murder around 7 a.m. By the time investigations began, less than two hours had elapsed. It was quite possible that the murderer would have had a bath at one of the hammams before fleeing.

I knew there was a hammam at the Crawford Market–Mohamed Ali Road junction. Around 9 a.m., I was driving past slowly when I spotted a young man in a yellow T-shirt crossing the road. He fit the description provided by the watchman. I arrested him. His terrified reaction confirmed my suspicion that he was the culprit. I brought him to the hotel and asked the watchman to identify whether he was the same person he had allowed entry into the Arab's room. When confronted with this fact, he confessed to his crime and also named his partner. We arrested his associate the same night. The case was pursued by SI Kandale and the accused were awarded life sentences.

11

THE BOMBAY POLICE ARE NOT BEGGARS

One morning when I was on station house duty, Bob Thomas, security officer at the Taj Mahal Hotel, called up to inform us about a possible murder there. I went to the hotel with a constable. In the lobby, the manager introduced me to a woman from the housekeeping department.

'What happened, Madam?'

'Sir, two days ago I had gone to the sixth floor suite to clean it. I was about to open the door with a duplicate set of keys when I noticed the 'do not disturb' sign on the door. I presumed that the guest would be asleep as it was early in the morning. I thought that the cleaning staff on duty in the afternoon would clean the suite. This morning, I saw the sign again on the door. A foul smell was emanating from inside. I thought something was wrong and contacted the manager.'

The manager handed the keys to me. We went to the sixth floor. An unbearable stench pervaded the floor. We were nauseated but had no choice except entering the room. An elderly Arab's body lay on the bed. I started examining the decomposing body and asked the manager if he knew who it was.

'Sir, he is a big shot. He is the owner of Hotel Al Khaja.' I was stunned. Hotel Al Khaja was a famous five-star hotel in the Saudi Arabian city of Al Khobar. Realizing the gravity of the matter, I informed PI Zende. My constable, who had been transferred to

Colaba police station from a rural area, was disoriented by what he had seen here and needed to be comforted. Since foul play had to be ruled out, I started examining the body for stab wounds and any other sign that may indicate if he had been smothered to death. I searched the room and started the inquest panchnama. There were seven big bags in the room, and some of them were half-open. The cupboards were also open. Senior officers from the Colaba police station had started arriving. I told them, 'I have conducted an inquest panchnama and am sending the body for post-mortem.'

One senior officer said, 'Bagwan, bablya, I know the procedure. You check the dead man's property. This is a very rich man. Verify each and every item.' The bags contained huge amounts of American dollars, Saudi Arabian riyals, Emirati dirhams, Indian currency notes, diamonds and diamond-studded jewellery, three to four expensive cameras, three-in-one tape recorders (a novelty in Bombay in those days) and costly artefacts purchased in New Delhi, Agra and Jaipur. The cupboards were also full of expensive items. This super-rich Arab, the owner of a five-star hotel in Saudi Arabia, was a regular traveller to India and always resided at the Taj Mahal Hotel. He would go all over the country to purchase expensive items for his hotel and family members. But fate had intervened and he had left this world forever.

'Sir, the entire property is very valuable. The *muddemal* panchnama . . .'

Before I could complete my sentence, one senior officer cut me off. 'I will show you what is to be included and what is to be left out of the panchnama. I know this better than you. I will show you what is to be shown and what is not to be shown. Prepare the panchnama as I tell you to.'

I was shocked to hear this order. The value of the property was worth several crores. I understood what was going on in his mind. I started praying to God to guide me through this. PI Zende's arrival saved the day.

In a loud voice, he instructed me, 'Bagwan, the muddemal panchnama must include each and every item. Nothing should escape your notice.' I took out a pen and pad and started making an inventory.

'The dead person has a right over each and every item that belonged to him. We have no right over it. Keep this in mind.' With this, PI Zende went away, casting a glance at my superior officer. Although the officer was his senior, he did not say a word to him. The panchnama took over seven hours to prepare.

We sent the body for post-mortem and informed the Arab's next of kin. We sealed all the property and took it into custody. The next day, the son of the deceased reached Bombay on a chartered flight and came to the police station. As per procedure, PI Zende handed over the body and the seven bags to him. The post-mortem report revealed that the Arab had died of a heart attack.

The son said, 'I am only interested in my father's body. You can keep the seven bags.'

This irked PI Zende. 'You can take your father's property outside the police station and donate it. You dare not leave even a pin here. The Bombay Police are not beggars!'

The Arab realized his mistake and apologized profusely. He left India with his father's body and property. This incident exemplified the disciplined nature and the noble character of Madhukar Zende. He had kept the pride of the Bombay Police and left his mark on many officers.

A salute to you, Sir!

12

MURDER OF A FAMOUS HOCKEY PLAYER

We received information that Surjeet Roy, a resident of the posh Bradys Flats on Sorab Bharucha Road, off Colaba Causeway, had been murdered. He was a well-known hockey player from Calcutta. In Bombay, he held a senior position with a well-known company. He lived alone. When we reached the crime scene, we discovered that his head had been battered with a heavy object while he was asleep. Since circumstantial evidence pointed towards this conclusion, we searched the house thoroughly. It was evident that robbery was the motive. The cupboards had been cleaned out. Since the door was locked from the inside, we wondered how the murderer had gained entry into the house. That was when we found one of the kitchen windows unbolted. The assailant may have climbed up a pipe and entered through the window at night. He might have smashed Surjeet's head with something heavy and then proceeded to loot all the valuables. Since Surjeet lived alone, there was no way of knowing the value of the stolen property. The police were informed about the murder by the servant, who could be a suspect. However, this was ruled out after he was questioned. The open window was the starting point of the investigation. It was definitely the work of an insider who was familiar with the flat. Accordingly, we interrogated the servant again and learnt that Surjeet had a Nepali cook, Jit Singh, aka Jitu, who had quit seven to eight months ago. What could have been the reason behind this? I then remembered that a complaint had been registered against Roy at Colaba police station. Jitu had complained that he had not been paid two months' salary. I went through the records for Jitu's address. But as expected, he was not to be found there. This was suspicious because people who come to this city for employment do not usually leave their residence unless something major happens. It was important to nab Jitu. I asked my informers to be on the lookout. A couple of days later, one of them told me that Jitu was working for Mohan Singh, a pimp. When I contacted Mohan Singh, he said that Jitu had worked for him but had to be dismissed because he got involved with one of his girls, Rani. I asked Rani about Jitu. At first she denied having anything to do with him. Since she wasn't willing to cooperate, I was forced to use another method. I gave her an idea about what she could expect if police action was taken against her for prostitution. Suddenly, she became very helpful.

'Sir, please don't lock me up. I will help you.'

She admitted that she was in a relationship with Jitu but did not know where he could be. Jitu called her from different locations to fix a rendezvous. I told her to tip me off whenever Jitu called next. Some days later, Rani gave me a call.

'Sir, Rani speaking. Jitu is meeting me at Hotel Infom today.'

Rani had kept her word. We nabbed Jitu. He denied having killed Surjeet. My gaze went to the palm of his hand. It had a fresh wound. When we grilled him, he admitted to his crime.

'Sir, I killed that son of a b★★★★.'

Not only did he confess to the crime but also helped us recover the stolen jewellery and Rs 4,28,000 in cash. The sole reason behind this gruesome murder was a tiff over two months' salary.

Sometimes, trivial matters can lead to something major. Had Roy paid Jitu his wages, he would have been alive. Later, PI Manohar Pawar, who was in charge of the case, completed the investigation. Jitu was charged with murder and robbery. The court sentenced him to life imprisonment.

13

GRAND AUTO THEFT IN COLABA: THE DOMAIN OF CAR THIEVES

Taj Mahal Hotel and Radio Club were popular venues for parties. People coming here would park their cars in the vicinity, only to find them stolen when they returned. Office-goers would park their cars in the day and find them missing in the evening. Every day, at least two to three such thefts were being reported at Colaba police station. Fiat cars were the favourite of the car thieves. The police were unable to do much to curb the string of thefts. ACP (A-Division) Raje Shirke was annoyed. He summoned me.

'Are you the detection officer or not? In such a small jurisdiction covered by Colaba police station, cars are being stolen every day. How can you afford to sleep? Is the government paying you to do nothing?'

His words stung. I decided to bring the car thieves to book. I prepared a chart to illustrate the number of cars stolen, their make, their colour, and the date and time of the theft. I got constables in plain clothes to keep an eye on the spots where the cars usually went missing from. In addition, I asked boot polish-wallahs, chai-wallahs and even beggar boys to keep a sharp lookout for potential thieves. I would often hand out some money to the beggar boys which made them more than willing to oblige. I even posed as a bhel-wallah and chana-wallah to keep watch at some places. Only time would tell if my methods would bear fruit or not.

It was a hot sunny day. I was keeping a close watch on the cars when I noticed a strongly built youth standing near one of them. He was smoking a cigarette and leaning against the driver's door. I wondered why he was smoking in the hot sun when there were plenty of trees around. I kept an eye on him. Suddenly, he opened the door of the car. I advanced towards him and caught him just as he was about to sit inside. He was strong and managed to push me away. He started to run. I gave chase and lunged at him, managing to catch him by his feet. My constables too came running and caught him.

This man was Ajay Kumar Handa, a notorious car thief. I recovered thirty-four cars from him, but many more were yet to be found. By the time our operation ended, thirteen more car thieves had been caught red-handed.

Another thief, Zia, was arrested in the same way. Zia's modus operandi was similar to Handa's. He would drive the stolen car straight to Dominic D'Souza's garage in the lane adjoining Radio Club. He would collect his share of the money and start hunting for another target. It was Zia who told us about D'Souza's involvement. D'Souza, however, was a tough nut to crack.

After much persuasion and intense interrogation, he finally broke his silence. He explained that he would change the registration number of the car, make some superficial changes and get them driven to Bangalore. 'Sir, I did this at the behest of Pravin Bhai. Only you can save me now.'

The mention of Pravin's name left the detection staff stunned. Pravin Kumar Thakkar, aka Pravin Bhai, was the owner of a petrol pump next to the Mantralaya. He regularly visited Colaba police station to meet the officers he shared a good rapport with. I informed Sr PI K.D. Pagare who said, 'Bagwan, take immediate action!'

I swung into action and went straight to Pravin Bhai's residence in Colaba to arrest him at the crack of dawn. PI Zende was overjoyed because Pravin, who had been arrested in another case, had previously managed to bribe people and take advantage of loopholes to get away. His interrogation revealed that the stolen cars were driven to a Fiat showroom owned by a man called Zakaria in Bangalore. I raided the showroom. Cars stolen from Bombay were driven to this showroom and alterations were made to the chassis and engine numbers. The original numbers were neatly cut out with a welding machine and replaced with fake ones. I recovered fourteen cars and hired drivers to drive them back to Bombay.

I had smashed the ring of car thieves and recovered 126 cars. DCP (Zone 1) Jal Contractor personally congratulated me and urged me to keep up the momentum. It felt like I had been given the licence to speed.

14

SUHAS NARAYAN BHATKAR, AKA POTYA

I had arrested members of a gang that was selling fake gold biscuits to unsuspecting women in Colaba on the pretext that they urgently needed money. I was taking the leader of this gang from Ulhasnagar to identify the dye used to make these fake biscuits. I was at the wheel, and in the jeep were Hawaldars Suryavanshi, Pawar and Parab, and the accused. It was 9.30 p.m. and we had just crossed Shivaji Park. Just then, a taxi came from the opposite direction and stopped in front of Sunrise Bar on Cadell Road. I noticed it because it had stopped all of a sudden. I saw some men armed with swords, iron rods and chains enter the bar. Soon, I heard bottles being smashed. And then one of the men dragged the barman out.

The gang beat him mercilessly. I drove the jeep towards them and purposely hit one of them. The man started abusing me. I stepped out of the jeep. The gangsters tried to escape as soon as they saw the police. I chased them along with Hawaldars Suryavanshi and Pawar, leaving Parab to guard the accused in the jeep. This drama was witnessed by some residents of Shivaji Park who were out for a walk. I managed to catch up with the man wielding a sword and grabbed him. As he fell to the ground, I managed to disarm him. The constables had already caught the other assailants. We brought them to our jeep and sent a wireless message. Soon, the Mahim police station wireless van arrived. On seeing one of them, PI Ansari of Mahim police station exclaimed, 'This is Potya!'

Suhas Narayan Bhatkar, aka Potya, had terrorized not only Dadar and Mahim but also Parel and Lalbaug. He had evaded arrest for a long time. He would extort money from beer bars and matka gambling dens. I had arrested Potya by accident. Gold chains and cash looted from gambling dens along with matka gambling chits were recovered from the gang. When Sr PI K.D. Pagare heard of Potya's arrest, he said to me, 'Bagwan, how did you attack Potya when he was armed with a sword? What if he hurt you?'

'Sir, what is written in one's destiny cannot be changed. I went to rescue the barman. How was I to know that this gangster was Potya?'

PI Pagare looked at me in wonder. Later, I received the Man of the Year award from the then Commissioner of Police, M.S. Kasbekar.

15

KEYS, PLEASE!

One day at Colaba police station, I received another call from Bob Thomas of Taj Mahal Hotel. He told me that the hotel was receiving a lot of complaints from guests about belongings being stolen from rooms. This was a major cause of embarrassment for the five-star hotel. It also reflected badly on India's image. When I reached the hotel, Thomas took me around and showed me the rooms where the thefts had been reported. He also mentioned that these robberies happened after the guests deposited their room keys at the reception counter. I positioned the detection staff in disguise at strategic places to keep a watch on the counter. A couple of days later, my suspicions were aroused by the strange behaviour of a man who was over fifty years of age. He was dressed in a fashionable suit. I noticed that he would strike up a conversation with the guests who came to deposit or collect their keys and then accompany them to the lift. I wondered how this person could spare so much time to just talk to tourists in a five-star hotel. Normally, the guests at such hotels are foreign tourists or business executives. There was always a possibility that this person was a member of the hotel staff. But Thomas told me that this person was not one of them. My suspicions were confirmed. There was also the possibility that he was a guest—confronting him could prove to be embarrassing.

Thomas also told me that this man spoke fluent English. I decided to approach him directly.

'Are you a member of the staff here?'

When confronted, the man appeared scared. I grabbed him by the scruff of his neck. A search revealed that he was in possession of the keys to one of the rooms in the hotel. His name was Ibrahim Ismail Patel.

Patel's modus operandi was simple. He would start chatting with the hotel guests and accompany them to the reception counter as they deposited their keys. Once they left, he would go to the counter and, posing as a senior executive of the hotel, ask for the keys. Once the staff would hand over the keys, he would confirm if the guests had actually left the hotel. He would then enter the room, wrap expensive items like cameras and watches in a cloth bag and leave. A search at his house led to the recovery of hundreds of keys to rooms at the Taj Mahal Hotel and Oberoi Hotel, along with the items he had stolen. Since the tourists had left India a long time ago, no one came back to claim their possessions.

The seized property is still gathering dust in Colaba police's custody.

16

OLD HABITS DIE HARD

Talking about tourists, here is another case. Colaba has been, and continues to be, a paradise for shoppers. The following incident happened in March 1977.

It was 11 a.m. The owner of Chida Kashi, a jewellery showroom behind Regal Cinema, was cleaning the showcases that had expensive merchandise on display. Just then, a beautiful girl, a middle-aged woman and a young man entered the showroom. The fragrance of their perfumes pervaded the air. Their trendy clothes made the owner feel that he had prospective customers.

'Yes, Madam!' He welcomed them cordially as he was sure that he would strike a deal early in the morning. He ordered his assistant to display the finest jewellery. The two women took their time in selecting the items. Sometimes, both of them would not approve of the jewellery, or one of them would like it but the other would not.

This went on for nearly an hour. The owner did not want to lose a customer and brought out more jewellery. The trio, however, did not select anything, politely apologized and left. The owner cursed his luck and started putting everything back into the showcases. That's when he realized that some of the jewellery was missing. He panicked and ran outside shouting, 'Chor! I have been robbed by three people!' His shouts drew the attention of the neighbouring shopkeepers. They started looking around and soon spotted the trio in a neighbouring street. They surrounded them and accused them of theft. The trio, however, denied all allegations. The drama attracted the attention of a patrolling constable who promptly brought them to the police station where I was on duty. The shopkeeper explained what had happened, but the young lady kept denying the allegations. I warned her, 'Madam, this is not your house. This is a police station.'

She soon calmed down. I then asked a woman constable to take her into another room and strip-search her. We were wondering what would happen if the search proved to be futile. But soon, the constable emerged with a smile and announced that the jewels had been found hidden in the woman's inner garments. The shopkeeper identified the items. This time, the trio didn't say anything. I got them photographed and sent the photos to the MOB for verification. I soon realized that they were serial robbers. Vera John Peter, the elder lady, Linda John Peter, her daughter, and her son John Peter were wanted for several other thefts. Their modus operandi was to enter an upmarket store on the pretext of buying expensive items and spending a lot of time inside. They would then distract the salesmen and hide some items in their inner garments. This Anglo-Indian trio, which hailed from Calcutta, had a number of cases registered against them in New Delhi, Calcutta, Madras and Bombay. Linda was a well-known cabaret dancer who had taken to robbery. She was earning a lot of money by performing in Calcutta but had developed a strange vice: shoplifting. They were arrested and later released on bail.

A year later, while serving at the Crime Branch, I had to arrest them again in a similar case. We were informed about diamond bangles having been robbed from a shop inside Oberoi Hotel. I showed the shopkeeper Linda, Vera and John Peter's photographs. His eyes lit up. 'Yes, Sir! These are the thieves.'

It was not difficult to locate them. I had meticulously maintained a diary that had details of their haunts in the city, the lodges where they stayed, the beauty parlours they visited, etc. One glance at the diary was enough. I immediately went to Bahari Lodge in Chembur and arrested them. They were sentenced in this case. As they say, a leopard never changes its spots.

17

BOMBAY'S FIRST DANCE
BAR: SONIYA MAHAL

'Sir, please wait for half an hour.'

'Why? What's the matter?'

'Sir, the dance bar is so packed that there is hardly any place for the girls to dance.'

'Oh! Our last train from Churchgate will leave soon.'

'Sir, I cannot help it.'

'Let us wait. I won't be able to sleep if I don't see her dance.'

Back in 1978, this was the scene at the entrance to Bombay's first dance bar. Soniya Mahal had opened on the first floor of Jolly Maker Apartment no. 2 at Nariman Point. Mr Vaswani, a Sindhi businessman, had come up with the idea of satisfying the sex-crazy citizens of this city and minting money in the process. He decorated the dance bar with mirrors across all walls and the ceiling, as if to emulate the sets of *Mughal-e-Azam*. The mirrors created the illusion of visual splendour when the girls danced. Well-known dancers presented their dancing skills before men who gathered here every evening. Soniya Mahal had a male dancer too, Salim, who supervised the other performers.

This new concept attracted the nouveau riche. By 10 p.m., the bar would be chock-a-bloc with diamond and gold merchants from Zaveri Bazaar. The dancing girls would be presented garlands of high denomination currency notes. This drama would go on till dawn.

Mr Vaswani kept getting richer. Not satisfied with this, he also offered a buffet lunch for office-goers during the day. At night, the scene would change dramatically. One night, when SIs Raja Tambat, Ashok Desai and I were on duty, the owner of Soniya Mahal walked into the police station with an elderly man.

'Sir, this gentleman is a retired railway officer. His daughter is one of the dancers at Soniya Mahal. Today, some people came and took her away by force.'

'Who were these people?'

'Sir, it was Samad Khan and Anjum Pahelwan.'

We knew exactly who these people were. Samad Khan was the nephew of Karim Lala and a notorious womanizer. We registered a case and informed PI (Crime) N.J. Manekshaw, who ordered us to take immediate action. The same night, SIs Tambat and Desai arrested Khan from the residence of his mistress. PI Manekshaw and I arrested Pahelwan from Jyoti Sadan on Marine Drive.

On questioning Khan and Pahelwan, we gathered that they had heard about the dancers of Soniya Mahal and decided to see for themselves. Khan's roving eye fell on the retired railway officer's daughter. He was fascinated by her beauty and began showering her with garlands of currency notes, but she did not pay any attention to him. This got Khan angry and he decided to take her away with Pahelwan's help. He simply lifted her off the dance floor and whisked her away in full view, leaving everyone gasping. After forcing himself on her, he drove away to the residence of his mistress in Versova.

Khan and Pahelwan confessed to the crime, but a lot of time had elapsed between the incidence of the crime and the confession. PI Manekshaw completed the investigation and presented all the evidence before the court. But all our efforts failed as the dancer never appeared to testify. Such was the terror of Karim Lala. Khan and Pahelwan went scot-free and continued to indulge in heinous crimes.

18

IQBAL ISMAIL SODAWALA: THE CATALYST FOR GANG WAR

One day, while on duty at the police station, I came to know that my informer Vinod Kunder, a taxi driver, had been stabbed. I reached the spot and got him admitted to a hospital. He had been attacked by Rehman, Rahim Lala's elder son and Karim Lala's nephew.

Colaba was frequented by a lot of foreign tourists who also demanded drugs. A clandestine drug business flourished on the first floor of Salvation Army Guest House in Red Shield House, next to Churchill Chambers on Mereweather Road. There were two rival gangs engaged in the drug business in Colaba. One gang consisted of Gopal Rajalingam Awaliya, Vithal Shetty and Raja. The other gang comprised Karim Lala's nephew, Rehman Abdul Rahim Khan, aka Pathan, Vinod Yadav and others.

Iqbal Ismail Sodawala, a resident of Nagpada, conducted his drug business under the facade of a dry fruit shop. But Nagpada did not interest him for long as foreigners only frequented Colaba. His ambition was to lord over the drug business there. He took help from Aziz Dilip of Dongri to get to know Vinod Kunder and Gopal Awaliya. Vinod helped Sodawala set up shop in Abbas building on Mereweather Road. This clashed with Rehman's business which was next door. Both the gangs clashed. Rehman's gang attacked Kunder with swords. Sodawala escaped unhurt.

We registered a case against Rehman and arrested him. Addl CP (Crime) and IPS offficer J.F. Ribeiro ordered us to take action against both gangs and rid Colaba of this menace. Sodawala started visiting Colaba police station regularly on the pretext of making inquiries about Vinod's case. He wanted to set up his drug business in Colaba by showing that he was helping the police with the investigation. But we were not fooled. Sodawala understood that he was being cornered. He started to plan how to trap me.

In 1977–78, Colaba attracted a lot of foreigners. It was the era of the hippy culture and drugs were easily available in back alleys. Mereweather Road behind Taj Mahal Hotel was swarming with foreigners sleeping in the awnings of buildings in a state of euphoria. Local social worker, Dr P. Navinkumar had requested Addl CP Ribeiro for help in this regard. With the Addl CP's support, I launched a full-scale operation against anti-social elements in the area. One of them was Sodawala and the other was Karim Lala's nephew and Samad Khan's elder brother, Rehman. I knew their networks, but I could not catch them red-handed. Sodawala had been visiting the police station regularly, hoping to be able to carry on his activities, but I always ignored him. One evening, as I was conducting a recovery panchnama of a case in the detection room, he came to see me.

'Salaam, Sahib.'

'What is it?'

Sodawala looked around to ensure that no one was there. He pulled out a bundle of currency notes from his pocket.

'Sir, here. Take this. It's Rs 3000.'

I lost my temper, caught him by the collar and dragged him out to the compound of the police station where I whacked him with a hockey stick. The other officers restrained me. Sodawala beat a hasty retreat. The next day I was told that I had been summoned by the ACB.

I wondered what the ACB wanted from me. I went to the office and presented myself before PI Mazumdar. 'Young man, you were saved. Yesterday, you survived!'

'What? I did not follow, Sir?'

PI Mazumdar explained. 'You had opened up a front against the illegal drug trade. Sodawala had been badly affected. He approached the ACB and alleged that you had demanded money to turn a Nelson's eye to his activities. Yesterday, my staff and I had laid a trap for you. Sodawala's currency notes had been marked. But instead of accepting the money, you thrashed him. The ACB team was watching this.'

'Sir, where were you hiding?'

PI Mazumdar smiled and said, 'People from the ACB go in disguise, but I will let you in on a secret. I was near the lock-up, disguised as the person providing meals to the detainees. I was the one wearing shorts.'

I told him about all the cases I had registered against Sodawala. 'Young officer, be clean and honest in your entire career,' he advised me before I left.

Sodawala stopped visiting Colaba police station and left the area. He shifted his den to Arab Gully in Nagpada, which I realized later. For his own advantage, he went on to spark enmity between Aziz Dilip and Rahim Khan, which led to a full-scale gang war.

19

DONGRI GANG WAR: AZIZ DILIP VS RAHIM KHAN

This was the era when Haji Mastan and Karim Lala held sway over the underworld. But a new figure was looming on the horizon, Aziz Dilip. Mastan and Lala had been rivals since 1976. The rivalry ended in 1986 when Samad Khan, Karim Lala's nephew, was murdered.

Aziz Dilip was a resident of Bachuwali building in Dongri. He was over six feet tall and strongly built. Even today, he is considered a legend in Dongri. He was the one to establish the illegal businesses of *patada* gambling, bootlegging, matka gambling dens and illicit liquor joints. He had two sons, Hamid and Majeed, who were also well-built. They were school dropouts who were inclined to a life of crime and lived luxuriously. I had encountered Hamid while investigating the Bahraini footballer's murder. Now, let me tell you about Majeed.

Ramzan Patel gave Bombay its first pub in Colaba. It was called Slip Disc. Every night, nearly 100 girls frequented this pub. They were commercial sex workers in the guise of dancers. Soon, Slip Disc became the largest pick-up centre in south Bombay. Its daily turnover was several lakhs. The day-to-day affairs were handled by a manager named Shapur Irani. Whenever the police would conduct a raid at Slip Disc, Patel, who wielded a lot of influence in the upper echelons of the police department, would put a lot of pressure on the police to back off. He was a member of the Radio Club, which was located beside the pub, and conducted all his financial transactions from its safe confines. Majeed had information that Patel had amassed great wealth in a short span of time. One day, he kidnapped Patel from the Radio Club. One of my informers tipped me off and I raided Majeed's den in Dongri. I rescued Patel who had been harassed and beaten up. I arrested Majeed for kidnapping and assault. But Patel was so terrified of Aziz Dilip that he refused to lodge a complaint against Majeed. I tried to convince him, but he declined. This is just one of the instances of Majeed's terror being unleashed based on the strength of his father's reputation.

Karim Lala's business activities were handled by his younger brother, Rahim Khan, aka Rahim Lala, and his manager, Babla. Rahim Khan had four sons: Rehman, Samad Khan, Ahmed Khan and Salaudin. They had terrorized the city. One example of Samad Khan's terror was the Soniya Mahal case. The seeds of bitterness between Aziz Dilip and Rahim Lala were sown by Iqbal Ismail Sodawala over the drug business. Their sons had clashed in the Colaba incident. After having suffered a beating, the over-ambitious Samad Khan planned to hit back. He hired a killer from Uttar Pradesh to get rid of Aziz Dilip. The 'matka king' of Dongri was attacked with a chopper at his den and killed. This signalled the beginning of a full-scale gang war.

Samad Khan's reputation was at an all-time high after Aziz Dilip's murder. Dilip's son, Hamid, was livid and hired a killer named Munna from Uttar Pradesh and another criminal called Mukhtar Lakdawala. The latter found mention in Bombay Crime Branch records for his bid to eliminate Rahim Lala, Samad Khan's father. These hired killers murdered Rahim Lala with choppers and guns when he was on his way home. This only added fuel to the fire. Enraged at the loss of their father, Rahim Lala's sons were thirsty for revenge.

Hamid, who had joined Dawood's gang by then, was killed at a bar in Navjeevan Society in Bombay Central. Majeed and Munna were also killed in quick succession. Having tasted success, Samad Khan was now brimming with confidence. He raised a war cry against Dawood. One day, he entered Dawood's den and opened fire on his brother, Iqbal Kaskar. Iqbal managed to escape, but only by a whisker.

Karim Lala understood that this gang war would only escalate. He tried to broker peace by talking things out with Dawood. On hearing about his uncle's peace overtures to Dawood, Samad Khan was angered further and went on to loot Dawood's smuggled goods that were being transported in a taxi near the Gateway of India. Samad Khan then tried to extort money from Dawood in return for his own goods. Dawood decided that he had had enough. He instructed Rama Naik's gang, which was working for him, to eliminate Samad Khan.

No one could have imagined that Sodawala would ignite such a fierce gang war that would splatter on to the streets of Bombay. I was attached to the Colaba police station till late 1979 and got an opportunity to handle serious cases of crime and learn about the denizens of the underworld. I managed to cultivate and develop a vast network of informers across the length and breadth of this great metropolis.

Then, I was transferred to Santacruz police station.

20

SABIR: DAWOOD'S ELDER BROTHER

In 1977, Nariman Point came under the jurisdiction of Colaba police station. I was posted as a beat officer there. During those days, evenings were all about relaxation and a sense of abandon. Boys with liquor and loud tape recorders were a common sight along the Queen's Necklace. With barely any monitoring arrangements in place, chain snatchings, robberies and general nuisance were common.

One evening, while I was patrolling the area, some loud music caught my attention. Initially, I thought the noise was coming from Oberoi Hotel. But as I approached the hotel, I saw four men sitting across the road from it, along the sea face, and consuming liquor. Mujra numbers blasted from the speakers of their dukker Fiat.

Assuming that they were local hoodlums, I decided to rough them up a little. As I tutored them about such activities being prohibited, one of them, drunk and tottering, slurred, 'Sahib, *jaane do na. Kayko vaanda karne ka?* (Sir, let it go. Why create trouble?)'

As I had little control over my temper, I caught hold of his collar and called for a taxi. I made the four of them get into it and told the driver to follow my motorcycle. I headed straight for the police station.

At the police station, they made a call. 'I am Sabir, let me go!' one of them kept repeating. I didn't pay any attention to this and booked all of them under the Prohibition Act. Their names were Sabir Kaskar, Rajji, Chota Kasu and Shakil Boss. After sometime, Jainabai made a dramatic entry into the police station. *'Arre, maaro dikro!* (Oh, my child)' she cried out. This caught everyone's attention, but I didn't entertain her. Jainabai called up the ACP and complained that I was being unjust and cruel towards the men in my custody. Her act worked and my senior ordered me to let the four men go. I did that. It wasn't long before I realized that these were members of Dawood's gang.

SANTACRUZ POLICE STATION

21

CHAIN SNATCHER'S ARREST
LEADS TO GOLD

ACP Jal Haradvala appointed me as the detection officer at Santacruz police station, perhaps after hearing about the cases I had handled at Colaba police station. This did not go down well with some of the other officers there.

I soon got down to the task of investigating chain-snatching cases and robberies that were on the rise. One day, while I was on duty as the relief officer, a woman entered crying. The duty officer told her, 'Madam, I will attend to you after I finish the work at hand.'

'Please sit down,' I told her. We had been trained to treat every complainant with kindness and a patient ear. Unfortunately, that is rare today. I asked the woman about her problem.

She said she was walking near the South Avenue and Ramakrishna Mission Marg junction when a person dressed in a shirt and pants came from behind her on a cycle. Before she could realize it, he had snatched her expensive necklace and *mangalsutra* (wedding necklace). She shouted at the top of her voice but no one came to her rescue as the road was deserted. She then made her way to the police station. I proceeded to the spot with my team and the woman in a jeep.

We started making inquiries but there were no eyewitnesses. I noticed a stall at the corner of the road and asked the vendor if he had seen anything.

'I have not seen anything or anybody.'

His tone aroused my suspicion. I repeated my question sternly.

'Sir, the cyclist crossed Swami Vivekananda Road and went straight ahead.'

I drove the jeep in the direction the vendor had indicated. Since the chain snatcher was on a bicycle, I decided to concentrate on cycle shops along the road. On spotting one such shop, I called out to the owner.

'Did any person wearing a shirt and pants come to your shop?'

'No, Sir.'

'Then have you seen any person like that take a bicycle on hire?'

When he denied any knowledge, I threatened him with dire consequences.

'Sir, some time back, one person named Babya Madrasi returned a bicycle he had taken on hire.'

'Where can I find Babya?'

'Sir, Babya and his boys are dangerous. They can be found playing cards in a hut by the side of the road.'

We located the hut made of tin and branches of coconut trees. We peeped inside and saw four men playing cards. I called out to them. Babya Madrasi came out brandishing a piece of tin. The hut had been surrounded from all sides. I caught hold of Babya and pushed him into the jeep. The woman recognized him as the man who had snatched her necklace.

Upon questioning, he revealed that he had snatched nearly thirty to forty chains in Santacruz, Khar, Bandra and Vakola. I decided to make a map of all the locations where he operated with information about the place, time and jurisdiction, including any cases that had been registered at other police stations. Later, we reached out to all the complainants to identify the chains that had been recovered.

I asked Babya, 'Who receives the stolen gold chains?'

'Sir, Champa Marwadi.'

'Where can I find Champa?'

'In Dharavi.'

We took Babya to Dharavi and arrested Popatlal Kothari, aka Champa Marwadi. Champa would purchase these stolen chains at low prices and melt them. He would also get small-time criminals from Dharavi to steal gutter covers and then sell them. I knew the modus operandi of this *malkhau* (the word used for a person who receives stolen property in the local language) and wanted to know the extent of his operations and the quantity of melted gold he had. We searched the premises and seized the gold in the presence of two *pancha*s. After obtaining court orders, we returned the gold to the victims. The seizure of such a huge quantity of gold caused a rift between Champa Marwadi and Babya Madrasi. I was sure that Champa would harm Babya once he was out on bail. I presented a chargesheet against Babya before the court. Babya was scared after I warned him about the danger ahead.

'Sir, what can I do?'

'Confess to your crime.'

Babya Madrasi agreed to do that. The court sentenced him to two years' imprisonment. The sentence was to run concurrently on each of the twelve to thirteen cases.

I found a new way of patrolling to prevent chain snatchings in the jurisdiction of Santacruz police station. I posted constables at strategic locations, which led to a fall in the number of such offences. However, other criminals remained active in the area. In order to bring them under control, I arrested some known offenders under the preventive sections of law. The business community in the area was overjoyed with the dip in crime rate.

22

ROBBERY ATTEMPT AT SHAKTI KAPOOR'S RESIDENCE

One day, when I was on relief duty at the police station, actor Shakti Kapoor came in looking panic-stricken. 'Sir, this is my domestic help, and he resides in my flat. I had left for a film shoot in the morning. He was alone in the house.' He asked the help to narrate what happened next.

The help said, 'It was evening when the doorbell rang. When I opened the door, I saw three strangers outside.

'I asked, "What do you want?"

'One of them said, "We have come with Shakti Kapoor in his car. He is talking to someone downstairs and told us to wait inside."'

Believing their story, the help ushered them in and went to the kitchen to get some water. In an instant, the three men locked the door from inside. They threatened him with choppers and demanded the cupboard keys. They grabbed the expensive tape recorder and all the other valuables they could lay their hands on. That was when the doorbell rang. The robbers thought it was Shakti Kapoor. They threw the loot on the floor and put a chopper to the help's neck, ordering him to open the door. The help had no option but to do so. It was the woman who lived in the neighbouring flat. She had come to borrow some sugar. Sighting an opportunity, the help rushed out of the house shouting 'Chor!'

The robbers panicked, pushed the woman aside and fled, leaving the loot behind.

I visited Shakti Kapoor's residence and saw all the items strewn on the floor. The robbery attempt had failed because of the woman's timely entry and the help's quick reaction. We conducted a panchnama of the spot.

23

THREAT TO AMITABH BACHCHAN

One day we got a call from actor Amitabh Bachchan's manager, Sheetal.

She said, 'Sir, this is a serious matter. Please come to Pratiksha [one of the actor's bungalows] as soon as possible.'

From her tone, I understood that something had happened. I went to the bungalow where I was received by Teji Bachchan and Jaya Bachchan, the actor's mother and wife. Both of them appeared frightened. They offered me a glass of lime juice.

'Madam, what has happened?'

They asked Sheetal to explain.

'Sir, we found this letter in the mail box.'

I opened the letter. Even I became tense after reading it.

'Four men from Raipur are going to kidnap Amitabh Bachchan from the bungalow.'

There was a possibility that this was a prank, but one could not rule out danger. I tried to instil some confidence in the Bachchans. There was one clue in the letter. It had been signed by Suresh Uchil. I remembered having seen that name somewhere. I thought for a while and realized that I had seen a signboard at a bhel-wallah's shop on Juhu Chowpatty. I traced him and quizzed him.

He said, 'Sir, I overheard four persons saying that since they had come all the way from Raipur, they must create a commotion, and the best way was to threaten Amitabh Bachchan and kidnap him.'

He was neither able to describe them nor was he able to tell me whether they had any weapons. I alerted my network of informers. I also conducted a combing operation in some parts of the city. When I returned to Pratiksha, it resembled a police camp. Many senior officers were at the bungalow with a huge contingent of armed policemen. Sheetal had informed Amitabh Bachchan about the threat while he was busy at a film shoot. Bachchan had responded by calling up the office of Indira Gandhi, the then prime minister. She, in turn, called up A.R. Antulay, the then chief minister of Maharashtra. The wheels of the government machinery had moved at a quick pace.

'Bablya, so you are here!' exclaimed a senior police officer. I explained to him all the possible leads I had followed. He turned to Amitabh Bachchan and said, 'Bagwan is a competent officer.'

Although we maintained heavy police bandobast at the bungalow, Amitabh Bachchan could not sleep and lay on his bed holding a licensed weapon in his hand. After further investigation, we realized that the letter was a prank, but it had managed to cause quite a sensation.

24

TERROR OF JUHU TAMED

One morning, a tall, well-built north Indian walked into the police station.

'Sir, please save me. My revolver has been stolen.' His name was Thakur and he had a flourishing milk supplying business in Wadala. He carried a licensed revolver for protection. Thakur had come to meet a relative in the Johnson and Johnson bungalow in front of Juhu Hotel on Juhu Tara Road. They were having a cup of tea at a stall along the road. His revolver was secured by a belt on his waist.

John Powda, a notorious goonda in Santacruz, had noticed the revolver and managed to snatch it from him. Powda extorted money from hawkers on Juhu Chowpatty by brandishing a knife. Such was the fear he had instilled in the hearts of people that no one could say anything against him or complain to the police.

This was a serious matter. If Powda used the gun, Thakur would be in the soup. The revolver had six bullets. Several people were likely to be harmed if Powda fired.

I reached the Johnson and Johnson bungalow with Constable Gaikwad. The bungalow belonged to a Parsi gentleman, but Powda had occupied it forcibly. We found him in an inebriated state. He brandished his newly acquired weapon on seeing us.

'You are new to this area. You don't know what I am capable of! Leave at once!'

The revolver was pointed at me, but I kept moving towards him. Constable Gaikwad was tense. He shouted, 'Sir, he is a dangerous criminal and will not hesitate to fire.'

I replied, 'I am not afraid of him or anyone else.'

I was not going to lose this opportunity to catch a dangerous criminal red-handed, that too with a stolen revolver. I kept looking at his glass filled with liquor to distract him and tried to emotionally blackmail him. 'If you shoot, your game is over, Powda! The Bombay Police will be behind you. I have come to talk to you, so you better calm down. Let us sit and talk.'

John shouted back, 'This is my last warning, officer! Don't come near me!'

I continued advancing. Powda fired, but it missed me. He was perplexed for a moment. Taking advantage of the situation, I lunged at him and jerked the gun out of his hand. I overpowered him and handcuffed him with help from Constable Gaikwad. The news of his arrest spread like wildfire. The entire business community and the hawkers in the area were overjoyed.

I worked at Santacruz police station for nearly a year. I got married in Baramati in November 1980, fulfilling my parents' and elder brother's wish. I returned to Bombay with my wife.

In the meantime, I was transferred to the Detection Crime Branch, CID.

DETECTION CRIME BRANCH, CID

DETECTION CRIME BRANCH CID

25

A KIDNAPPING IN BROAD DAYLIGHT

When I was transferred from Santacruz police station to Detection Crime Branch, CID, there were a number of senior and seasoned police officers working there. There was hardly any place to sit and work. A special squad had just been formed under PI Ratnakar R. Kolekar. One night, I was allotted the work of station house night duty officer. The duties included collecting messages about crimes committed at night, passing on the information to senior officers, updating the lock-up register, examining the accused in the lock-up and compiling a list of serious crimes reported by police stations across Greater Bombay.

As I was winding up my work, my informer from Colaba, Jumbo, told me that a businessman had been kidnapped from Churchgate in the afternoon and taken to a closed room on the first floor of Bandukwala building in Nagpada's Arab Gully. Jumbo's tip-offs were always accurate, but I was in a dilemma. I did not know whom I should convey this information to as I had worked in the Crime Branch for barely a week. I was the youngest officer there. Driver Kamble and Hawaldar Rane were on night duty with me. I got into a jeep with them and drove straight to Dongri. In those days, SI Raja Tambat was staying in the residential quarters of Dongri police station. Having worked together at Colaba police station, I shared a good rapport with him.

I explained everything to him and he readily agreed to come with me to Nagpada. At the location, Jumbo said, 'Sir, the businessman is locked in a room next to the common toilet.'

Jumbo then vanished. We found that the main gate was locked from inside. We failed to find any other entrance. That was when we noticed that the building had a balcony running along the length of the first floor. This would be the only way to gain entry. We parked the jeep close to the building. Climbing on to the hood of the jeep, I jumped and caught the balcony railing, using it to leap on to the gallery. I managed to enter the building and came down the staircase to open the main gate from inside. My team made its way towards the common toilet and opened room no. 14. In the dim light, we saw three people sleeping. One of them was the victim. We arrested the other two: Abrar Ahmed and Israr Ahmed. Abrar had murdered a youth named Kokvai in broad daylight in Kamatipura on 16 July 1981. He had jumped bail and was wanted by the police. He confessed to kidnapping the businessman.

We searched the room and recovered charas, morphine and *surine* (charas packed in small plastic bottles), three revolvers, swords and choppers. When interrogated, Abrar and Israr revealed that they had one more associate, Iqbal, who lived on one of the upper floors of the same building. I ran up the staircase and knocked at Iqbal's door. His wife opened the door. I asked her about Iqbal's whereabouts. Iqbal, meanwhile, woke up and could be heard swearing loudly.

'Who has come to disturb me at this hour?'

Rubbing his eyes, he came to the door. When I saw him, I was shocked.

'Iqbal!'

'Bagwan Sahib!'

It was Iqbal Ismail Sodawala, aka Pistawala or Charoli. I remembered the time I had thrashed him when he had tried to bribe me and failed.

Today, I had arrested Sodawala again. He confessed to the kidnapping. The businessman regularly walked from Churchgate to Azad Maidan. Sodawala and his associates kept a watch on his movements. One day, they stabbed him in the back and abducted him in a taxi. They robbed him of all his belongings. The stab wound was deep and the businessman kept slipping into unconsciousness. Sodawala had forced Dr Tony Dias to give him first-aid at knifepoint. Dr Dias had a clinic in the red light area of Kamatipura and was known for treating prostitutes. The businessman was still critically ill when I got him admitted to a hospital.

Sodawala's associates—Abrar Ahmed, Ejaj Ahmed, Israr Ahmed, Mohamed Shahid, aka Chota Shahid, and Mukhtar Ahmed—were arrested. Shahid had stabbing and extortion cases registered against him and had committed a murder in Pydhonie while out on bail. We brought them to the Crime Branch along with the seized weapons and drugs. After locking them up, I began preparing a panchnama. Another officer, whom I would not like to name, walked in. He was slightly senior to me. He congratulated me and said, 'You have worked all night and must be tired. Go home and rest. I will take care of all the paperwork. Don't worry. You deserve to rest after all your hard work.'

After being assured by this senior officer, I left for home as it was almost dawn. I witnessed a dramatic scene when I returned the next morning. I saw the arrested persons being brought out of the press room in burqas, escorted by a new team of constables. I immediately rushed to my senior officer, R.R. Kolekar, and told him the whole story. He understood what had happened and asked me to accompany him to the office of the Assistant Commissioner, Crime Branch, Ranbir Leekha, on the first floor of the CID building. He asked me to explain and understood that the other senior officer had tried to steal the credit from my team. I told him that he could question the arrested persons to identify the policemen who had arrested them. Assistant Commissioner

Leekha then ordered the criminals to be paraded before him. He asked them, 'Who arrested you?'

All of them pointed to me. Assistant Commissioner Leekha was furious and called for the other officer. He did not stop at reprimanding him. Instead, he marched down to our office on the ground floor where all inspectors of the Detection Crime Branch were present (C.O. Samagond, L. Kurdikar, Ramdas Kamat, Pimpalkar, P.W. Sawant and Narayan Nikam). Assistant Commissioner Leekha ordered one of the officers to clear his table and said, 'Bagwan, from today you will sit here.'

I was elated to hear this. I had a separate table and a separate team of constables who would report to me. Now, I could work among the stalwarts of the Crime Branch. Taking advantage of me being a rookie, my senior had tried to rob me of my achievements. Had I not returned early, he would have succeeded. I was extremely fortunate that my work got noticed and I earned respect in the department.

26

RASHID ARBA: THE KING OF SMUGGLING

The 1970s and '80s saw the number of cases of gold smuggling and the drug trade increasing in the city. Rashid Arba was the kingpin of gold smuggling. He was called Arba because of his close links with Arab gold suppliers. His main supplier, Abdulla Galadhari, was based in Dubai. His den was located at old Musafir Khana in Crawford Market.

Arba would connive with his suppliers to smuggle in gold, silver, textiles, tape recorders and watches from Dubai. These goods would arrive at the Bombay docks. Some goods would also come by air. The city's coastline provided excellent landing spots for these smuggled goods.

The trade was controlled from Musafir Khana where the goods were sorted and dispatched to places outside Bombay. In order to prevent these goods from being stolen, and recovery of money in case of non-payment, a small army of gangsters was necessary. This muscle power was provided by Dawood, his elder brother Sabir, younger brothers Noora and Anees, Sayed Miya and Umar Baxi. This was the era of Haji Mastan and Karim Lala. Even Dawood and his henchmen addressed them as 'uncle'.

Karim Lala: The King of Pathans

Karim Lala and his brother had been carrying on their illegal activities from Jail Road, Dongri, before Independence. Lala provided shelter to all fellow Pathans coming in from Afghanistan, the North-West Frontier Province and Kashmir. The Pathans were employed by landlords to collect rent on their behalf.

This was the time when charas was sold openly in Bombay. The police would register cases under the Prohibition Act, which was a bailable offence. The Pathans would come out of jail soon and continue their business. Babla was Lala and his brother Rahim Lala's manager.

Haji Mastan's smuggling business, meanwhile, did not clash with Lala's. There was no conflict of interest and they respected each other. They clashed only after Samad Khan's rash behaviour. Both of them had big gangs and were involved in settling land disputes and recovering debts. This is how I came in contact with Lala and Mastan.

Interestingly, Lala and Mastan had a healthy respect for the police, and the latter could locate them any time they wished to.

Lala's Arrest

Babya Khopde, aka Chandrakant Khopde, was the leader of the Golden gang in Parel. Babya had threatened a prominent industrialist regarding a land deal. When Commissioner J.F. Ribeiro came to know of this, he ordered a case to be registered against Babya at Gamdevi police station. The Crime Branch was entrusted with the task of arresting Babya. We tapped our network of informers for tip-offs and nabbed him. He confessed that he had been given *supari* (money paid to a hitman) by Karim Lala who was looking to make a fortune out of this.

I was ordered to arrest Lala. When I went to his penthouse in Baida Gully, he was sitting in a lungi. I arrested him like that. Commissioner Ribeiro was pleased. But the next day, Lala was out on bail. All cases against him fell flat in court because neither the witnesses nor the complainants came forward to testify. Such was Lala's terror.

27

HAJI MASTAN: THE DON OF BOMBAY

In 1981, cricketer and industrialist Madhav Apte was looking to sell some property he owned in front of Bhavan's College near Girgaum Chowpatty. Haji Mastan showed an interest in buying it and approached Apte through brokers. Apte, however, was determined not to let the property fall into the hands of a notorious smuggler.

Mastan soon gave up attempts to purchase it since he was aware that it could be dangerous to try and push Apte, who was also the president of the Bombay Cricket Association and a prominent member of society. Some months later, Apte sold the property to the Sumer Group. That was when Mastan decided to make his move.

On 10 March 1981, two partners of the Sumer Group—Kishoremal Shah and his nephew Ramesh Shah—left for their office at 10 a.m. Mastan's gang blocked their Fiat car, kidnapped them and took them to their den at Bombay Garage near Babulnath Temple. They beat them mercilessly and forced them to sign a document stating that they had sold the property to Mastan. They were then released.

Back home, the duo narrated the ordeal to their family. Kishoremal Shah's son-in-law, Mangal Prabhat Lodha, who is now a BJP MLA, was the son of a judge of the Rajasthan High Court, Gumaanmalji Lodha. When Lodha told his father about this incident, the judge called up the then Commissioner of Police, K.P. Medhekar, who ordered Sr PI, Detection of Crime Branch, V.Y. Dange to investigate. He, in turn, asked me to take action.

That very night, I went to Mastan's residence in Baitul Suroor, a building located in a lane off Peddar Road. Mastan was not at home, but we brought one of his relatives, his driver Nabab Khan and his elderly manager, Dawood, to the Crime Branch. The next morning, Mastan came to the office of PI (Administration), Crime Branch, Y. Tarte. When PI Tarte asked me about the case, I requested him to hand over Mastan to me for further questioning.

PI Tarte ordered me to hold an identification parade for the complainants and the accused in the presence of witnesses. Kishoremal Shah and Ramesh Shah could not identify the accused. I had no option but to release Mastan's associates.

Later, leaving the office triumphantly, Mastan looked at me and said, 'You are very young. I thought you would be older.'

28

RAJJI: DAWOOD'S AIDE

It was 1981, when I was posted with the Crime Branch. The Royal Enfield Bullet was quite an eye-catcher back then. I loved how it thundered through the streets and grabbed the attention of the passers-by.

One day, I was crossing the busy Mohammed Ali Road with SI Raja Tambat on the pillion. I felt a sense of pride as the motorcycle roared through the streets. That was when I saw a man looking at me.

I slammed the brakes and stopped at the petrol pump where he was seated. SI Tambat was puzzled. Without looking away, I walked up and held him by the collar. I had recently seen his photo in the Crime Branch files. He was seated in a chair along with some accomplices. All of them looked astonished.

I said, '*Chal, saale. Tu Crime Branch mein wanted hai*. (Come on. You are wanted by the Crime Branch)' The man was Rajji, one of the main members of the Dawood gang. He was also the right hand man of Jainabai, the city's woman don.

'You are wanted under Section 307,' I told him as I held him by the neck. SI Tambat, meanwhile, kept Rajji's men away from me.

Rajji had recognized me. '*Arey, Sahib, aap toh Gabbar Singh ho. Kyu pakda hai mujhe? Jaane do na.* (Sir, you are no less than Gabbar Singh. Why have you caught me? Let me go.)'

One of his men ran to a shop nearby to seek help. Minutes later, I got into a verbal tiff with Rajji and his accomplices, even as a crowd gathered. Just then, a Honda Accent stopped near my bike. A well-dressed man in a kurta-pajama walked out. The crowd started whispering, 'Dawood Bhai. Dawood Bhai *aaye hain*. (Dawood is here.)'

The man walked up to me. '*Sahib, apna aadmi hai. Chod do isse. Meri baat tumhare department se ho gayi hai. Jaane do isko.* (Sir, this is my man. Let him go. I have spoken to your seniors.)'

I didn't budge. Just then, Jainabai also arrived. '*Mere bachhe ko chod do!* (Leave my child alone)'. She sent Peeru Bhai, her son-in-law, to call the Crime Branch.

Jainabai caught my hand and started pulling me away saying there was a call for me from the Crime Branch.

I handed Rajji over to SI Tambat before going to take the call at a shop nearby. It was a senior officer from the Crime Branch. He said that he needed Rajji to be let off and told me to release him. Without a second thought, I did that. Cutting through the crowd, SI Tambat and I got back on the motorcycle and left.

Later, I got to know that my 'encounter cop' image had got Dawood and Jainabai worried. They took me to be a hot-headed man. I don't think they were wrong.

29

THE SPARK THAT TRIGGERED
A GANG WAR

In 1977, Sabir, Dawood, Rajji, Bada Shakeel, Bose, Sher Khan
and Khalid Pahelwan took orders from Haji Mastan. Amirzada,
Alamzeb, Iqbal Tempo, Shahzada, Ayub Lala, Liaquat and Sayeed
Batla were part of the Pathan gang controlled by Karim Lala. Since
both the gangs were involved in smuggling and drugs, their rivalry
led to violence at times. Tension kept brewing between them.

Iqbal Natik, the editor of Urdu weekly *Raazdaar*, published
articles exposing Amirzada's gang.

Acting on the leads from the *Raazdaar* report, Nagpada police
station launched proceedings against Amirzada, Alamzeb and
Iqbal Tempo as the police already had their criminal records.
Members of the Pathan gang were called to the station to record
their statements. Members of Dawood's gang, too, were called
at the same time for some reason. The Pathan gang suspected
that Dawood's gang was hand in glove with the police. They
had an altercation and later the gangs clashed with swords and
guns in broad daylight. The police had to be called in to bring the
situation under control. Amirzada, Ayub Lala and Sayeed Batla
decided to teach Dawood a lesson. They suspected that Dawood's
gang was providing information to Natik against them. On 2 July
1977, they kidnapped Natik from his residence in Dongri. Even
before a case could be registered, Natik's body was hacked and

thrown into the Dharavi Creek. This is how the Pathans vented their anger against Natik. Ayub Lala and Sayeed Batla immediately went underground.

Dawood thus found an advantageous opportunity against the Pathan gang, which was on the run, and decided to target Lala and Batla at once.

Dawood's gang managed to locate Batla and cut off his fingers. He was admitted to a hospital. The police, meanwhile, arrested him for Iqbal Natik's murder. The police also arrested Lala later. The rivalry between the two gangs intensified with every passing day.

Sayyad Miya was the cause of another major flare-up. During 1979–80, Miya and his partner Umar Baxi ran a smuggling racket. Gold would be smuggled into Bombay from Dubai by air. This was done in connivance with some Customs officers. Investigations revealed that one of the officers involved was Koppikar. A carrier, while passing through Customs, would inform him where in the aircraft he had placed the jacket full of gold biscuits. Koppikar would then wear the jacket under his uniform, walk out of the airport and hand it over to Miya. Koppikar had gained Miya's confidence by carrying out this operation three or four times. But one day, he told Miya that a consignment worth Rs 6 lakh was not to be found in the aircraft. Miya made his own inquiries and realized that Koppikar had lied. He asked Dawood's gang to get Koppikar to confess and to recover the consignment. He even asked Dawood to use his father's influence, who was a policeman.

Dawood refused to take up the job as Koppikar was a Customs officer and it would be risky to use their methods on him. Miya, however, was not willing to give up. He asked Amirzada to recover the gold. Amirzada had no such qualms. He used his might and recovered the gold from Koppikar. The moment Dawood came to know of this, he confronted Miya and warned him of dire consequences if he engaged with his rival again. He compelled him to swear that he would never give any other such job to Amirzada.

Dawood had established his supremacy in Dongri by attacking Sayeed Batla and even soured the relationship between Miya and Amirzada. This didn't go down well with the Pathan gang. With their business being affected, Amirzada and Alamzeb were left enraged. They decided to attack. Their target was Dawood's elder brother Sabir, the brain behind Dawood's gang.

30

GANG WAR ESCALATES: DAWOOD DEALS A BODY BLOW

The Amirzada gang decided to target Sabir using the principle 'the enemy's enemy is your friend'. They found a common enemy in the form of Jaffer Jamal Siddique. Dawood's associate Chota Kasu ran a matka gambling den in Pydhonie and was well-experienced when it came to smuggling. Jaffer had murdered Chota Kasu's cousin and been arrested. The matter was pending before a court.

Chota Kasu, with help from Rajji, another of Dawood's associates, had tried his best to get Jaffer convicted. Jaffer was ultimately awarded a life sentence. In jail, Jaffer met gangster Manya Surve. The two became close friends. Soon after, both of them feigned illness and had to be admitted to a hospital from where they escaped. Jaffer returned to Pydhonie to continue his criminal activities, his influence having become stronger after the murder of Chota Kasu's cousin and his friendship with Surve. One day, Chota Kasu received information that Jaffer and Surve had been seen in Bhendi Bazaar. Chota Kasu, along with Rajji, Sher Khan and Bada Shakeel, attacked them with swords and guns.

Jaffer was shot, but Surve, showing presence of mind, helped him board a bus and managed to escape. Manya took Jaffer to Thane and used his medical knowledge to extract the bullet from his body. Their friendship grew stronger. Jaffer, meanwhile, was seething with anger and sought revenge.

At this point, Amirzada extended a hand of friendship. Jaffer joined the Amirzada–Alamzeb gang. Now, Dawood and Sabir were their common enemies. They decided to leave for Kanpur to procure weapons and contacted Bully Pahelwan, the local don.

Pahelwan was an old friend of Karim Lala. He took Amirzada to the Chambal Valley and used his good offices with the notorious dacoit Mustakeem to get him nine new imported weapons, including Mauser rifles, pistols, revolvers, three other guns and 400–500 cartridges. Armed to the teeth, the Amirzada–Alamzeb gang was ready to take on Dawood's gang.

The gang had information that Sabir, who was fond of women, had recently become involved with a *mujra* dancer named Chitra. They selected 11 February 1981 as the day that they would attack Sabir.

Late that night, Amirzada, Alamzeb, Jaffer, Liaquat and Rafique watched Sabir leave Congress House with Chitra in a Fiat car. They followed him. Sabir stopped at a petrol pump in Prabhadevi around midnight and handed over the keys to the pump attendant. The gang decided that this was the right moment to strike. Alamzeb jumped in front of the car and Jaffer and Amirzada surrounded it from both sides. They pumped a volley of bullets into Sabir's body. He sank in the driver's seat.

The bloodthirsty gang then proceeded to hack the body. A ghastly sight indeed! Chitra was witness to their first target being eliminated. In the heat of the moment, they decided to eliminate their second target too—Dawood. They sped towards Bohri Mohalla, Dawood's den at Musafir Khana on Pakmodia Street, and opened fire at his residence from below. Dawood's associates and Khalid Pahelwan retaliated with gunfire. One of the bullets from Pahelwan's .12-bore gun hit Amirzada in the waist. Realizing that Amirzada could be fatally wounded, Jaffer pushed him into the Ambassador car and drove away as fast as possible. He suggested that Amirzada be treated in Thane, but Amirzada and Alamzeb refused as they did not trust Jaffer. They dropped him off at Thane and, along with Liaquat and Rafique, drove to Baroda in Gujarat. They tried getting Amirzada, whose condition was worsening, treated at the Baroda Government Hospital, but the doctors there grew suspicious. Alamzeb and his boys then took Amirzada to get him treated elsewhere in secrecy. They are rumoured to have sought refuge under infamous gangster Abdul Latif, on whom the movie *Raees* is based. It was Latif, who was friends with Alamzeb and Amirzada, who helped Amirzada recover.

Amirzada became obsessed with the thought of killing Dawood. He was still baying for his blood. After about eight months, his sources told him that Dawood was planning to go on a Hajj pilgrimage. In those days, pilgrims reached the airport in buses that left from the Musafir Khana at Crawford Market. Dawood was to travel in one such bus which Amirzada planned to stop at Mahim. He kept a watch on all the buses leaving Crawford Market. Every bus was packed, but there was no sign of Dawood.

Dawood was shrewd and did not board a bus. He went to the airport in a car and left for the pilgrimage unharmed. Some months later, the Amirzada–Alamzeb gang learnt from one of their trusted informers, Hanif Seven, that Dawood would go to Ahmedabad to attend a hearing in a Customs case in which he was an accused. The gang decided to wait for Dawood in Ahmedabad and kill him on the road leading to the court. They maintained complete secrecy. When Dawood's car, with its tinted glasses, was spotted making its way to the court, they overtook it and blocked it. They proceeded to attack him with all the firepower they possessed. Dawood was shocked for a moment, but showing great presence of mind, he ducked behind the door of the car and escaped with just an arm injury. His driver, however, was not so lucky. Dawood had escaped death for the third time. The news spread throughout Bombay—Dawood was invincible.

31

RICH BOY GONE ASTRAY

It was 24 February 1981. I was discussing a case with PI V.Y. Dange when a gentleman, about fifty years of age, came in with a woman. They looked terrified. PI Bhaskar Satam spoke to them.

'What is the matter? Please try to relax and tell us.'

'Sir, our son has been kidnapped.'

'Please tell us the details.'

'Sir, my name is Jeetubhai Shah, and this is my wife. We live on Marine Drive with our son, Uday. We own a cloth store, Sonali, in the Oberoi Shopping Centre. On the twenty-first of this month, I received a call at home from a person who asked if Uday was around. When I said that he wasn't, the caller promptly disconnected. The next day, I closed my shop at 8.30 p.m. and was looking for a taxi. Uday was with me. He said he had to meet somebody near Delhi Darbar Hotel in front of Regal Cinema. I went with him and waited till 10 p.m. but no one turned up. My son did not tell me who he had to meet. The next day, I left for the shop in the morning. Uday was still at home. My wife will tell you what happened next.'

Mrs Shah spoke in fluent Marathi. 'Around 11 a.m., I wanted to go shopping and asked Uday to accompany me. We hired a taxi and Uday directed the driver towards Sukh Sagar Restaurant at Girgaum Chowpatty. I told Uday that since we'd had breakfast at home there was no need to go to a restaurant. However, he said that he had to meet someone there at 11.30 a.m. By the time I paid the taxi driver, Uday was talking to someone near the restaurant. He asked me to wait for ten minutes. I waited for quite some time, but Uday did not turn up. I assumed that he had gone with his friend as he does not like to accompany me when I go shopping.'

'How do you know that he has been kidnapped?'

Mr Shah said, 'Sir, I was not aware of what had happened in the morning. But after I returned home, the phone rang and the caller said, "We have Uday. If you value his life, pay us Rs 5 lakh."'

'Why did you not inform the police immediately?'

'We were worried for our son's safety and were under great pressure.'

PI Satam registered a case of kidnapping. There were two possibilities. Uday may have staged his own kidnapping to extort money from his parents or he had actually been kidnapped for ransom. Since the kidnappers had used the telephone to communicate, we decided to focus on the phone at the Shahs' residence. The kidnappers had not indicated when and where the ransom was to be brought. They would definitely contact the Shahs with instructions. We decided to tap their telephone. We advised the Shahs on what should be said when the kidnappers called next. A team of policemen in plain clothes camped at the residence. The same afternoon, the telephone rang. Mr Shah spoke to the caller, 'Whoever you are, please do not harm my son. I am willing to pay you, but I do not have the full amount at the moment. Please give me at least two days to arrange for the money.'

We started tracing the calls to determine the location. They had originated from Gowalia Tank, Byculla and Nagpada. I put my informers to work at various public telephone booths. The Shahs were beginning to panic more and more. I tried my best to boost their flagging spirits. On the third day, the telephone rang again and Shah quickly picked it up. As soon as the caller disconnected,

I called up the same number to determine the location. It turned out to be a public booth in Kalanagar, Bandra (East).

We rushed to Bandra and conducted a house-to-house search in the vicinity of the phone booth. We found Uday Shah in a room on the first floor of a chawl nearby. He had been tied up and was very weak. I shifted him to a safe place and questioned him about the kidnappers. He said it was the work of Abdul Majid. I was intrigued because Majid was a resident of Ibrahim Mansion in Byculla and a member of the Asad Khan-Phundan Khan gang. What could be the connection between Uday and Majid? Who had told Majid of the Shah family's wealth?

I then laid a trap at Majid's house. We arrested Abdul Nasir Ghulam Gawas Khan, another member of Asad Khan's gang. He helped us trace Majid and Vinod Singh. Since Uday was the prime witness, we questioned him thoroughly. His revelations shocked us.

Uday Shah, a twenty-one-year-old who lived in the posh area of Marine Drive, had grown up in the lap of luxury. He had given up studies after the SSC examination and helped his father with the business. Fascinated with the underworld, he became friends with Majid, who informed Asad Khan and Phundan Khan about the wealthy Shahs. Asad Khan took advantage of this fact and asked Uday to shell out money whenever required to get his gang members out on bail. Uday would oblige. Majid knew that he had found a golden goose.

One day Majid asked Uday for Rs 5000, which was a large amount in those days. Uday could not arrange it. This got Majid's criminal mind ticking and he decided to kidnap Uday. On 21 February 1981, when he called the Shah residence, Uday's father picked up. The next day, Majid called Uday at the shop and told him that Asad Khan wanted to meet him at Delhi Darbar Hotel.

That night, Uday's father was with him, which is why Majid decided to put off the kidnapping plan. On 23 February, he told

Uday to meet him at Sukh Sagar Restaurant. One of the gang members met him there and took him to Cozy Juice Centre at Gowalia Tank. This was the haunt of the Asad Khan-Phundan Khan gang. Uday had fallen for the trap.

Uday Shah was rescued in time. I shudder to think of what could have happened to him had that not been the case.

32

SAVED IN THE NICK OF TIME

On 11 May 1982, a Crime Branch team went to Pakmodia Street in search of a suspect in a robbery case. When we reached Musafir Khana, we heard someone screaming from one of the buildings. This was the den of Dawood's gang. We rushed into the building and saw a man hanging upside down in one of the rooms. He was being beaten by Mohamed Areef, Abdul Rehman Rashid Khan, Mehmood Khan, Chota Shakeel, Hanif Kutta, Taufique Takla, Abdul Kadar Ibrahim, Taufique Shaikh and Ali Abdul Antulay (Dawood's cousin). They were armed with swords and sticks. We disarmed and arrested them. The victim, twenty-two-year-old Sureshkumar Pran Nagarkar, was rescued and a case was registered.

Nagarkar was a resident of Sakinaka and worked in the flight catering section of Hotel Plaza near Santacruz airport on a salary of Rs 800 per month. His duties included handling breakfast and lunch packets for passengers travelling in Indian Airlines and Gulf Air planes. He had a colleague named Mohammed Kazi. Nagarkar had noticed that Mohammed was a spendthrift and lived a luxurious life. One day, he asked Mohammed the secret behind his lavish lifestyle. Mohammed said, 'Suresh, in order to live life king-sized, one has to take risks. You can earn a lot of money if you are willing to take risks.'

Mohammed told him that he was involved in smuggling gold coming in from Dubai on Gulf Air flights. He even explained the modus operandi to him. In those days, gold smuggling was at an all-time high. The air route was the preferred mode of bringing in gold. The smugglers, referred to as carriers, strapped on a jacket laden with gold biscuits provided to them at Dubai airport. When the flight landed in Bombay, the carrier would be the last person to leave the aircraft after depositing the jacket in the dustbin in the toilet and covering it up with paper napkins. The carrier would then leave the airport after going through the immigration check. An airport staff member would then board the plane on the pretext of cleaning it, pick up the jacket and wear it under his uniform. Since they do not need to clear the Customs channel, they would leave the airport and hand over the jacket to Dawood's gang members who would be waiting outside. Nagarkar decided to make a quick buck. Mohammed Kazi introduced him to a person named Mohammed, who explained the plan to him. There was just one hitch. Although Nagarkar was a supervisor, he was not authorized to board an aircraft. Nagarkar took Vijay Kesurani, who had the authority to enter an aircraft, into confidence and tempted him with money. Vijay agreed to help him. After a flight landed, he brought the jacket hidden in the toilet to Nagarkar, who delivered it to Mohammed who was waiting outside the airport.

On 28 March 1982, the first consignment of fifty gold biscuits landed. There were two jackets, each containing twenty-five biscuits. Each biscuit weighed 100 grams. As per the plan, Vijay played his part. Nagarkar then handed over the jackets to Mohammed who was waiting for him at Juhu Beach. Mohammed paid Nagarkar Rs 18,000 for his services. Nagarkar gave Vijay Rs 10,000 from this. On 10 April, a consignment of sixty biscuits landed. Mohammed gave Nagarkar Rs 18,000 on delivery. Nagarkar paid Vijay Rs 13,000 this time.

On 17 April 1982, a consignment of 100 biscuits arrived. Mohammed gave Nagarkar Rs 20,000. Nagarkar gave Vijay

Rs 13,000 for doing his bit. On 9 May, another Gulf Air flight landed in Bombay at 5.35 a.m. This time, it was a consignment of 100 biscuits in four jackets. As usual, Vijay went to get the jackets from the aircraft. Mohammed, meanwhile, was waiting for Nagarkar at Juhu Beach. Hours passed by and Mohammed was losing patience. He called Nagarkar.

'Nagarkar Bhai, is the work done?'

'What work? Your carrier didn't deposit the consignment in the toilet.'

'What?'

Mohammed was shocked to hear this. He had received confirmation that the gold had been loaded on to the aircraft in Dubai. Nagarkar, however, had denied this. Mohammed then called Nagarkar to Andheri. He and four other gangsters told Nagarkar to take them to Vijay's house and asked him to call him downstairs. The gang took Nagarkar and Vijay to a building near Jaslok Hospital and threatened them with dire consequences if the gold was not returned. The duo stuck to their version of the story. On 11 May 1982, Mohammed called Nagarkar to Vile Parle railway station at 3 p.m. Nagarkar kept his appointment. He was then brought to the Musafir Khana on Pakmodia Street where Dawood's gang members tortured him to get him to confess. We had managed to rescue Nagarkar in the nick of time. The case was handed over to Customs, who recovered the gold from Musafir Khana in Nagpada.

Nagarkar's lust for wealth had made him double-cross the dangerous Dawood gang. He had risked his life for money despite having a respectable job.

33

FLAMBOYANT PATHAN BROUGHT TO JUSTICE

One afternoon, when I was finishing paperwork at the office, a man entered with his arm in a bandage. I asked him, 'What is the matter?'

He replied, 'I am a trader from Malkapur. I had gone to Nagpada to buy some *patra*s (tin boxes) when an open jeep abruptly came to a halt near me. There were three young men and two fair girls seated in it. One of the men ordered me to hand over my bag. When I refused to do so, he whipped out a knife and slashed my arm before snatching my bag and driving away. The bag contained Rs 98,000. I was attacked and robbed in broad daylight. No one came to my rescue.'

I was wondering why he had come to me instead of approaching the nearest police station. His next statement made things clear. 'Sir, I went to a doctor at the corner of the street. He bandaged my arm and advised me to contact you.'

He had noted the registration number of the jeep. Based on the description of the attackers he gave, I concluded that this was the work of the Asad Khan-Phundan Khan gang.

Phundan Khan was a former associate of Karim Lala. He was a powerful ganglord from Rampur who loved charas. I knew his son Asad Khan, a tall and well-built Pathan, as I had arrested him in connection with a car theft case when I was posted at Colaba police station. His father had got him released as he was still a minor then.

The starting point of the case in question was the jeep. I asked my informers to keep a lookout for it. Within an hour, one of them had located it and confirmed that it belonged to Asad Khan, whose den was Cozy Juice Centre at Gowalia Tank. I went to the spot and saw him, dressed in a Pathani suit, sipping a tall glass of juice.

The moment he saw me, he took to his heels shouting, 'Police! Police!'

I went after him. The chase continued through Pan Gully to Kemps Corner and towards the Parsi Tower of Silence before he decided to go on to Kemps Corner flyover. He jumped off it and landed on the main road, a good seven to eight feet below. I jumped after him. Being an athlete and trained in judo and karate, I landed on my feet like a cat. Asad Khan did not have this advantage and fell flat. He tried to get up and run again, but I caught him.

I paraded him through the streets he had terrorized. The shopkeepers heaved a sigh of relief. Asad Khan and his gang would regularly extort money from them. He wore a bandana around his forehead and an armband. He looked like a Bollywood don. He drove around in an open jeep. His flamboyant style had attracted two Parsi girls from Gowalia Tank who roamed around with him in the jeep. Asad Khan would flaunt them like trophies. His associates Jardulla Khan and Kader Mohamed were arrested later.

That night, Jardulla Khan took the aluminium cup kept in the lock-up for drinking water and managed to compress it into a cone that he used to injure himself with. In the court the next day, he alleged that I had beaten him up and forced him to confess. His advocate, Rashid Matdar, also tried to raise a hue and cry about police brutality but the court saw through this game and sent them to further police custody. I recovered all the stolen property and submitted a chargesheet in the court. The investigation in this case also led to four other cases being solved. This included the case of a stolen jeep.

This episode meant the end of this gang in Bombay.

34

FIRST ENCOUNTER IN THE HISTORY OF BOMBAY POLICE

Manohar Arjun Surve, aka Manya Surve, attended school in Pinto Villa, Dadar, around 1969. He turned to a life of crime because of his brother, Bhargav Surve. Bhargav ran a matka gambling den in Dadar and was a rival of the Date–Dandekar gang. Bhargav and Manya killed Dandekar and were arrested by PI Dabholkar of Dadar police station. In order to end the terror Bhargav and Manya had unleashed, PI Dabholkar turned Manya's associate Charles into the state's witness. The result was that Justice Gupte sentenced Manya and Bhargav to life imprisonment for murdering Dandekar. On hearing the verdict, an enraged Manya threatened to kill PI Dabholkar. This happened in the presence of a judge and the government pleader.

Manya was sent to Yerwada Jail in Pune. He planned his escape by feigning illness. He was admitted to Sassoon General Hospital for intensive care, but under police supervision. Manya's friends Bajya Sawant and Shaikh Munir helped him escape. The police conducted a manhunt, but every time they would be about to nab him, he would manage to get away. Manya also started threatening PI Dabholkar over the telephone, and even went to the extent of stalking him. Such was the impact on PI Dabholkar that he moved to New Delhi to live with his daughter.

Manya's sworn enemy, Suhas Narayan Bhatkar, aka Potya, operated in Dadar's Agar Bazaar. Their rivalry was because of the extortion money (*hafta*) to be collected from matka gambling dens and illicit liquor joints. A war erupted between the two. On 4 March 1977, Manya fell into a trap set by the Crime Branch and was sent to Yerwada Jail again. Potya, too, was serving a sentence in Yerwada. Both of them came to blows frequently and, consequently, Manya was shifted to Ratnagiri Jail. There, Manya went on a hunger strike. There was no option but to shift him to a government hospital. Of course, Manya had thought of this in advance and was waiting for an opportunity to escape.

On 14 November 1979, Manya managed to flee from the hospital despite an armed police escort being present. Once outside, he formed a new gang consisting of Prakash, aka Shendi Misal, Uday Shetty, Bajya Sawant, Shaikh Munir, Ravi Kamathi and Kishore Sawant and spread a reign of terror in Bombay and its surrounding towns.

The gang looted hotels, bars and matka gambling dens in broad daylight. And then Manya dealt a blow to the police by planning an attack on Vijay, a convict in police custody, who happened to be an enemy of Shendi Misal. Manya's gang overtook the police jeep carrying Vijay and stopped it. When the two constables in the jeep got out, Manya stabbed them with a *gupti* (dagger). The driver of the jeep sped away and Vijay survived. The stabbing of the policemen caused a furore. On 24 April 1980, Manya and his gang looted Rs 1,50,000 from a milk supply van in Mahim. On 28 April 1980, they looted Rs 1,60,000 in Navi Mumbai. The police launched a full-scale war against Manya's gang and arrested Krishna, Chandu and Kishore. Manya, however, remained absconding. He had now armed himself with a new weapon: acid. Being a student of science, he was aware of its lethal effects and ways to procure it.

In one case, Manya entered the office of Ashok Mastakar of Mastakar Travels in Dadar and threw acid on him for not meeting his demands. This was despite the fact that Ashok was his classmate in school. A grievously injured Ashok had to be rushed to Sion Hospital. A police escort was stationed there. But Manya had the audacity to enter the hospital in the guise of a doctor and threaten Mastakar there too. Another of Manya's victims was Mangal, a provision storekeeper. Mangal, however, succumbed to his injuries in hospital. Manya then targeted Slimwell Gymnasium in Mahim, which was owned by one Pappi Patil.

Patil, a bodybuilder, refused to give in to Manya's threats. Manya responded by shooting at Patil with a pistol in his gym. The bullet hit Patil in the thigh. While Manya fled from there, his double game worked out just as planned. An injured Patil was more likely to pay up and a lethal attack on a famous bodybuilder would send a message to the others to either pay up or face the consequences.

Manya knew that he was on the police's hit list. PI Yashwant Bhide of the Crime Branch had come to know that Manya often used stolen cars and had taken a known car thief into confidence. The thief informed PI Bhide that he would give Manya a car at 1.30 p.m. on 11 January 1982 near Ambedkar College in Wadala. Manya and his gang were planning to use it to loot a bank in Vashi. Operation Manya Surve was set into motion at the Crime Branch under the supervision of PI Issac Samson. I had gone to the office as usual on that day and had no inkling about any of it. Being a junior officer, I was assigned the mundane work of filling in details of senior officers' insurance policies. While I was immersed in the paperwork, PI Samson happened to glance at me and said, 'Take Bagwan into our team. We need someone who looks like a college boy.'

I had put in seven to eight years of service but still looked boyish. Two teams were formed. One team consisted of SIs Raja

Tambat, Sanjay Parande, Vilas Shirke, PI Yashwant Bhide and me. Our team was supposed to lay a trap outside Ambedkar College and nab Manya. The second team, led by PI Shivaji Sawant, was supposed to lay a trap in Vashi. This was to ensure that Manya would be caught at Vashi in case he escaped from Wadala. Manya was always armed with a Mauser revolver, grenades and acid bulbs. He was known to attack without warning. We decided to keep watch in a private car outside Ambedkar College.

As Operation Manya Surve was being streamlined, I told PI Samson, 'Sir, please let me drive the car.'

He studied me for a second and then said, 'Okay, done!'

PI Samson had acquired a golden Hillman car from a mechanic, Vikas, who had a garage in Dhobi Talao's Wellington Terrace. We left for our mission. I was driving with SI Tambat seated next to me. The other three officers were seated behind us. Our informer had told us exactly where the car was to be parked near Ambedkar College. We parked some distance away from that spot, next to a bus stop. Around 1.30 p.m., a taxi stopped a little ahead of us. Manya was sitting inside with a woman. PI Bhide was the only officer who could identify him. We had been instructed to be patient. The taxi door opened and the woman got out to cross the road. I came out of the car and sat on the bonnet. I held a few books in my right hand with a revolver hidden under them. I was playing the part of a college boy waiting for his girlfriend, but my eyes were fixed at the college gate. My colleagues, too, were waiting. At this moment, the woman walked past our car, throwing a casual look at me. She walked up to the Fiat provided by the car thief and examined it before walking back towards the taxi. She walked past our car and sat inside the taxi. She was the scout sent to check if everything was all right for Manya to step out. Some seconds went by. A man dressed in a white shirt and trousers stepped out of the taxi. PI Bhide confirmed that it was Manya.

I was still seated on the bonnet. Manya walked past me. For a moment, I considered grabbing him by the waist. But Manya appeared to be strongly built and it would not be wise to do so. Every second was important. He had barely walked two to three steps away from me when I moved quickly to take position behind him. I called out, '*Aye,* Manya, *thaamb!* (stop)'

Shocked, Manya turned around, losing his balance. Trying to take advantage of his position, he reached for his Mauser that was tucked inside his sock. He fired at me. The bullets missed me by inches. Just then a BEST bus arrived at the bus stop. The conductor stepped out to see what was happening and was injured because of Manya's random firing.

I, meanwhile, positioned myself to take the perfect shot. I fired at Manya from just six feet. The bullet found its mark. 'Raja, fire!' I shouted.

SI Tambat, too, fired at Manya. He was wounded but didn't stop abusing the police. The moment he sank to the ground, Hawaldar Bargude and Constable Pawar caught him.

Just then, the college bell rang and students started pouring out of the gate. PI Samson and the constables had a tough time controlling the crowd. We rushed the wounded conductor and Manya to Sion Hospital. Manya was declared dead on arrival.

We wanted to arrest Manya Surve alive. Had he not opened fire at us, he would have been alive.

This incident was recorded as the first encounter in the history of the Bombay Police.

Every police officer dreams of getting a chance to fire at least once in his lifetime. The Manya Surve encounter gave me a chance to do so very early in my career. PI Bhide, SI Raja Tambat and I were awarded the police medal for gallantry by the then Governor of Maharashtra, Air Chief Marshal (retd) I.H. Latif.

35

RAJ BHAVAN SMUGGLING CASE

It was 1982. Smuggling in Bombay was at an all-time high. There was great demand for imported goods that were sold as soon as they landed. Contraband was smuggled into the city through various routes. One of the most daring and innovative methods adopted was to land smuggled goods on the exclusive beach of Raj Bhavan, the residence of the Governor of Maharashtra. Goods smuggled across the Arabian Sea in mechanized dhows were offloaded into small boats and brought to the Raj Bhavan beach. Of course, this was done in connivance with some employees at Raj Bhavan and Gamdevi police station. The then Commissioner of Police (Greater Bombay) J.F. Ribeiro refused to turn a blind eye to this activity. At midnight, a resident of Walkeshwar informed the police control room that smuggled goods were being unloaded at the Raj Bhavan beach.

The police rushed to the spot and seized the contraband. When Commissioner Ribeiro heard a wireless message about smuggled goods being seized, he ordered the Crime Branch to conduct a raid at Raj Bhavan. We did so under the supervision of PI R.R. Kolekar.

A gate next to the Consulate General of Afghanistan, which led to Raj Bhavan, was guarded by SRPF constables. We found gold hidden in the lunch boxes of these constables. Their bags, which hung from the trees, were filled with expensive watches and silver.

We arrested them. Two police officers from Gamdevi police station were also suspended. The raid made headlines and caused a furore. Since this was a smuggling case, the Crime Branch handed over the case to the Bombay Customs.

It was common knowledge that the mastermind and kingpin behind this was Keshav Bhogle (name changed). He was a landing contractor for smuggling operations and wielded a lot of influence in the police and Customs circles, many of whom were on his payroll.

The news kicked up such a storm that the Customs authorities were left with no option but to pursue the case. When they raided Bhogle's residence on the ground floor of Mansarovar building, they found nothing. Bhogle himself was untraceable. The media continued to mount pressure with headlines like: 'Raj Bhavan: A smuggler's haven'. The Customs department was forced to issue a non-bailable warrant against Bhogle. The execution of this warrant was the duty of the Crime Branch (CID), Bombay.

The police had some information on Bhogle as he had served as a constable during 1979–80, till he was dismissed from service for his involvement in the illicit liquor trade. Bhogle had then entered the political arena under the tutelage of A.R. Antulay, then chief minister of Maharashtra. He became the Youth Congress president for Bombay. He indulged in smuggling under the cover of his political umbrella. He even travelled in Antulay's official car, with the security entourage and media in tow. Bhogle took the chief minister for a guided tour of the illicit liquor distilleries that operated in Dharavi. The nocturnal visit did not go unreported. Mr Ribeiro, who was then the Addl CP (Crime), had to bear the brunt of it all. It paved the way for his transfer to the newly created post of DIG of Police (Railways), Maharashtra, a far cry from the coveted position of chief of the Crime Branch (CID), Bombay.

This transfer had led to a lot of resentment building up within the Bombay Police. An upright and honest officer of Mr Ribeiro's calibre had been shunted out while Bhogle continued to indulge in smuggling with political patronage. It was high time that his criminal activities were exposed.

This was not 1979, it was 1982. Mr Ribeiro had returned as the Commissioner of Police (Greater Bombay), and there was a new chief minister at the helm. This was a golden opportunity for Commissioner Ribeiro to bring the culprit to book. He formed a special squad, members of which he hand-picked, to crack down on Bhogle's activities. Bhogle owned a bar called Banjara in Byculla. Raids were conducted at Banjara Bar and his residence in Mansarovar building opposite the Maharashtra chief minister's bungalow, Varsha.

'Bagwan. Get me Keshav Bhogle,' Commissioner Ribeiro told me. He called me 'hot boy' at times because, according to him, I was a slightly hot-headed young man. I left in the Detection Crime Branch Ambassador car with two constables. We reached Bhogle's residence where his domestic help opened the door.

'Is Keshav Bhogle at home?'

'Sahib is not at home.'

'Is Mrs Bhogle at home?'

Before the help could answer, Mrs Bhogle appeared at the door. I showed her the warrant and explained what it said. She agreed to allow us to search the premises, but we found nothing. A thought struck me. While leaving, I put my hand on the help's shoulder and said, 'Mr Bhogle and I are on good terms, which is why I am here. We are not going to show anything in the panchnama. Our work is done. There is just one thing lacking, and that is Keshavrao's ['Rao' is a Marathi suffix used to show respect] signature. After that, your boss will be freed of this problem permanently.'

The servant relaxed.

'It is very important that Keshavrao signs this paper. It will be excellent if you can tell me where he is.'

The servant probably thought that I was one of the police officers who were close friends with his boss. He seemed more than willing to help. 'Nothing will happen to my boss?'

I put an arm around his shoulder and reassured him. 'Once he signs this paper, I am leaving.'

'Come. I will take you to the boss.'

We got into our car and drove away. A little distance away, the help pointed to a bungalow. 'Sir, boss is in there.'

We were astonished. This was the residence of a minister, Nanabhau Yembedwar. The security personnel on duty told us that the minister was working inside. I knocked on the door and was ushered in. I saw Keshav Bhogle, wearing a crisp white safari suit, sitting in front of the minister. I spoke to the minister.

'Sir, I am SI Isaque Bagwan from the Detection Crime Branch, CID. I have to question Mr Bhogle about an important matter.'

'I am busy in a meeting. I will come to your office later. You may leave,' Bhogle replied.

I addressed the minister again. 'The matter is of utmost importance. I will not be able to leave without questioning him. Please send him outside for two minutes.'

Bhogle tried to intimidate me. 'Wait outside! Can't you see I'm busy with Sahib?'

I did not budge. 'This is urgent. We need to talk now.'

The minister spoke to Bhogle. 'Bhogle, go and see what he wants. One should not come in the way of government work.'

Bhogle was left with no choice but to step outside. As soon as he came out, I showed him the warrant and held his hand tight. He was not willing to cooperate. I pulled him along and pushed him into our jeep before rushing back to the Crime Branch. Commissioner Ribeiro had come down from his office and was waiting in Sr PI (Administration) Y. Tarte's cabin. On seeing me, he exclaimed, 'Well done, my boy.'

In the press conference which followed, Commissioner Ribeiro said, 'The brain behind the Raj Bhavan smuggling, Keshav Bhogle, was arrested at a minister's bungalow.'

The news sent the political circles into a frenzy. Vasantdada Patil, then chief minister of Maharashtra, called Commissioner Ribeiro to find out how Bhogle had been arrested. He then asked the commissioner to visit Yembedwar at the Mantralaya. Commissioner Ribeiro asked me to accompany him. When we met the minister, he greeted us with folded hands. 'I was speaking to him [Bhogle] as a party functionary. How was I to know what crimes have been committed by the people visiting me? Whatever action your officer has taken is correct. But I request you to change your statement. Show that he was arrested somewhere else.'

Commissioner Ribeiro agreed. As we were leaving, he patted me on the back and said, 'Bagwan, see how this minister was requesting us to obfuscate facts. This happened because of an officer like you.'

'Keep it up, my hot boy!' I will never forget what my idol, Commissioner Ribeiro, said that day.

36

BELGIAN DIAMOND ROBBERY

In 1982, Parmanand Patel, an MP from Madhya Pradesh, was in Bombay to attend a wedding. He was accompanied by his friend Diwanji Joshi. After the function was over, Patel left for Jabalpur by air. Before leaving, he left a bag with Joshi who was to leave by the Gitanjali Express the same night. Joshi placed the bag with his own luggage in the coach and stepped out of the train to meet those who had come to bid him goodbye. He boarded the train when the whistle blew. Just as it was about to leave, he realized that Patel's bag was missing. He raised an alarm because the bag contained family jewels, including Belgian diamonds, gold necklaces and other jewellery. He contacted Patel to inform him about the loss.

Patel was a powerful political figure, and the government machinery swung into action swiftly. An FIR was lodged at the VT railway police station. The total value of the stolen goods was over Rs 50 lakh. A week passed by but the railway police was unable to manage a breakthrough. All investigations led to a dead end. The Crime Branch was entrusted with a parallel inquiry but, as a matter of fact, the entire police department was pursuing the matter. Fifteen days passed, but there was no clue.

One morning, while PI Kolekar and I were working in the office, Hawaldar Pandit entered with a person. 'Sir, this is my informer, Pande. He lives in the area that comes under

Lokmanya Tilak Marg police station. Please listen to what he has to say.'

Pande spoke. 'Sir, the other day, I was sitting in a bar in Pydhonie. I overheard two persons talking and what they said made me suspicious.'

'What were they saying?'

'They were talking about selling gold, but they were looking for a goldsmith who was willing to take risks and ask no questions. I felt that they were trying to sell stolen property.' Pande told us that one of them was a regular customer at the bar. I went there with Hawaldar Pandit, Constable Deshmukh and Pande. We maintained surveillance for over a week. After about eight days, the suspect was spotted entering the bar alone. Pande pointed him out to us. We arrested him. Initially, he refused to confess. But after intense interrogation, he said his name was Hussain and that a person named Imran had given him gold necklaces. We then arrested Imran and recovered all the stolen jewellery. MP Patel came to Bombay to identify his jewellery. He was so happy that he announced a cash reward of Rs 10,000 to the Crime Branch and also made a huge donation to the Police Welfare Fund.

This case exemplifies the invaluable role played by informers in solving baffling cases.

37

STENCH OF A GUTTER: CLUE TO A KIDNAPPING

I worked in the Crime Branch under the direct supervision of PI Madhukar Zende and handled complicated cases of chain-snatching, housebreaking, theft, robberies and murder. On 24 September 1982, a constable informed us about the arrival of thespian Dilip Kumar at the commissioner's office. We thought that such a famous actor must have come to see the commissioner for the renewal of his gun licence or some other security matter. But that was not the case. Within a few minutes, Commissioner Ribeiro had summoned PI Zende to his office. He asked me to come with him.

When we reached the commissioner's office, we saw Dilip Kumar sitting with two other people. Commissioner Ribeiro said, 'This is Mr Mushir and Mr Riaz.'

Then he spoke to the two men. 'These are my super cops. You can tell them everything.'

One of them turned to us. 'My name is Mushir. I am the producer of a film called *Shakti*. Two days ago, I left my office, M.R. Productions, with my friend Harish. We were in my car. I was driving towards Haji Ali. I dropped Harish at his office behind Poddar Hospital in Worli. Just as I approached Haji Ali, a white Ambassador car overtook mine and blocked it. I was forced to stop. Three men emerged from the car and pulled me out. They were armed and pushed me into their car after blindfolding me. They pushed me to the floor of the car, took me to their hideout and demanded Rs 20 lakh. I requested Harish to give me Rs 2 lakh urgently. I promised to pay the remaining Rs 18 lakh as soon as possible. That was when they set me free.'

We heard him out but had no clue about who was behind it all. Since Mushir was blindfolded, he could not identify the kidnappers or tell us where they had taken him. I wanted to ask him a couple of questions but was not sure whether I should do so in front of the commissioner. PI Zende saw me hesitate. 'Bagwan, do you have any clue? Any questions or suggestions?'

'Sir, if you permit me, may I ask Mushir some questions?'

'Go ahead. You can ask any question. Don't hesitate.'

'Mushirbhai, they blindfolded you at Haji Ali?'

'Yes, Sir.'

'How much time did it take you to reach the room where you were confined?'

'Approximately ten to twelve minutes.'

The only likely places within ten to twelve minutes from Haji Ali were Nagpada or Dongri.

'What happened then?'

'After we stepped out of the car, they made me walk on a gutter.'

'If you were blindfolded, how did you know it was a gutter?'

'Sir, I know from the stench that assailed my nostrils.'

I suspected the place to be Nagpada as such gutters were to be found there in those days.

'How long did it take you to reach the building after crossing the gutter?'

'The building was close to it.'

'How did you climb the stairs? Did the kidnappers help you?'

'I slipped once, after which one of them took my hand and placed it on the railing.'

'On which side was the railing: right or left?'

'On the right side.'

'How many steps did you climb?'

'About ten to twelve steps.'

'You must have stopped on the first floor. Did you turn to the left or to the right?'

'I turned to the right.'

'Did they immediately take you to a room or did you have to climb some more steps?'

'No, Sir. After reaching the first floor, I had to walk a few steps. Perhaps it was the passage of the building.'

My suspicions were confirmed. This was a chawl in Nagpada. 'Then what happened?'

'Sir, while I was in the passage, I could hear the voices of children. They were reading verses from the Koran.'

'Then what happened?'

'They took me to a room, locked it from inside, removed my blindfold and started threatening me with dire consequences.'

'What did you see in the room?'

'The room was empty except for two chairs, and there was a photo frame with a picture of Mecca and Medina above the door.'

Mushir's description suggested that the room was in Nagpada. I was aware of Koran classes being conducted there.

I got up. 'Sir, I have a clue.'

'Go ahead, Bagwan,' said Commissioner Ribeiro, smiling.

I went to Nagpada to look for a building which had a gutter next to it and a staircase on the right side. Our team went to the fifth lane in Nagpada. The first building was Cheena building, but that was not the one we were looking for. Next to it was Kadar building, and it had railings on the right. We went up to the first floor. In the first room on the left was a classroom for children. We realized that we were on the right track. I turned right as described by Mushir. I passed two rooms and found the third room latched.

I unlocked it and saw two chairs inside. When I looked up, I saw the photo Mushir had spoken of.

In the meantime, a crowd gathered. The entry of the police had caused a sensation. Amidst the crowd, I saw Salim, the only male dancer at Soniya Mahal. I asked him, 'Who does this room belong to?'

'Sir, this is the inquiry room of the Amirzada–Alamzeb gang.'

I called PI Zende and informed him of the development. Naik Pansare of the Crime Branch told him that this was Kadar building. This information was like music to his ears. He knew which gang operated where.

PI Zende ordered me to take action immediately. Now, I had to confront the Pathan gang. I would have to tread carefully, but I had nothing to fear as I had complete support from Commissioner Ribeiro and PI Zende. Unfortunately, such support from seniors is lacking today.

I went to Temkar Mohalla near Do Tanki to gather information about Amirzada and Alamzeb from Bastar, a resident of the area. He was an informer for Dawood's gang and had already become a part of my network too. He regularly updated me about pickpocket gangs in the city. He said, 'After the murder of Sabirbhai, there has been a lot of tension in the area. All members of the underworld have gone underground.'

Amirzada, Alamzeb and Jaffer Ismail Siddique had been absconding since Sabir's murder. That they had kidnapped Mushir even while they were wanted by the police indicated that they had a hideout near Bombay. Rumour had it that they were holed up under the refuge of two local bigwigs—MLA Liaquat Rafiq and gangster Abdul Latif who enjoyed his fifteen minutes of fame when Shah Rukh Khan played him in the movie *Raees*.

'Take me to the den of any one of them.'

'Sir, Alamzeb can be found on the second floor of Ali building on Duncan Road.'

I took Bastar to Duncan Road. Alamzeb was not to be found at home, but I met his father, Jangrez Khan. I also arrested a young man, Salim, who I thought was suspicious. The moment we left Ali building, I asked a constable to keep Salim at a distance. I walked to our Ambassador car which was parked at a distance. Bastar was sitting inside with his face covered. 'Sir, the boy you have arrested is Salim Bhangi, aka Sanya. He is an associate of Alamzeb's brother, Shahzada, and is involved in the murder of Abu Kaliya.'

I went back to Salim and asked him, 'Salim, where are Amirzada and Alamzeb?'

It wasn't long before Salim confessed to his role in kidnapping Mushir and said that Amirzada and Alamzeb had fled to Kalapur in Ahmedabad to seek refuge under MLA Rafiq. He added that Shahzada had gone to Shegaon.

PI Zende formed two teams. One comprised SIs Bawiskar and Jeremiah and Hawaldars More and Narayan Parab, who left for Ahmedabad. The other team comprising PI Bhaskar Satam and me left for Malkapur by the Nagpur Express to look for Shahzada. We took a taxi from Malkapur to Shegaon but could not locate him. Later, we came to know that Shahzada had given Salim false information to mislead the police. We returned to Bombay empty-handed. But the team that went to Ahmedabad had better luck. They were combing through Kalapur when Constable Parab spotted a white Ambassador car parked outside a gambling den. Parab identified the car and Amirzada. Soon, Amirzada was arrested and brought to Bombay. When I was interrogating him, he said, 'Sir, we got a tip-off about Mushir from one Ahmed Sayad Khan, a resident of Wanja Wadi in Mahim.'

The same day, I went to Chappra building in Mahim and arrested Khan. His father also accompanied us to the Crime Branch. At the same time, Amirzada's father, Nabab Khan, was also brought in for questioning. In the detention room, while we were busy with paperwork, Hawaldar Parab noticed Amirzada's father slipping a piece of paper into Khan's father's hand. He took it and showed it to PI Zende. Amirzada's father had addressed a note to his son-in-law, Nasir Pathan, in Urdu. It read: 'Ahmed has been arrested by the police. Go to the rear of the building and remove all the weapons buried in the ground.' PI Zende ordered some of the officers to seize this important evidence.

Khan's interrogation around his involvement in Mushir's kidnapping revealed the following facts:

Twenty-nine-year-old Ahmed Sayad Khan lived with his parents in Chappra building in Wanja Wadi. He had two brothers, Mohammed Salim and Abdul Wahab. Both were married and lived in Rustom Manzil near Mount Mary Church in Bandra. Abdul Wahab was a film artist and Ahmed was a production manager. Ahmed had a very close friend, Abu Bakar, a resident of Mahim. One day, Abu took Ahmed to Bhendi Bazaar and introduced him to Amirzada who invited him to his sister's wedding. Ahmed was impressed that Amirzada, a well-known figure of the underworld, had invited him so cordially. Amirzada then introduced him to Alamzeb, Shahzada and Mehmood Kaliya.

Ahmed was overawed to be in the company of dons. Amirzada and Ahmed's friendship blossomed and they started meeting regularly. Ahmed started distancing himself when he came to know that the Amirzada gang was involved in recovering money and extortion. Some months passed. One day, before 1982, Alamzeb came to Ahmed's house. When Ahmed inquired about Amirzada's role in Sabir's murder, Alamzeb remained silent. In July 1982, Amirzada and Alamzeb again paid Ahmed a visit. Ahmed was frightened. 'We have come to you because you are in the film industry. You have to show us some party whose money is stuck in the business and is having difficulties recovering it. Show us someone who has black money. You must do this for us.'

Ahmed was scared, but he had no option but to help the gang. That is when he remembered Harish. Harish had a well-furnished office, 'Glamour Colour', from where he did publicity work for Bollywood. Harish had done some work for Ahmed's film *Tajurba*. About a month earlier, Ahmed's brother Mohammed had gone with Harish to Studio Chandrakant in Mahim. During this meeting, Ahmed had come to know that there was Rs 90 lakh belonging to Mushir in Harish's office. Ahmed desperately wanted to extricate himself from the clutches of this gang and was happy to share this information with Amirzada.

Amirzada had met Harish at a trial show. He had found an easy target.

On 23 September 1982, Shahzada, Liaquat and two others kidnapped Mushir. Since Mushir did not have the full amount with him, they beat him mercilessly. When he could not bear it any longer, he took Harish's name. Shahzada and Liaquat asked Amirzada to confirm with Ahmed if Harish had the money. Once Amirzada gave the go-ahead, Shahzada and Liaquat went to Harish's residence in Madhav building near Shivaji Park. They took Rs 2 lakh from him. Mushir promised to pay the balance amount of Rs 18 lakh soon. He was released after that.

We were left wondering why the Amirzada–Alamzeb gang had resorted to kidnapping to extort money. In those days, the gang had unleashed a reign of terror and managed to extort money with ease. There was no need to kidnap Mushir.

Once the whole picture was taken into consideration, we realized that all attempts to kill Dawood had taken a heavy toll on the financial resources of the gang. They desperately needed funds, which is why they had forced Ahmed Sayyad Khan to identify rich targets in the film industry, who in turn led them to Mushir.

38

JAFFER JAMAL SIDDIQUE

With Amirzada's arrest, the Sabir murder case had been solved by the team comprising PI Bhaskar Satam, SIs Suresh Bawiskar, Jeremiah and myself, under the supervision of PI Madhukar Zende. However, one accused, Jaffer Jamal Siddique, was still at large. When we questioned Amirzada about his whereabouts, he said, 'After murdering Sabir at Prabhadevi, we went to Dawood's den at Musafir Khana. We came under heavy gunfire and I was wounded. Jaffer put me in the car and started driving towards Ahmedabad, but he got off before we left Bombay. I lost track of him that day.'

This was a clue that Jaffer was still in Bombay. His had become a dreaded name in Pydhonie after he murdered Chota Kasu's cousin and Sabir. He had been extorting large amounts of money in the area. I wondered who was collecting the extortion money and how it was being delivered to Jaffer. I alerted my informers. Soon, one of them told me that Gani, one of Jaffer's close friends, collected the extortion money and handed it over to him. It would be difficult to turn Gani against his friend, and attempting to do so also meant risking that Gani might alert Jaffer. I thought of using one of Gani's friends, Nizam, aka Nizam Don, to convince him to lead us to Jaffer. I had earlier arrested Nizam in the Shafi Toofani case.

'Look, Nizam, you introduce me to Gani and I swear that no one will touch a single hair of yours.'

'Sir, I have implicit faith in you but the matter is complicated. However, I will try my best.'

Soon, Nizam arranged a meeting with Gani. I tried to gain Gani's confidence, but he was hesitant. Nizam told him, 'Gani, I know Bagwan Sahib very well. Today, if you do something for him, tomorrow he will reward you and your future will be bright.'

Gani said, 'Since Bagwan Sahib has come to the Crime Branch, I have heard a lot of good things about him. But the problem is that if I lead him to Jaffer and he gets arrested and suspects me, I will be a dead man.'

There was truth in what Gani was saying. Everyone in the underworld knew that Jaffer was a close friend of Manya Surve's and a man with a mean streak. If Jaffer was to escape from jail as he had done in the past, Gani's days would be numbered. 'Gani, you give me Jaffer and I will arrest you with him to ward off any suspicion. I leave it to you to decide.'

Gani appeared convinced. 'Sir, I will make an effort.'

I kept coaxing him. 'Gani, you have never worked with me until today. Just try.'

I returned to the office and told PI Zende about the developments. He told me to stay in touch with Gani. It was the morning of 7 November 1982. My wife handed over my wallet and handkerchief to me as I headed out.

'Will you be able to come home early this evening?' she asked.

'Why? Are we going out?'

She pointed to the calendar. It was my son, Sohail's, second birthday. I had forgotten. 'Sorry, I forgot. Don't worry, we will celebrate Sohail's birthday on a grand scale at Apollo Hotel. I will invite PI Zende and the other officers.'

I left home after kissing Sohail goodbye and went straight to Apollo Hotel. On reaching office, I invited PI Zende and my colleagues. Just then, the phone rang. It was Gani.

'Sir, Gani speaking. Jaffer is going to meet me around 8.30–9 a.m. tomorrow near Mulund Civil Hospital.' When PI Zende was informed, he was pleased but reminded me of the party in the evening. We held the party as planned. After it was over, I went to Mulund in my trusted informer Gopal's taxi to reconnoitre the area where the meeting was scheduled. Gani accompanied us. Despite the heavy rain and a breakdown, we reached Mulund.

Gani said, 'Jaffer is a very careful man. When I meet him on the street, he will pass me and keep walking ahead. If he is satisfied that there is no threat, he will come back towards me. But if he suspects anything, he will simply walk away.'

By the time we returned to the office, it was 4 a.m. I assembled all the staff and selected the best for our team. I also decided to go to PI Zende's residence. It was 5 a.m. when we reached there.

'Bagwan, any problem?'

'No, Sir. But I request you to come with us because Jaffer and Gani will be together, and there is always a possibility that there will be others with them.' He readily agreed to join us. When we reached Mulund, we went to the first floor of the hospital to watch over the area. Seasoned criminals like Jaffer can spot policemen in a fraction of a second. I did not want to take any risk, particularly in the case of a dangerous criminal like Jaffer. Our team took positions. PI Zende and I positioned ourselves behind parked cars on opposite sides of the road. The clock kept ticking. Soon, it was nearly 11 p.m. We were watching Gani very carefully. Suddenly, he took out a handkerchief from his pocket and let it fall to the ground. This was a predetermined signal. He was asked to drop the handkerchief the moment Jaffer crossed him.

Jaffer, meanwhile, continued walking and then suddenly looked behind. There were two men behind him. He then walked back to Gani and both of them began walking together, followed by the two men. PI Zende and I started moving towards them. He asked me to grab Jaffer and said that he would tackle the two men. Able-bodied and strongly built, PI Zende got into action.

He grabbed the two men by their collars. Jaffer, meanwhile, tried to make a run for it. Now was the right time to catch him. When I got close enough, I pushed him hard. He fell to the ground and quickly rolled under a parked car. His hand went straight to his weapon. I leapt to the ground and put my revolver to his head. 'Jaffer, I am Isaque Bagwan, Detection Officer, Crime Branch. Stop your nonsense or I will fire!'

On hearing this, PI Zende shouted, 'Bagwan, don't shoot him.'

Hearing PI Zende's booming voice and seeing my weapon on his head, Jaffer was stunned. Taking advantage of this confusion, I snatched the five-chambered brass revolver from his hand. Jaffer realized that there was no way out and quietly came out from under the car. Our team had surrounded it. Having jumped parole, Jaffer had been absconding for over one and a half years. We brought him to the Crime Branch. PI Zende was so elated that he repeatedly struck the steering wheel of the jeep with his baton, blowing the horn continuously and attracting the attention of the entire unit. Every single person came out to see what the commotion was about. They gathered all around us. 'Look, we have brought Jaffer!'

This was indeed an achievement, given that Jaffer was a terror in Pydhonie and Dongri. Most officers congratulated me, but a few of them murmured amongst themselves. 'Jaffer must have surrendered,' they said.

This remark got PI Zende visibly furious. He told them off by saying that he himself was a witness to Jaffer's capture. With this, all the accused in the Sabir murder case had been arrested.

39

AMIRZADA'S BRAVADO

We had to take Amirzada to different parts of the city to collect evidence in Mushir's kidnapping case. Two interesting incidents took place while we were going around Bombay with him.

One day, we were on our way to Santacruz when a blue car overtook us at Mahim. Amirzada said, 'Sir, that is Anjum's car, Anjum Pahelwan of Dawood's gang.'

Amirzada requested me to overtake the car and block it. I did not understand why he wanted me to do so. 'Sir, please block his car and watch the fun.'

'What are you going to do?'

Showing me his handcuffs, he said, 'What can I do? You are armed with two revolvers. Please stop his car and watch. It will be worth it.'

I decided to speed up. A mustachioed six-and-a-half foot tall man stepped out of the car in anger which melted away the moment he saw Amirzada. Amirzada let loose a torrent of abuses, but Anjum stood as quiet as a mouse. 'What can I do for you?'

'The police are here now, but wait until you meet me in the lock-up.' Anjum was left stunned.

We drove away towards Juhu. 'Sir, he is a member of D-Company, but you saw how he cowers in front of me.'

The second incident happened in the court. I had taken Amirzada there with an armed police escort to seek remand.

The court was packed with members of the Pathan gang, led by Amirzada's father, Nabab Khan. His partner, Madhoo Bhai Matkewala, stepped forward and said, 'Brother, today the opposite party has also come to court. That is why we are here in full strength.'

Dawood's Singapore smuggling case was being heard on the second floor. Most members of his gang were also in court. They came down when they realized that Amirzada's case was being heard on the first floor. While we were taking Amirzada to the court room, his path crossed Dawood's, who started abusing him incessantly.

Amirzada said, 'I am the son of a Pathan. Sir, please remove my handcuffs. I promise I will not run away. I only want to teach him a lesson with these chains.'

'They have weapons,' I said.

'Sir, I am not afraid. A man does not die because of mere bullets.'

The atmosphere was charged. There was tension in the air with both the groups face-to-face. Matkewala was acting smart in front of Dawood and his gang. Dawood slapped him hard across the face. The gangs clashed.

Dawood's gang member Hanif Kutta attacked Amirzada's informer Hanif Seven who had given him information about Dawood's Ahmedabad visit. The gang lifted Hanif Seven and were about to carry him away. That was when I pulled my revolver out.

'Stop this nonsense or I will fire.'

Dawood's gang let go of Hanif Seven. The situation had been diffused. By the grace of God, the day went by peacefully.

This rivalry had to be seen to be believed. I had saved Hanif Seven's life, and he never forgot this favour. Later, he told me about the whereabouts of a notorious chain snatcher, Jabbar Zabardast, which helped investigate the Professor Shantadevi murder case and several other cases related to drugs.

40

ROMANCE INTERRUPTED AND A BROKEN TOOTH

In 1983, Nariman Point, Girgaum Chowpatty, Marine Drive, Hanging Gardens and Malabar Hill were frequented by couples at night. The police often heard about instances where couples would be robbed, but no one ever came forward to register a complaint.

One of my informers told me, 'Sir, yesterday I was sitting in a bar when four people at an adjoining table were talking about couples sitting at Chowpatty beach.' When I offered him a generous amount of money, he said, 'These people loot couples and then go to Foras Road, near the stables at Pila House.'

To verify this information, my staff and I kept watch at Pila House. We maintained vigil for over a week. Finally, the suspects came to the stables in an inebriated state. We watched them climb on to the loft and waited for them to fall asleep. After an hour, we raided the loft and arrested all of them—ringleader Govind Sarkar and his associates Nishikant Deshpande, Raju Shelar and Ramesh Shukla.

We recovered seven to eight stolen cars from Bustan Apartments in Nagpada. They confessed to robbing thirteen to fourteen couples and stealing cars. The next day, the newspapers splashed the news of the arrest and evoked a good response from many couples who had been looted. Many of them turned up for the identification parade. One girl showed us a broken tooth which she had preserved. One of the accused, Shelar, had clamped his hand on her mouth to keep her from shouting. She had bitten him in an attempt to get away. In order to free himself, he pulled his arm away forcefully, causing her tooth to break. The wound on Shelar's arm was still fresh. We got the accused and the victim medically examined. The accused were awarded long sentences. Had the girl not preserved her tooth, a vital piece of evidence would have been lost.

41

SHAIKH MUNIR'S THREAT

It was June 1983. I was in the office when the telephone rang.

'I am Shaikh Munir, Manya's friend. You killed my brother, and I will not let you live. I will blow you and your motorcycle up with a bomb. If you are not a coward, come and face me!'

I was angry and took up the challenge. 'Where are you? I will come there and show you what Isaque Bagwan is made of.'

'If you are so eager to die, come to Bombay Central.'

'Wait there. I am on my way.'

I went to Bombay Central with a constable on my Royal Enfield motorcycle. We searched the entire station, but Munir was nowhere to be found.

Later, PI Zende calmed me down, but the thought of Shaikh Munir kept hovering in my mind.

42

JAFFER JAMAL SIDDIQUE'S
ESCAPE FROM JAIL

Jaffer had been detained at the Thane jail. He had managed to flee from judicial custody on 15 May 1983 with two other prisoners. D. Ramachandran, the then commissioner of police, had suspended two police officers and four constables. But that was not going to solve the problem at hand. The media was keeping the pressure up. Every day, wild allegations were being levelled against the police. Newspapers printed headlines like 'Criminals escaped or were allowed to flee?'

I was upset. My informer Gani's life was in danger. Commissioner Ramachandran called me and said, 'Bagwan, Jaffer has fled from judicial custody and the police are being blamed. You had arrested him before when he was wanted. Go after him and arrest him again. I want Jaffer behind bars.'

I had participated in the Manya Surve operation when Commissioner Ramachandran was the Addl CP (Crime), Bombay. I started planning how to get Jaffer again. I got in touch with my informers, including Gani.

On hearing of Jaffer's escape, Dawood's associates Chota Kasu and Rajji came to my office and offered me two heavy gold rings. 'Sir, we know that you are looking for Jaffer. We are offering you Rs 7 lakh as a reward to kill him in an encounter. We are willing to pay any amount of money.'

I lost my temper. 'Don't try to buy the police. Get out of here.'

Sensing my anger, they apologized and left.

Jaffer had feigned illness and got himself admitted to the government hospital. Ashok, aka Munna Philips or Chikna Munna, had also escaped with him. Munna ran a charas joint in Thane. I decided to concentrate on him. Gani, who had helped me arrest Jaffer earlier, came forward to help again. He informed me that Munna would arrive outside a particular hotel in Malad at 11 a.m. on 3 July 1983. We laid a trap around the hotel. It was decided that the moment Gani would spot Munna, he would remove his chappal and act as if the strap had come off. The moment Munna arrived in a rickshaw, Gani signalled to us.

I caught hold of Munna and locked him up at Colaba police station instead of the Crime Branch so that Jaffer would not know of his arrest. After intense interrogation, Munna revealed that he was on his way to Hotel Surya in Mangalore with a revolver and Rs 10,000. Jaffer was to call him the same day from an unknown location.

'What is the code word?'

'Work has been done.'

The reply 'work not done' would indicate that Munna had been caught or there was danger. At great risk, I took Munna to Mangalore. Jaffer rang up at the pre-decided time.

'Munna, is the work done?'

'Yes, brother! It's done!'

I informed my superiors of the developments. Addl CP (Crime) N.C. Venkatachalam, said, 'Bagwan, you operate alone each time. This time a dangerous criminal like Munna is with you. Take someone along. Just one SI and two constables are not sufficient.'

When PI Zende sensed my reluctance, he said, 'Bagwan, the boss is annoyed. Do not disobey his orders. Just take an inspector with you.'

PI Sonar was ordered to accompany me. He had only worked in rural areas and was not familiar with the ways of the Bombay underworld. He would not be of much use. We travelled to Mangalore by bus.

All this while, something sinister was being planned against me in Bombay.

43

AN ATTEMPT TO KILL ME

It was 5 July 1983. I had informed my wife that I was going to Mangalore. Around noon, when she was busy in the house, the doorbell rang. She opened the small window next to the main door. A stranger stood outside.

'What do you want?'

'Mr Bagwan has met with an accident.'

'Where?'

'Near Regal Cinema. I have come to take you.'

My wife, however, was suspicious as I had told her that I was leaving for Mangalore. She decided to test him.

'What was he wearing?'

The man fumbled, and my wife shut the window. She rang up PI Zende and told him about the incident. He sent some policemen to my residence at once, but the stranger had fled. Within an hour of this incident, all police stations were informed of a shootout in which a hawaldar on duty at the Prabhadevi traffic signal had been injured. There was a link between both incidents.

In order to avenge Manya Surve's killing, his associates Shaikh Munir, Bajya Sawant, Ravi Kamathi and Shendi Misal had been waiting in a taxi below my residence. On a usual day, I would leave my house around 10 a.m. and ride to office on my motorcycle. They had planned to attack me then but failed as I was away in Mangalore. Then they decided to kidnap my wife, but she foiled their plan B.

On their way back, they vented their frustration by firing at the hawaldar at Prabhadevi junction.

44

JAFFER JAMAL SIDDIQUE REARRESTED

In Mangalore, we booked room numbers 8 and 9 in Hotel Surya. PI Sonar and my constables were in room no. 9 with Chikna Munna. I waited in room no. 8.

Jaffer called the hotel and asked for Munna. I got Munna to confirm the meeting. Jaffer arrived in an autorickshaw and headed straight for the room. Just as he was entering, I pushed him inside and held him in a tight grip. PI Sonar and the others arrested him.

On seeing me, Jaffer said, 'I was sure that if anyone were to catch me, it was going to be you. No one but Bagwan Sahib would have the guts to catch me. You have got me again!'

This was a certificate from a master criminal. Mission successful!

Commissioner D. Ramachandran and PI Zende were informed. We left for Bombay with Jaffer in a bus.

Incidentally, one of our co-passengers was a well-known heart surgeon from Baramati, Dr Bhoite, who had recently got married and was returning from his honeymoon.

All through the journey, Jaffer told me about his life. We reached Bombay the next day. As we crossed Dadar, Jaffer said, 'Sir, do you want to see who I really am? I will give you a glimpse.'

'What do you mean?'

'Everyone in Bombay thinks that D-company is the strongest, but they are blind. Do you wish to see who is more powerful?' The bus was about to reach Bhendi Bazaar.

'What is it that you want to show me?'

Jaffer started laughing. 'Sir, ahead, on the left is Mandvi Police Colony. Further ahead, at the corner of Murgi Gully, is Mayur Transport Company. Please tell the driver to halt for two minutes.'

My curiosity aroused, I asked the driver to halt. Jaffer leant out of the window and let loose a barrage of abuses at Dawood's aide Rajji. Murgi Gully was Rajji's domain, but the sight of Jaffer caused a pandemonium. Shopkeepers pulled the shutters down and tables and chairs at roadside shops were knocked over. It was like a stampede.

'Run! Jaffer is here!'

Jaffer said triumphantly, 'Sir, see how these D-company people are terrified of me.'

Jaffer had shown that it was he who was the real don of Pydhonie, where just the mention of his name was enough to strike terror in the hearts of residents and goons. Later, I locked Jaffer and Munna up in the Crime Branch lock-up. I was about to go home when one of my informers told me about Shaikh Munir's plan to kill me.

45

SHOT IN THE DOCK

The Sabir murder case was being heard in the sessions court of Bombay. It was presided over by Judge S.Y. Joshi. Only one accused, Alamzeb, was still absconding. Amirzada and Jaffer Jamal Siddique were represented by a battery of lawyers: advocates Adhik Shirodkar, Chari, Chotubhai Shah and Yamunabai Kale. The government pleader was Mr Pawar. I used to take all the witnesses to court every day. As many as fourteen to fifteen witnesses had already been examined but had turned hostile because of the fear of Amirzada. One of the witnesses even collapsed after seeing him in court. Such was his terror.

The most important witness in the case, mujra dancer Chitra, who was Sabir's mistress and was with him in the car when he was shot at, had assured us that she would tell the truth before the court. However, on seeing Amirzada and Jaffer, she turned hostile. This was the result of the Pathan gang's threats. 'I did not see anything. I don't remember. When the firing was going on, I closed my eyes,' she told the court.

The judge was watching everything silently, but his hands were tied. This was a travesty of justice, but he could do nothing. Amirzada lost no time in taunting me, 'What happened to your witnesses? Your efforts have been in vain. Remember, no one is going to testify against me.'

I was so exasperated that I told PI Zende too that all our efforts had gone waste. All the accused were going scot-free. Mushir's kidnapping case was also finished.

We had seized eleven revolvers of different makes: two rifles and a big gun with a single barrel along with 300 cartridges. We presented these as evidence before the court. Amirzada confessed to having purchased these from the dacoit Mustakeem with help from Bully Pahelwan. As this confession needed to be supported by evidence, defence advocate Shirodkar took great pleasure in taunting me, 'Bagwan, have you bought the weapons from some drama company? I hope you have not included your own service revolver as evidence against my client.' The crowd burst out laughing. I was furious but kept mum.

Despite strong evidence, the court castigated the police. I was crestfallen. Only PI Zende could console me. It was 5 September 1983. That night, the Amirzada and Arun Gawli gangs clashed in Arthur Road jail. To teach Amirzada a lesson, the Gawli gang had stabbed him in the buttocks. In those days, gangsters always stabbed their rivals' buttocks so that they would remember them whenever they used the toilet. But Amirzada looked cheerful despite being in pain because he was sure that he would be exonerated.

I was feeling depressed and spoke to PI Zende. 'Sir, the Sabir case is also going to fail. From the petrol pump attendant to Chitra, everyone has turned hostile. Only two witnesses remain: the police surgeon and me. What is the use of our testimony?'

'Bagwan, I understand your reaction. I also feel the same way, but we have done our duty. The law will take its own course. The judge will pronounce his judgment. But remember, even if we do not get justice in this court, we will get justice in the court of God. We will be rewarded. He is more concerned about this case than all of us.'

PI Zende had left it to God. I felt so disheartened that I told him, 'Sir, tomorrow I will not come to the court.' Hearing this, SI Jeremiah chuckled.

This enraged PI Zende. 'Jeremiah, all you do is sit in the office and do nothing. No one else is attending the court hearings except Bagwan because it is his case, but this case concerns the entire Crime Branch.'

He then ordered SI Jeremiah to accompany me to court every day.

The morning of 6 September 1983 dawned. I went to the office feeling sombre, picked up all the case papers and reached the court at 11.15 a.m. Amirzada and Jaffer were brought under armed escort. Amirzada did not spare the opportunity to taunt me. 'Sir, now only your testimony remains, along with that of the police surgeon. After the judge hears both of you, I will be a free man. After that you will never catch me again.' He was so elated that he seemed to have forgotten his stab wounds.

Amirzada's father, Nabab Khan, and his relatives, accompanied by Jaffer's relatives, were present in the court. At 11.40 a.m., the judge ordered the proceedings to begin. Dr Khade, who had performed Sabir's post-mortem, was examined. There was pin-drop silence. The defence advocates had requested the court's permission for me to sit outside. I sat on a bench with the case papers in my hand. My mind was clouded with thoughts. I was anxious about the outcome. Inside the court, the *karkoon* called out Dr Khade's name. He stepped into the witness box. Once he had testified, the police prosecutor called me. He said, 'Bagwan, the original papers of the post-mortem of the deceased, Sabir, are to be shown to the court.'

I started taking out the relevant papers. That was when I heard four shots being fired. Amirzada screamed. I looked up to see a young man in a T-shirt and baggy pants firing at Amirzada inside the court room.

Shocked, people dived under tables and benches. Taking advantage of the chaos, the shooter ran towards the bench reserved for constables, threatened the policeman sitting there and tried to jump out of the window. I moved swiftly and, within a fraction of a second, fired two shots at him. One bullet pierced his thigh and he fell. The policemen in the court pinned the wounded man to the ground. The court's doors were locked from inside to prevent any more untoward incidents. In the meantime, ASI Yeshwant Parab took away the shooter's .38 bore revolver and handed it over to me. He was identified as David Pardeshi.

Amirzada was rushed to hospital by his father and the police but was declared dead on arrival. News of the firing reached the police headquarters. Commissioner J.F. Ribeiro rushed to the spot with other senior officers. I narrated the sequence of events to him. At the same moment, principal judge of the sessions court, Mr Jahagirdar came up to the commissioner and said, 'Your officer has done a very good job. If he had not stopped the assailant in his tracks . . .' Before the judge could say more, the commissioner said, 'the nose of the police department would have been cut!'

The commissioner congratulated me and said that he would recommend my name for the police medal for gallantry. This would be my second gallantry award.

Later, during interrogation, Pardeshi told me, 'Luck favoured you that day otherwise I would have jumped out of the window. Alibhai and Ballu were waiting for me in a *dukker* Fiat. Your aim was good, otherwise I would have escaped.' In those days, dukker Fiat was slang for an old Fiat car that had a round and stout bonnet. The word 'dukker' itself means 'pig'.

According to their plan, Bada Rajan's associates Ali Abdulla Antulay and Balaram, aka Ballu, were waiting for Pardeshi in a dukker Fiat. But God had other plans. He had closed Amirzada's case. David Pardeshi was awarded life imprisonment and sent to Thane jail. Two years later, he escaped from prison and remained absconding for a long time. This was until Amirzada's brother, Shahzada, Alamzeb and gangster Abdul Latif found him in Ahmedabad. He probably felt a surge of emotions when he saw them: a mix of frustration, anger, betrayal and fear. They must have seen this in his eyes when they killed him right there.

Bada Rajan's name had featured for the first time in this case. Pardeshi had revealed during interrogation that Dawood, wanting to take revenge for Sabir's murder, had joined hands with Bada Rajan and asked him to plot Amirzada's murder. Bada Rajan had hired Pardeshi for the job. Dawood was the brain behind the plan. A case was registered against him at Colaba police station. A combing operation was conducted to arrest him. The investigation officer in this case was PI Rajaram Garkal.

Dawood applied for anticipatory bail in Judge Sonar's sessions court. The public prosecutor, Mr Pawar, raised strong objection against the bail application. At one stage, the judge himself visited Dawood's den at Musafir Khana along with the public prosecutor.

Despite all this, it was surprising that Dawood managed to get anticipatory bail. Advocate Ram Jethmalani, who appeared for him, used all his legal acumen in ensuring that he remained free.

Amirzada's murder had cast a pall of gloom over the Bombay underworld. There was an unearthly silence on the surface but a storm was brewing underneath. The events that unfolded a month later were indicators of an intensifying gang war.

46

SHOOTOUT AT ESPLANADE COURT

On 30 September 1983, the police had brought Bada Rajan to Esplanade Court in connection with a case of extortion and were granted further remand. Before he could be put in a police van, Chandrashekar Safaliga, disguised in naval uniform, opened fire at Bada Rajan and killed him. There was pandemonium outside the court. The police crime conference in the adjoining Police Club had just ended. Sr PI (Azad Maidan) Shashikant Guru, who had just come down the club's stairs, caught hold of Safaliga and took away his .38 bore revolver. He was later awarded the police medal for gallantry and rose to be an ACP. Safaliga, meanwhile, was handed over to the Crime Branch. Investigation revealed that it was Rajan's close friend, Abdul P. Kunju, who had given supari for him to be killed.

Kunju was a dark, strongly built don who operated in the Chembur–Tilak Nagar area. He had a lot of cases registered against him for serious crimes. He had committed three murders for the Bada Rajan gang, but they had a fallout over extortion money. While he was in Nashik Jail, serving a sentence under the NSA, he was plotting against Bada Rajan. On one occasion, Kunju was brought to Bombay for a case being heard in the high court. While returning to Nashik, he escaped from the Bombay Central State Transport Depot. The Nagpada police registered a case of runaway from custody against him.

Kunju picked up twenty-two-year-old Safaliga from Tilak Nagar and brainwashed him into working for him. He took him to the hills of Ulva village in Raigad district's Uran taluka and trained him in how to use a revolver. Soon, Safaliga became an expert marksman. Kunju then asked him to kill Bada Rajan. He sent Safaliga in a Navy officer's uniform to Esplanade Court with a loaded revolver. Safaliga, who had no crime record, killed Bada Rajan.

Once this fact came to light, the police and Rajan's heir, Rajendra Nikhalje, aka Chota Rajan, started hunting for Kunju. The police learnt that Arvind Dholakia was Kunju's 'godfather'. Based on this information, we raided Arvind's brother, Lalit Dholakia's, office near Alankar Cinema on Sandhurst Road but could not find anything. We then raided Caesar's Palace Disco on Linking Road, Khar, owned by the Dholakia brothers. We learnt that the manager and other employees had orders to take care of Kunju's financial needs. I managed to convince one of the employees to tip me off about Kunju.

On 9 October 1983, SI Shankar Desai and I, under the supervision of PI Zende, laid a trap for him on 20th Road, Khar. Kunju was there to hire a tourist car. He knew that he was being hunted by the police and Chota Rajan and decided to escape from the city. We arrested him. Later, the Chota Rajan gang killed him in broad daylight while he was playing volleyball in Tilak Nagar.

Another gang war was on in full swing in Bombay!

47

THE HAND OF GOD

After Amirzada was killed, his father swore that he would take revenge. He formed a new gang, inducting gangsters from Ahmedabad and his younger son, Shahzada.

Shahzada reached out to Abdul Latif, the dreaded gangster from Gujarat and Amirzada's friend. Along with old accomplices Azim Pahelwan, Liaquat and Kanwaljit Singh, who was an aide of Madhoo Matkewala, they hatched a plan to bring down Rashid Arba, the king of smuggling and Dawood's mentor. They began tracking him.

Arba had excellent contacts in the Gulf. An attack on him would be a direct blow to Dawood.

One night, Arba was driving from Dongri to Worli accompanied by a religious leader, a pir. They stopped at a petrol pump next to Asha Daan Centre in Worli. It was 1.30 a.m. The gang opened fire at Arba with .38 and 9 mm weapons. The moment the first bullet hit Rashid, he slumped and started praying, holding the pir's hand. Seeing him slump, the assailants thought their work was done. They fled. The pir, who was unhurt, rushed Arba to Jaslok Hospital. Soon after, PI Zende and I reached the petrol pump and saw the car riddled with bullets. There was a pool of blood inside. 'Sir, Rashid must have died.'

'I also feel the same. Let us go to the hospital.'

When we reached the hospital, we were in for a surprise. 'Zende Sahib, how are you? How are you doing, Bagwan?'

Rashid greeted us with a smile. He had survived the shootout miraculously. When we saw the X-ray reports, we were stunned to see thirteen bullets embedded in his ribs, chest and shoulders.

'How did you survive such an attack?'

'If God is on your side, no one can kill you!'

Arba thanked the pir too for the miracle. Shahzada, Latif, Singh and Rafiq were arrested by the Gujarat Police and handed over to the Bombay Police for interrogation in the Rashid Arba shootout case.

Arba died in 2010.

48

THE IRON PIPE ESCAPE ARTISTE

Shafi Toofani, a notorious gangster with several cases filed against him, had fired at API Ravi Naik of Pydhonie police station. Unit I of Detection Crime Branch and the local police were combing the city to nab him. On 2 April 1984, we received information that Toofani would soon visit the third floor of a building in Nizam Street.

I, along with SI Shankar Desai, Constable Chandu Khanvilkar, Naiks Sahadeo Appa Naik, Pawar and Pasi laid siege at his hideout. We formed two teams, one comprising SI Desai and Naiks Pasi and Pawar, and the other comprising Constable Khanvilkar and me. Toofani entered the area with an accomplice, but soon sensed our presence and vanished into one of the buildings. We started searching all the buildings in the area, but there was no sign of him. Then Khanvilkar spotted a person running away and started shouting. We chased him through Kazi Sayed Street and saw him running towards Panjrapole. I was sure that we would catch him since Panjrapole Street led to a dead end. He fired two rounds in our direction. The bullets missed us by a whisker. He brandished his gun and threatened us not to advance. I identified myself and, with my gun ready, kept moving towards him, taking advantage of the darkness. I spotted a handcart and hid behind it to come within firing range. I pushed the cart towards him. It hit him hard. Taken by surprise, he lost his balance. I lunged at him and grabbed the German-make pistol from him. But this person was not Shafi, it was Mohamed Farooq, an associate of Toofani who was wanted in a number of robbery and assault cases registered at Pydhonie and other police stations. We arrested him and put him in jail after registering a case of attempt to murder by firing at the police. The Crime Branch rewarded me with a commendatory note and cash.

Toofani had escaped that night, but I kept up efforts to arrest him. Four months later, I received information that Shafi would return to the same building on Kazi Sayed Street. I planned to arrest him before he got there. All roads leading to the building were dotted with policemen in plain clothes. We managed to arrest him around 3 a.m. He was armed with a .38 bore revolver.

During interrogation, I asked him how he had escaped the last time. He said, 'Sir, each time, an iron pipe helped me escape.'

Shafi had fixed an iron pipe below the parapet of the window in his room. At the first sign of danger, he would climb out and hang on to that pipe. He had also fixed support for his feet on this pipe so that he could stay there for hours. If any one looked outside the window, they could not make out that there was a pipe under the parapet. Action was taken against Toofani under the NSA. But while Toofani and Farooq had been arrested, one of their associates—Mohamed Ayyaz—remained at large. One evening, while I was returning from Haji Ali, the car stopped at a traffic signal near Ratan Tata Institute on Hughes Road. I was looking around when I noticed a person sitting in a Fiat car, trying to cover his face with a handkerchief. Since it was a hot day, I grew suspicious. I started following the car. The driver of the Fiat realized that he was being followed. He accelerated, but I continued to give chase. The car stopped at Pan Gully near Kemps Corner Bridge, and the man got out and started running.

I chased him and arrested him. This was Ayyaz. He was armed with a revolver and was on his way to commit a robbery. He was also involved in a number of robberies reported from the airport. By the grace of God, another criminal had fallen into our hands.

49

GANG WAR ERUPTS

Around 1984, gangs had established a firm foothold in Bombay, the city of gold. They had realized that Bombay was a money-making haven. Everyone was out to make a fast buck. Each gang wanted to outdo the other. Amassing wealth had become a prestige issue.

On 17 September 1984, a wireless message was received at the Crime Branch about an individual opening fire on Shahid Khan of Jal Bungalow on Arab Lane in Nagpada. Apparently, handmade crude grenades, called bombs by these gangsters, had been used in the attack. Even as I was informing PI Zende about the incident, another message was received about sporadic firing outside Dawood's building at Musafir Khana on Pakmodia Street.

'Bagwan, go to the bungalow with your staff,' PI Zende told me. When I reached Arab Lane with SI Desai and constables Pawar and Pasi, there was a lot of tension in the area. Shahid Khan, who was wounded in the firing, had already been rushed to J.J. Hospital by his sister with help from Shakir and Naeem Sayyed, aka Chote. By the time PI Zende arrived, we learnt that Shahid had been declared dead on arrival at the hospital. We began inspecting the spot and recovered empty cartridges and shrapnel. We then went to Musafir Khana. The place looked like a battlefield with windows broken and the doors and walls of the buildings sprayed with bullets. We recovered empty cartridges and examined them. The residents were terrified. There was no one to tell us anything.

'Bagwan, what is your opinion of both these incidents?'

'Sir, both instances were to hurt Dawood.'

'Yes, you are right. Shahid was the chief of all of Dawood's smuggling operations and other criminal activities, and Pakmodia Street is his headquarters.'

'Sir, both attacks have been carried out by more than one gang and more than one person.'

'Why?'

'Sir, the empty cartridges suggest that.'

'A very good observation, Bagwan.'

The empty shells recovered from both places had been fired from different weapons. PI Zende was of the same opinion.

'Bagwan, what steps are you going to take?'

'Sir, my regular sources.'

He laughed heartily. He knew I would put my network of informers on the job. Since both the attacks had targeted Dawood, I contacted my source in his gang. I learnt that Dawood's establishments had been attacked by Karim Lala's nephew, Samad Khan, and his henchmen Shahenshah and Ziya. Samad Khan had used an AK-47 to shower Dawood's door with bullets. One of them had missed his younger brother, Iqbal, by a whisker. The bullet had grazed past his ear.

In the other incident on Arab Lane, Maqbool, Abdul Atta, Mehmood Kaliya and his brother, Yusuf Kaliya, had fired at Jal Bungalow.

Dawood and Kaliya did not get along. Kaliya had once thrown a handmade grenade at a funeral procession moving through Bhendi Bazaar. In the Jal Bungalow incident, too, a similar grenade had been used. The associates of Khalid Pahelwan, one of Dawood's gang members, were seriously wounded. Dawood's gang had chased Kaliya but he had managed to get away. The gang was just waiting for an opportunity to take revenge and was keeping a watch on Kaliya.

Dawood's younger brother, Anees Kaskar, along with Chota Shakeel, Taufique Takla and Iqbal Jogeshwari attacked Kaliya with a .45 revolver at the Tardeo AC Market when he was visiting a passport agency there. Kaliya escaped by ducking under a table, with the bullets hitting the wall. He then ran down the building, firing from a pistol and chasing away his assailants. I informed PI Zende of the developments. He asked me to hunt down Samad Khan, Shahenshah, Ziya and Kaliya.

I received information that Kaliya's brother, Yusuf Kaliya, Maqbool Usman Ali Shabdi and Abdulla were at Meena Lodge near Alankar Talkies in Pune. PI Zende and I conducted a raid there and arrested them.

By this time, Dawood had already fled to Dubai. His underworld empire was being looked after by Anees, along with his henchmen Chota Shakeel, Iqbal Jogeshwari, Taufique Takla and Shahid Hasan Gulam. This was the 'D-company' that had established its stronghold over Bombay.

Gulam, aka Shahidbhai, and his younger brother, Zahid, aka Chote, ran matka gambling dens, *chakri* and other gambling activities from Jal Bungalow. Thanks to Dawood, Shahid was rolling in wealth. He was living life king-size and was addicted to wine and women. On the night of 16 September 1984, Shahid was drinking with Hasan Haji Ali Vager, Abdul Majeed, Rehman Sheikh, Akbar Khan, Mehmood Khan, Dilip Dharadhar and Naeem, aka Kalu. As the night advanced, one of them suggested that they visit a dance bar.

This sentiment was echoed by the others. Shahid, who was already in an inebriated state, asked them for their choice of dance girl. They replied in unison, 'Let us go to Nargis.'

Nargis performed at Haji Ismail chawl. Her beauty and dance found many admirers. Shahid and his gang entered the dance hall where she was performing and spotted Maqbool Usman Ali Shabdi sitting on a white *gaddi* (mattress). Maqbool was a wealthy shop owner in Crawford Market and a gangster. Seeing him, Shahid flew into a rage. Nargis was terrified as the two rich and powerful rival gangsters confronted each other. However, she soon regained her composure and greeted them. She requested them to sit and enjoy the dance. But the tension was building.

Suddenly, Shahid abused Maqbool and slapped him. There was silence. Shahid was tall and well built, while Maqbool was short and sturdy. Noticing that he was outnumbered, Maqbool chose to keep his cool. Shahid and his men caught him by his ear and made him do sit-ups. Humiliated, Maqbool left. Soon after, Shahid and his gang too left the dance bar. It was 2.30 a.m. when they returned to Jal Bungalow. Shahid was feeling on top of the world at having humiliated Maqbool and wanted to celebrate some more. 'Naeem, get some more scotch for everyone.'

Naeem did so with pleasure and filled everyone's glasses. The party was on in full swing. About an hour later, Kalu, who was guarding the gate, shouted that someone had come to the bungalow. Shahid came out to see who it was. He was astonished to see Maqbool, Abdul Atta, Mehmood Kaliya and Yusuf Kaliya. Shahid realized what was happening. Maqbool had brought Mehmood Kaliya to take revenge for his humiliation.

Shahid lowered his voice and said, 'Mehmood Bhai, we are part of one family. There are no issues between us. Why are you involving yourself in this minor scuffle?' Kaliya, however, was in no mood for a discussion. He simply emptied his pistol into Shahid. The silence of the night was punctuated by the sound of gunshots and Shahid's screams. His gang rushed out with weapons but Kaliya quickly flung four hand grenades at them. He had got these from a young boy named Munna in Madhya Pradesh, who had accompanied him to Jal Bungalow.

The grenades caused panic among Shahid's men. In the resulting confusion, Kaliya and his associates fled from the spot in a car that was waiting for them. Later, Nargis identified the accused. Kaliya told the court that he was attending a function in Kanpur on that day. The court granted him anticipatory bail. Out on bail, he went to Dubai for a holiday with his friends, one of whom leaked information about this visit to Dawood, who too was in Dubai.

Dawood moved quickly. Kaliya was shot dead in an encounter with SIs Emanuel Amolik and Suryavanshi at the Bombay airport when he returned. The officers faced departmental inquiries for this encounter. Kaliya, the terror of the underworld, had been silenced forever. A chargesheet was filed in the court. However, all eyewitnesses turned hostile because of which the main accused, Maqbool Shabdi and Abdul Atta, and some others were acquitted. Two of the accused in the Shahid murder case had been shot dead.

Some days later, Mehmood Kaliya's brother, Yusuf Kaliya, was granted bail. He was shot dead by Dawood's gang at a clandestine brothel in Simla House on Nepean Sea Road. Samad Khan was still absconding.

50

THE END OF AN ERA OF PATHAN TERROR

Gang war was at its height in Bombay when a pimp, Dharma, came to my desk and showed me a photo of an AK-47 rifle. 'Sir, the weapon in the photo belongs to Samad Khan. He will visit Mumtaz's brothel in Simla House on Nepean Sea Road to meet Tina around 4–4.30 p.m.' Incidentally, Tina was the reason Dharma held a grudge against Samad Khan. He liked her and didn't appreciate Samad's closeness with her.

I was aware that Mumtaz ran a brothel in Simla House, which is in the posh Malabar Hill area. I informed PI Zende about this development. He had full faith that I could nab Samad Khan, but before that he brought it to the attention of M.T. Gupte, ACP (Crime Branch, CID).

ACP Gupte said, 'Bagwan, your tip-off may be perfect but one has to take into account the fact that Samad will not surrender without a fight. He may open fire with his AK–47. Also, remember that there are girls there. If something untoward happens, then what? In addition, we are in the midst of the Ganapati festival. If something goes wrong, we will all have to answer for it. It is better to defer action for a few days.'

It was not possible to act against the advice of a senior officer.

The Ganapati festival ended and the Dussehra festivities were about to begin. That was when Samad Khan's body, riddled with bullets, was found in a pool of blood on the footpath in front of a building in Sikka Nagar area of Girgaum, a few steps away from the Vithalbhai Patel Road police station. Khan had enraged Dawood after firing at his den. His brother, Iqbal, had escaped death by an inch. Dawood had fled to Dubai, but he was out to take revenge. Eventually, he got the Rama Naik gang, which included Rama Naik himself, Babu Reshim, Chota Rajan, Tanya Koli, Sanjay Raggad and Sada Pawle, to kill Khan.

A day before Dussehra, Khan had spent the night with a Kashmiri girl at a Gujarati friend's flat in Sikka Nagar. Dawood had information about this and got in touch with Naik's gang. He told them that Khan was armed with an AK–47 rifle and wore a bulletproof jacket. Naik's hit team comprising Babu Reshim, Chota Babu and Sanjay Raggad, disguised themselves as *patti*-wallahs with baskets and turbans on their heads. They hid their weapons inside the baskets and positioned themselves strategically around the building, patiently waiting for Khan to step out.

Around 6 a.m., Khan stepped down the stairs with his AK–47 wrapped in a lungi only to be greeted with a spray of bullets. On the day of Dussehra, the city heaved a sigh of relief as Khan's reign of terror came to an end. He was wanted in a number of cases including rape, S.K. Jain's murder at Bandra's Sea Rock Hotel and countless others. Dawood had got his revenge. The era of Pathan terror under Samad Khan was over.

51

THE ONE THAT GOT AWAY

It was around 6 p.m. on the evening of 1 October 1982. Devchand Gala boarded a taxi at Tardeo to head towards Lamington Road, now called Dr D.B. Marg. He was carrying Rs 1 lakh in an old bag to avoid drawing attention to it. As soon as the taxi stopped at a traffic signal, a group of gangsters surrounded it and kidnapped Devchand. A case was registered. The needle of suspicion pointed towards the Kundan Dubey gang which was active in Tardeo.

Dubey was a notorious criminal who lived in Tardeo's Panchayat chawl. He had been sentenced in a murder case but had jumped parole. He sought refuge under Bhai Thakur in the Vasai–Virar area where a large number of wanted criminals from other states also sought shelter. Dubey's associates were his younger brother, Shivdatt Kedarnath Dubey, Nizamuddin Shamsuddin Sheikh, aka Nizam Don, and Appa Rama Patil. Patil was a known stabber and had a number of cases of rape, murder and assault registered against him.

Dubey's gang was a rival of Rama Naik's ever since Naik's associate had been murdered by Dubey and Parasnath Pandey. In an act of revenge, Naik's gang had killed Pandey. On receiving information that Dubey was in the Tardeo AC Market, the Crime Branch conducted a raid. But it failed because information about it was leaked beforehand. A constable posted at Agripada police station, who regularly visited the Crime Branch, caught a whiff of the impending raid and told Dubey. PI Kulkarni of Tardeo police station had been monitoring the gang's activities. On 25 October 1982, he had information that Dubey would visit Bhatia Hospital in Tardeo.

PI Kulkarni and his team surrounded the hospital. The hot October afternoon had taken a toll on the policemen. PI Kulkarni tried his best to boost their morale. The sun set but there was still no sign of Dubey. Finally, around 9.30 p.m., he came with his gang. Realizing that he was about to be intercepted by the police, he launched an attack. Suddenly, the street lights went out and the whole area was plunged in darkness. Taking advantage of the ensuing chaos, Dubey and his gang slipped away. The blackout had been staged to allow him to flee. A case was registered at Tardeo police station.

PI Zende was upset by this turn of events because wild allegations had been levelled against the police. He entrusted me with the task and asked me to double my efforts to arrest Dubey. I knew that Rama Naik could give me a tip-off about his whereabouts. My logic was: 'An enemy's enemy is my friend.' Naik informed me that he was hiding in room no. 3 of Camp no. 4 in sector 26 of Ulhasnagar, and that he was heavily armed. His associate Nizam Don always slept with a sword in each hand and did not hesitate to attack at the slightest provocation. We reached the spot late at night. It was a *wada*, an open courtyard, surrounded by a huge stone wall. One of our constables climbed over and opened the main gate. Tackling Nizam was a hazardous proposition. We had to stand on his hands to prevent him from reaching for the swords. Several swords and choppers were seized from the gang. We did not find Dubey there but managed to arrest Shivdatta Dubey, Nizam Don and Appa Rama Patil.

52

SABRINA TRAPS
A KILLER: SHAIKH MUNIR

Professor Shantadevi had been murdered in a local train on the Western Railway. The case was being investigated by the GRP and had hit the headlines. There was a hue and cry in the media as there had been no breakthrough for a long time. A.R. Antulay, the then chief minister of Maharashtra, decided to hand over the case to the Detection of Crime Branch, Bombay CID.

After going through all the papers, I realized that this was the work of a chain snatcher. The scene of offence pointed in that direction. I started gathering information about all the chain snatchers who operated on trains and their modus operandi.

We were patrolling the city when I spotted a man who appeared nervous on seeing our vehicle. I stopped the car and grabbed him. As soon as he realized that he had been caught he began to talk. 'Sahib, my name is Ramzan Jumma Sheikh. I am a chain snatcher on trains, but I did not kill Prof. Shantadevi.'

Sheikh was a history-sheeter as per the railway crime records. We solved twenty-eight chain-snatching cases with his arrest. He would sell the chains to goldsmiths who would melt the gold. This would help them avoid being caught.

Cases had been registered against Sheikh at various police stations. We took note of all of them and called all the women who had filed complaints. We took permission from the court and returned their jewellery. The women were pleasantly surprised. Some of them were so happy that they performed an *aarti* (prayers of blessings) for my team and me. I can never forget the respect and blessings they bestowed upon us. Sheikh was awarded four years' imprisonment.

A week later, one of my informers from the Rama Naik gang told me that the murder had been committed by Shankar, aka Kayyum, a known chain snatcher whose den was in Byculla. Naik conducted a matka gambling den in the MHADA colony in the area. I parked my jeep close to it. The punters saw me. One of them came forward and asked, 'Sir, what brings you to our area today? Is there any problem?' I told him to call Naik. I got out of the jeep and sat on the bonnet. Naik soon came out to meet me.

'Sir, I am surprised to see you. If only you had called me, I would have come to your office.'

'Rama, the matter is such that I had to come and meet you in person.'

'Sir, what is the matter?'

'Rama, I want Kayyum.'

I told Naik that he was a prime suspect in the Prof. Shantadevi murder case. Just then, one of the punters came running and whispered into Naik's ear.

'Sir, I will give you Kayyum by evening but please do not wait here any longer. I will stay true to my word. I will give you Kayyum, but I beg you to leave immediately.'

I could not understand why he wanted me to leave, but I considered him to be reliable and true to his word. In those days, chain snatchers and petty thieves depended on local *dada*s (dons) like Naik for protection. In cases of pickpocketing and robbery, the police would contact the local dada to facilitate the surrender of the accused and the stolen property. Since Rama had not called till late in the evening, I decided to call him to my office.

'What happened about Kayyum?'

'Forget about Kayyum, Sir. I will get him to surrender soon, but consider yourself lucky. Shaikh Munir bears a grudge against you and was going to kill you today. He was in my den when you came to meet me. My boys told him that I was talking to you outside. In an instant, he pulled out his gun and loaded it. My boys pounced on him and restrained him, telling him that they did not want any untoward incident or the Crime Branch would make life miserable for me.'

It was Munir who had threatened to kill me and had even come right to my doorstep to do so. I had completely forgotten about him, but destiny had brought him back into my life. I decided to hunt for him. His history sheet read as follows: he was originally a chain snatcher who operated in trains and had at least seventeen to eighteen cases registered against him. The GRP had arrested him and the trial was in progress at the Railway Court on the first floor of the old building at the end of Victoria Terminus Station. The police had to bring him handcuffed since he was a hardened criminal. They put him in the dock after removing the handcuffs.

When Munir realized that the sentence was going to be delivered, he addressed the judge. 'Are you going to announce the sentence or not, Judge Sahib?'

The court was surprised by this statement. The judge had already decided to sentence him but was confused. Taking advantage of this momentary confusion, Munir rushed to the window and leapt out. Before anyone could react, he had jumped on to a passing train. A case of 'runaway from police custody' was registered against him. One case of rape had already been registered against him. He had terrorized the south Indian community of Dharavi and extorted large amounts of money from them. While

Isaque Bagwan receiving his first
police medal for gallantry from
the then Maharashtra Governor,
Air Chief Marshal (retd)
I.H. Latif, on 26 January 1984.

Bagwan receiving his second
police medal for gallantry from
the then Maharashtra Governor,
Air Chief Marshal (retd)
I.H. Latif, on 26 January 1985.

Bagwan receiving his third police medal for
gallantry from the then Maharashtra Governor,
V. Shankaranand, on 28 January 2009.

Haji Mastan

Karim Lala

Tiger Memon

Dawood Ibrahim Kaskar

Jaffer Jamal Siddique

Alamzeb Jangrez Khan

Amirzada Nawab Khan

Sabir Ibrahim Kaskar

Weapons seized from Amirzada's gang after Sabir Kaskar's murder.

Friends who turned into bloodthirsty foes (from left to right):
Amirzada, Samad Khan, Dawood and Alamzeb.

(From left to right) Hawaldar Waghmare, Amirzada Nawab Khan, SI Isaque Bagwan, Ahmed Sayad Khan and Naik Pasi.

The kidnapping of producer Mushir, who made films like *Shakti*, led to Amirzada–Alamzeb's gang being busted.

Sharpshooter David Pardeshi.

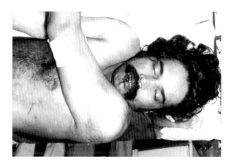

Amirzada, after being shot dead by Pardeshi in a sessions court.

Mehmood Kaliya

Shehzada Nawab Khan,
Amirzada's younger brother.

Azim Pahelwan, Abdul Latif and
Kanwaljit Singh after being arrested
for shooting at Rashid Arba.

The witness dock where
Amirzada was shot dead.

Manya Surve   Shaikh Munir

Subhash Bhatkar, aka Potya.

Weapons seized from Manya Surve.

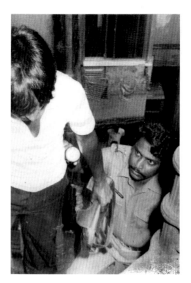 

SI Isaque Bagwan recreating a crime scene as per court orders.

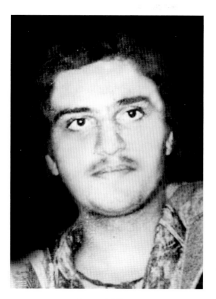

Samad Khan

Hamid (above), the son of Dongri's 'matka king' Aziz Dilip,
was murdered by Samad Khan's associates.

Abdul Kunju

Bada Rajan

Sharpshooter Chandrashekar Safaliga
dressed as a naval officer.

Rama Naik

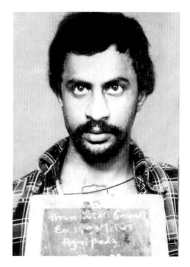

Arun Gawli

Babu Reshim

Sada Pawle

Ravindra Sawant

PI R.R. Kolekar (second from left), SI Isaque Bagwan (centre)
and ACP Ranbir Leekha (extreme right).

(From left to right) Addl CP A.K. Ankola, SI Isaque Bagwan and
other officers of the Crime Branch (Drugs Control) with
the narcotics seized from Aga Khan.

Mandrax seized from a factory after the arrest of
Shaikh Abdullah Akhtar (centre).

(From left to right) Addl CP S.M. Shangari, Commissioner V.K. Saraf and SI Isaque Bagwan with the brown sugar seized from Pakistani drug dealer Jamal.

Deputy CM and Home Minister R.R. Patil being served food by Commissioner A.N. Roy and Sr PI Isaque Bagwan.

Narcotics king Aga Khan.

Pakistani smuggler Haji Gani.

ACP Isaque Bagwan pointing to a grenade pin in the hands of one of the terrorists inside Nariman House.

Another of the terrorists killed inside Nariman House.

(Left) The grenade pin in the terrorist's hands, (right) ACP Isaque Bagwan pointing to the grenade that was still live.

Nariman House, also known as Chabad House.

Bodies found tied up inside Nariman House, (inset) a bullet mark on a photo frame.

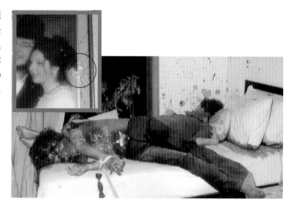

Bodies piled up inside Nariman House.

in jail, he had become a close friend of Manya Surve who liked his daring attitude and recruited him into his gang.

I received information that Munir had a friend named Pushkin Marlbrose who was about twenty-eight years old and a resident of Baithi chawl in Versova's Dadabhai Naoroji Nagar. Both were chain snatchers. Munir visited Pushkin residence regularly. I kept a watch on Pushkin's residence for two weeks. I learnt that he lived with his mother and sister, Sabrina. I was sure that I had heard her name at some point. Eventually, I remembered that Sabrina was a prostitute in Colaba. She plied her trade outside Jehangir Art Gallery in Kala Ghoda. When she saw a prospective customer, she would tell him that her husband had abandoned her and that she had no option but to prostitute herself to make ends meet. I had known Sabrina during my stint at Colaba police station.

I contacted her.

'Sir, what brings you here?'

'Sabrina, I want Pushkin.'

'Why? Has he picked your relative's pocket?'

'Sabrina, your brother has a close friend, Shaikh Munir. I want him.' On hearing his name, she appeared frightened.

'Sir, who is Shaikh Munir? What has he to do with my brother? I do not know where Pushkin is!'

Knowing that money moves mountains, I gave her a hefty amount and tried to gain her confidence.

'Look, Sabrina, I am only interested in Shaikh Munir. I promise you, no harm will come to Pushkin.'

'Sir, I know you are true to your word, and I trust you. I will try to convince Pushkin, but please give me time.'

A couple of days later, while I was discussing a case with Sr PI I.K. Rajguru and SI Gaokar of Unit IV, Sabrina came into the office.

'Sir, my brother has been arrested by the Dadabhai Naoroji Nagar police for no fault of his. Please get him out on bail.' I learnt that he had been picked up by the police on suspicion. The court had granted him bail, but he had no surety and no money for the bail. Although Pushkin was a pickpocket, he was going to help me trap a dangerous criminal. I decided to help him and made arrangements to pay for his bail of Rs 1500. As soon as Pushkin was released, I accompanied him to his residence with Sabrina. In the presence of his mother, I firmly told Pushkin to help me. At first, he was reluctant, but agreed to help after getting a tongue-lashing from his mother and sister. He promised to inform me when Munir would come to enjoy his mother's fish curry and rice, for which he had developed a fondness.

Four days later, Sabrina came to the office in a rage.

'You people have arrested Pushkin again!'

SI Gaokar had arrested Pushkin the previous night to ferret out information about Munir. I approached Sr PI Rajguru and said, 'Sir, I have been making efforts to cultivate Pushkin so that he can tip us off about Shaikh Munir. He has been arrested by SI Gaokar. Please discharge him.'

He understood what was happening and thundered, 'Bagwan has been cultivating Pushkin in order to catch a dangerous criminal. You release him right now and assist Bagwan in the matter.'

SI Gaokar had thought that he could extract information from Pushkin by putting pressure on him. This was not the way to deal with an informer. An informer has to be carefully cultivated. SI Gaokar did not have the faintest idea about how to do that. I got Pushkin released and kept in touch with him.

On 17 February 1984, the telephone rang in the office and was picked up by Sr PI Rajguru.

'Is Mr Bagwan there?'

'No, Bagwan has gone home after night duty. Who is speaking?'

'Please ask him to phone Pushkin Marlbrose.'

Sr PI Rajguru knew who the caller was.

'Is there any message for him?'

'Please tell Mr Bagwan to call me urgently.'

As soon as Pushkin put down the phone, the Sr PI called me and sent his jeep to pick me up. The moment I reached the office, I called Pushkin. 'Sir, Munir had come to my house last night. He is going to come today in the afternoon.'

'But Pushkin, are you aware of the dangers of trapping him at your house?'

Pushkin interrupted me. 'Sir, I have already taken that into consideration. I have told him that I have to attend court in Bandra and that he should wait in a garage in the Ganga Bhavan building in our area.' Pushkin had made a smart move to ward off any suspicion from him. I congratulated him for taking this initiative. 'Sir, I have something more to tell you. There is construction work going on in Ganga Bhavan building, and the garage is at the back. Shaikh is supposed to meet me there. Salim will be accompanying him. Sabrina will lead you to Ganga Bhavan, but please take care of her.'

When I informed Sr PI Sahasrabuddhe about the developments, he said, 'Bagwan, don't be trigger-happy! Try not to fire, but if the situation demands then it's a different story. Give someone else a chance to fire this time.'

'Okay, Sir!'

We made preparations on a war footing. Sr PI Rajguru was also going to participate. The team also included SIs Fateh Singh Gaikwad, Ashok Desai, Raja Tambat, Naresh Talwalkar and Gaokar. In the meantime, Sabrina joined us. We parked our vehicles at Seven Bungalows and proceeded to Versova. We hired three autorickshaws. The two teams sat in two different rickshaws and Sabrina, SI Gaokar and I sat in another. Sabrina was dressed in a burqa to conceal her identity. The plan was to surround Ganga Bhavan. SI Gaokar and I were to enter from the main gate and challenge Munir. The teams positioned themselves strategically. As the autorickshaw approached Ganga Bhavan, SI Gaonkar asked the driver to stop. With sweat dripping from his forehead, he got off and said, 'I've never taken part in such a risky operation, and I haven't fired at anyone in my life. I'm not going any further. You carry on, Bagwan.' I realized that he was scared and let him go. Once our autorickshaw entered the front gate, Sabrina exclaimed, 'Sir, there is Munir standing inside the front gate.'

The moment I set eyes on him, I could feel the adrenaline racing through my veins. I instinctively reached for my weapon. This was the criminal who had tried to kill me, but Sr PI Sahasrabuddhe's words resonated in my ears. What was I to do? The other teams were still behind. To have waited for them would have meant giving the criminal a chance to flee. I decided to challenge Munir alone till the others arrived. I stepped out of the autorickshaw and shouted, 'Surrender, Munir! Our police team has surrounded the building. Do not resist and do not try any tricks. Come with me peacefully.'

Munir was both shocked and frightened to see me. He immediately reached for his revolver and was about to fire. It was an instinctive reflex as I shot at Munir. Before he could raise his weapon, Munir had fallen to the ground.

DETECTION CRIME
BRANCH: OTHER CASES

DETECTION CRIME
BRANCH: OTHER CASES

53

MURDER AT THOMSON GENERAL STORES

Around 8.30 p.m. on 12 February 1982, I was at Fit Well tailors on Wodehouse Road, Colaba, when I received a message that Oliver D'Souza, a partner of Thomson General Stores in Meherzin building on the same road, had been killed after being shot at by an unidentified man. I rushed to the crime scene. PIs N.J. Manekshaw and Karande of Colaba police station were already there with their team. PI Manekshaw narrated the series of events:

'Around 8.30 p.m., Ratilal Hansraj Ruparel and Oliver D'Souza, partners of Thomson General Stores, had stepped out of the store. As they pulled the shutters down, two unidentified men tried to enter forcefully. When D'Souza attempted to stop them saying "the store is shut for the day", one of them pulled out a gun and shot at him. Taking advantage of the distraction, the second man entered the store and fled with the cash box. D'Souza's partner Ratilal then rushed to Colaba police station.'

PI Manekshaw asked for my opinion. 'Bagwan, this is what happened. What are your thoughts? You should look into this matter.'

As I surveyed the crime scene, I found circular, stained, thick cardboard lids within the empty bullet shells. The cardboard lids covered the tip of the cartridges. Showing them to him, I said, 'Sir, the shells indicate that the shots were fired from a *katta* (a countrymade gun). In my opinion, some people from Uttar Pradesh seem to be involved. We should look into the case from that angle.'

Another officer present there said, 'On the basis of ballistic experts' reports, we can investigate the case from that angle. But for now, this murder seems to have taken place due to a property dispute.'

The Colaba police were of the opinion that D'Souza's murder was the fallout of a property dispute and was being masked as a robbery. They began investigating it from that perspective. A parallel investigation was launched by Unit II of the Crime Branch. One of the officers had an informer, a thirty-eight-year-old taxi driver named Abdul Wahab Wahid Ali. I recognized him because all officers sat together at the Crime Branch. He often came to meet this officer.

Experts had confirmed the use of a *gaothi* katta in the D'Souza murder case. Such weapons were brought from Uttar Pradesh. If it was a case of robbery, it was the job of a gang from UP. If it was murder, then the question arose as to who gave the contract for the killing? With these two angles in mind, the officer was questioning his informer, taxi driver Abdul Wahab. However, no clue had surfaced so far.

One day, my informer, Shantaram Mehetre, came to meet me with regard to another case. I casually mentioned the Thomson General Stores murder case and that I was looking at the involvement of a gang from UP. After a momentary pause, Mehetre said, 'Sahib, you are talking about the matter involving the store on Wodehouse Road, right?'

As I nodded, he continued, 'Sahib, right opposite that store is a small lane, Pandey Road. At the corner of that lane is a fruit vendor who hails from UP. His name is Shaukat Ali. He resides in the Geeta Nagar slums. Keep an eye on him.'

'Shantya, what could possibly be his involvement in this matter?'

'Shaukat Ali is a simple man, but he helps us receive messages from our village. A lot of people from UP visit him regularly.' Shantaram had made a valid point. I got an informer to keep a watch on Shaukat Ali's fruit stall and his house. Two to three days later, the informer told me, 'A taxiwallah visits Shaukat Ali's hut every night. He stays there for half an hour to one hour and leaves in his taxi.'

'Taxi number and driver's description?'

'Sahib, the taxiwalla comes in the night, so I couldn't see him properly. But I noted the taxi number.'

I took down the number and asked one of my informers, who washed taxis, to tell me about the one in question. Two days later, he gave me the following information. 'Sahib, the taxi guy you are looking for goes to a saloon in Byculla every morning.'

I waited outside the Byculla saloon. Almost as if on cue, a taxi came and halted in front of it. I was shocked to see the taxi driver. It was Abdul Wahab. I faced a dilemma: if I picked up Abdul, then my fellow officer might think I was shutting off his source, and if I did not question Abdul, how would I solve the case? If Abdul was not involved, why did he visit the fruit vendor's hut every night? If his intention was only to meet Shaukat, he could have done that at his fruit stall as well. If Abdul called himself a police informer, why wasn't he giving any information to my fellow officer about D'Souza's murder? Going by the logic of 'better safe than sorry', I took Abdul Wahab into custody. No sooner had we reached the Crime Branch than Abdul declared he had 'police friends' and created a scene. My fellow officers were confused when I pointed out the number of times Abdul had visited Shaukat Ali's house and how long he stayed there. Finally, he confessed, 'Sahib, the Thomson Store guy was murdered by our gang.' My colleagues were astonished to hear this.

Abdul began to give an account of all his crimes. Four months ago, Abdul had got Mubarak Alimuddin, Shaukat Ali,

Abdul Kadar, Kallu, alias Bobby, Jamil, Irshad Pahelwan and two notorious dacoits—Shahid and Kazi—from Haraswada village of Nizamabad taluka in UP's Bijnor district to Bombay and formed a gang. Abdul confessed to having murdered one of the partners of Thomson General Stores with help from this gang. He also revealed that his gang members resided at Lakda Bandar in Sewri. I went with my colleague SI Shankar Desai and arrested all the gang members. They, too, confessed to their crimes.

Abdul's gang members visited Shaukat Ali at his fruit stall regularly. It was there that they noticed that Thompson General Stores always had customers. This indicated a thriving business and a full cash box. They hatched a plan. The gang reached the store as the partners were wrapping up for the day. After firing at D'Souza, they took away the cash box containing almost Rs 65,000 and fled in the taxi parked outside. Except Irshad Pahelwan, all the other gang members had been taken into custody. Further interrogation led Alimuddin to confess that, after committing the Thompson General Stores crime, Pahelwan and the others had fled to UP and been killed in a police encounter soon after. He was wanted in many robbery cases in the state. We were confident that interrogation of this gang's members would solve several other cases too.

On the night of 14 January 1982, the owner of Rajmahal wine shop on Reay Road, near the Dockyard railway station in Mazagaon, had stepped out with his servant. Just as the servant began pulling the shutters down, the gang reached the shop on the pretext of buying liquor. The owner asked his servant to open the shutter halfway and went in to get the liquor bottles. Seizing this opportunity, the gang members pulled the servant inside the shop and stole Rs 40,000 cash at gunpoint. The gang then locked the owner and servant inside the shop and fled in Abdul's taxi.

On the night of 27 January 1982, around 8.30 p.m., this gang went to Palace Jewellery shop on R.A. Kidwai Road in Wadala.

They fired at the owner, Nakshatra Kumar Jain, robbed the shop and fled in Abdul's taxi. A case was filed. On 9 April 1982, a man attempted to snatch a young woman's chain after threatening her with a chopper. The girl was trained in martial arts and fought back. Seeing her courage, passers-by came forward to help her and caught hold of the thief. The commissioner of police gave her an award for her courage. The chain snatcher was Mubarak Alimuddin.

In Andheri, the gang opened fire in the middle of a road and stole a businessman's bag. They had plotted the robbery in a bar on Reay Road. We confiscated three kattas and live bullets from them. We also succeeded in retrieving most of the stolen cash and goods. After I had caught all the accused, PI Manekshaw of Colaba police station visited the Crime Branch. As soon as he saw the gaothi kattas, he said to me, 'Bloody Bablya, you were right that day when you said that a 12 bore gun was used to kill D'Souza!'

Two of the accused in this case were sentenced to life imprisonment while the others were sentenced to eight years in jail.

54

A PAKISTANI SMUGGLER ESCAPES

The area outside the Maratha Mandir cinema in Bombay Central is always bustling with activity. It was no different at 2 p.m. on 16 December 1982. Taxi drivers, hawkers, shopkeepers, all were involved in their daily business. Suddenly, shots were heard.

'Thief! Catch him!'

'He has shot a man and is running away!'

A man was running down the road with a revolver in one hand and a big bag in the other. Some people ran after him. The moment he realized that the crowd was about to catch up with him, he threw the bag into the air. Currency notes came showering down. The crowd's attention was diverted. Rich and poor alike began to fight to grab as much money as they could. This led to a traffic jam and complete chaos. Within minutes, news reached the Crime Branch that DRI Superintendent, Mr Iyengar, had been shot at Maratha Mandir. The news left us shocked. The DRI branch of the Customs department was similar to the police's Crime Branch.

The DRI worked to identify smugglers and investigate hawala rackets involving the illegal transfer of foreign currency, gold and silver, and crimes that affect the national economy. Mr Iyengar was a senior officer. He was responsible for the Intelligence Department. He was known as an extremely sincere, intelligent and courageous officer. A Crime Branch team led by PI Zende left for the crime scene. Mr Iyengar had been rushed to Nair hospital.

He had been shot in the mouth by a person sitting inside a white Fiat. The attacker had managed to escape after creating a diversion by scattering currency notes on the road. Who was it? We rushed to Nair Hospital. Mr Iyengar's colleagues, Mr Sawant, Mr Patankar and Mr Kulkarni, informed us that his condition was serious. They gave us an account of the incident.

In those days in Bombay, smuggling of gold and silver would take place on a large scale. Though operations in the city were carried out by local smugglers, the brain behind it all was still a mystery. Who was the don of this gold–silver smuggling racket? Mr Iyengar had decided to solve this mystery. He had found out that Haji Gani, alias Bawa, a Pakistani national, was heading the smuggling racket, and that Gani visited Bombay via Dubai only when there was a very big deal to crack. Mr Iyengar wanted him behind bars. He had decided to uproot the tree rather than break the branches. Not everyone in the Customs department believed in this strategy, which is why Mr Iyengar had maintained total secrecy.

In Bombay, Mohammed Ahmed Umar Dossa and others would receive Gani. They had purchased a flat in the name of Mohamed Hasan Ahmed in Nagpada's Bustan Apartments. They conducted all smuggling activities from there. To avoid suspicion, they had set up a cloth business in Manish Market as a front. They had one more partner, Mushtaq, alias Tiger Memon. Gani, Mohamed Hasan and Mohammed Dossa had planned to meet near Maratha Mandir on 16 December to conduct a large transaction involving gold. Mr Iyengar had found out about this after tapping a telephonic conversation. Based on this input, he had laid a trap at Bombay Central.

The moment Gani arrived in his Fiat car, Mohamed Hasan and Mohammed Dossa went to give him a bag containing Rs 30–35 lakh and placed it on the passenger seat. Gani was in the driver's seat. As soon as the deal was done, Mohamed Hasan and

Mohammed Dossa left. Mr Iyengar decided that these two could be caught anytime, but Gani was a big fish. He moved in to arrest Gani. He moved from behind Gani's car and reached the driver's side. He pushed his head inside the window and pointed his gun at Gani.

Gani was taken aback for a moment, but in the next instant he whipped out a foreign-made pistol and fired at Mr Iyengar. The rest of the DRI team watched him collapse and tried to stop Gani. He threw the bag full of money into the air. Taking advantage of the consequent commotion, Gani succeeded in escaping. But Mr Iyengar's team managed to catch Mohamed Hasan. Having received information about the incident, the Nagpada police sent a wireless van to the spot. The DRI team handed over Mohamed Hasan to them. Upon interrogation, he revealed that he was a Pakistani national, and that the smuggling operations were carried out from Bustan Apartments. The flat was sealed.

Mr Iyengar recovered several days later. We also came to know that the Dossa brothers —Mustafa Dossa and Mohammed Dossa—were involved in this case. Mohammed Dossa was arrested.

How had Mohamed Hasan, a Pakistani citizen, managed to live in Bustan Apartments without anyone getting to know? This became a topic of heated debate in the 1980s. In 1993, Bombay witnessed a series of devastating bomb blasts. The seeds of Pakistan's plan to wreak havoc in the city had been sown long ago.

55

TIGER MEMON

In February 1993, I was promoted to the rank of a PI and posted with the Protection Branch. Around 8 or 9 March, I was on sick leave. I had gone to meet a colleague in Millat Nagar, Andheri. He was a year junior to me. We had become friends while serving together at Colaba police station in 1977. We were discussing our work and family when my colleague mentioned that he was under pressure to crack a firearms case as he was part of a special squad led by DCP Arup Patnaik and had to deliver soon. He asked me for help, given my experience in solving similar cases at the Crime Branch. I assured him that I would help if I came across any information. We chatted for a while and then stepped out for a drive in my Maruti van. I was driving when I saw a maroon Maruti Esteem halt at Yaari Road junction. I looked at the driver. He, too, glanced at me and ducked. He placed his handkerchief across his face and drove away at full speed.

I shouted, 'Tiger!' I gave chase, but he was as quick as lightning and disappeared in a matter of seconds.

'Didn't you just ask me about cracking a firearms case? Well, you're in luck.' I told my colleague that the man in the Esteem was Tiger Memon, aka Mushtaq, a smuggler who had Customs, extortion and assault cases registered against him. He sped away because he remembered me from when PI Zende had arrested him. I had information that he carried an AK–47. He was definitely active on the crime scene. He worked through the night and could be found at his residence in Hussaini building opposite Mahim police station. 'You better nab this guy before we lose track of him. I'm sure Patnaik Sahib will be pleased with you if you catch him.' My colleague nodded and thanked me for sharing such vital information. Days passed, and I forgot about this.

On 12 March 1993, the city bled because of a chain of bomb blasts. Investigations were underway and, in no time, Tiger Memon was declared as the main accused.

The next time I met my colleague, I admonished him for his complacence. Had he arrested Tiger then, he could have foiled his plans and prevented the blasts. My colleague simply hung his head in shame.

I was later part of the special squad that was formed to look into the terror attack. My team traced the scooter which was used. I also arrested Raj Koli, a fisherman from Shekhadi, a coastal village in Maharashtra's Konkan district. The RDX used in the bombs was smuggled into the country through Shekhadi. I was willing to give it my best to bring the perpetrators to justice until DCP Rakhale's (name changed) statement incited communal hatred. There were more like him in the department who considered this to be a religious issue rather than the handiwork of some criminal minds.

I can never forget one meeting during these troubled times that I was part of, the one in which DCP Rakhale himself announced specific instructions for his men. It did not sound like an official statement when he said,

'Yeh Muslims *ka* economy *todna chahiye, in logo ka sab do number ka paisa hai* [We must break the economy of the Muslims, their earnings are black money]. That is our responsibility now. Bring in these guys now, hammer them, every little pawn and *uchakka* [petty criminal] you guys have dealt with or brought to task. It is time. Let's make sure their money is burnt, just the way they planned these bomb blasts. Muslims *ne karwaya hai yeh sab* [Muslims are responsible for this].'

But this is rubbish, it is wrong, I thought. Today, they have a term for it: it is most popular during airport security checks. Even Shah Rukh Khan was subjected to it. It's called racial or selective profiling.

I declined all duties during this time. This included anything that involved hauling and rounding-up suspects because I knew what was going on. If this was the attitude of the authorities, of those in charge, what could you expect from their minions on the road?

56

USHA KIRAN: CARMICHAEL ROAD MURDER CASE

Usha Kiran building on Carmichael Road is known to all. At one point, it was famous as the tallest building in Bombay. Some of the wealthiest families lived there. One such family was that of Beniprasad Agarwal. He lived in a 4000 square feet apartment on the first floor of the building with his wife, Sarla, their thirteen-year-old son and eleven-year-old daughter. Agarwal and his brothers dealt in steel with the Birla Group. They had a few domestic helps working in the house. Tight security was maintained at Usha Kiran building. It was impossible for a stranger to enter.

One day, Agarwal's son returned from school as usual. He rang the doorbell. When he did not receive a response, he contacted the watchman. Since the house was on the first floor, the guard got a ladder and the boy entered the house through the balcony. He was shocked to see his mother lying on the floor in a pool of blood. He called his father. The boy's father, uncle and other relatives rushed home. They contacted Gamdevi police station. Soon, the police arrived. Looking at the messy state of the bedroom and wardrobe, the police gathered that the plan included robbery after killing Sarla. She had been stabbed nearly sixteen times. There was a deep slash on her neck and her stomach had been ripped open. Owing to the seriousness of the matter, the Gamdevi police alerted the Crime Branch. As soon as we received the message, PI Zende, SI Shankar Desai and I rushed to the crime scene.

The Gamdevi police had begun the panchnama and other procedures. Ramu, the domestic help who lived with the Agarwal family, was missing. He was the prime suspect. The police tried to get information about him from the security guards and other domestic help, but they couldn't get a clue. The murder had caused a sensation and the Crime Branch was conducting a parallel inquiry. How would we locate Ramu? Who had recommended him to the Agarwals? Where was his village? The Agarwal family was asked several such questions. Trying to come to terms with the loss, the family could only tell us that Ramu was from UP. He was hired as a house help two to three months before the unfortunate incident. However, they could not remember who had recommended him to them.

In those days, people who migrated to Bombay from UP drove taxis, washed cars, became porters or fruit sellers. This scenario hasn't changed even today. Keeping this in mind, I began to gather information about the areas where such migrants lived in large numbers. Dongri was one such place. I made inquiries if any of them had left the city after the murder. Ramu may have committed the murder and fled, but his relatives might still be in Dongri. Usually a criminal flees to his village after committing a crime. The police then pull up the relatives for information. It was also probable that Ramu's relatives, too, had fled the city. I was proved right. In Dongri, I met Gulam Rasul who washed cars and drove a taxi to earn a living. I talked to him about this case. He told me, 'Sir, the murder that you are talking about, I came to know of it last night from taxi driver Kesari Prasad.'

I questioned Rasul about Prasad and his connection with the incident. Rasul told me that Prasad was Ramu's maternal uncle and was worried after reading about the murder in the newspaper. He knew that the police would come, which is why he decided to leave Bombay. He had coaxed Rasul to drive his taxi for a few days. I asked Rasul, 'When did Kesari Prasad leave for his village?'

'Sir, he took the Lucknow Express last night and will reach after three days.'

It was crucial to catch Prasad in order to get to Ramu. After taking permission from my seniors, I reached the airport with constables Pawar, Pasi and Rasul who could identify Prasad. We boarded the Bombay–Delhi flight. Sarla's brother-in-law, Prakash Agarwal, and his son, who were on their way to Varanasi to immerse her ashes in the Ganga, were on the same flight. They recognized me and showed me the urn containing the ashes. With tears in his eyes, Agarwal said, 'Sir, you will surely succeed in catching the criminal with my *bhabhi*'s blessings.'

We reached Delhi in a few hours. From there, we took the Delhi–Lucknow flight. At Lucknow railway station, we kept a watch on all the exits. Rasul was with us to identify Prasad. Soon, we had him in custody. Seeing Rasul with us, Prasad understood why he had been caught. We searched him and found a copy of the *Navbharat Times* which carried a report on the murder. He had carried the newspaper with him for three days which confirmed that I was on the right track.

We had successfully completed one stage of our investigation. We went to Prasad's house in Lucknow and found bundles of currency notes. There were dried blood stains on the bundle of Rs 20 notes. From this, I gathered that Ramu had already visited his maternal uncle's house. Prasad and his wife accepted the fact that Ramu had come to their house. Prasad further revealed that Ramu's actual name was Hridayram, alias Ramprasad Bhagwati Prasad Gudiya. Prasad's wife told us that Ramu had gone to his village, Kansi Simli, near Gandara.

We were faced with two major problems. First, where would we keep Prasad when we went looking for Ramu? Second, there was a curfew in the city on account of then prime minister Indira

Gandhi's assassination. The Lucknow Police tried to stop us at one of the nakas, but let us go after we identified ourselves. We handed Prasad over to the local police.

Kansi Simli was situated near Gandara village, which was 9 km off the main highway in Bahrai taluka. There was a curfew there too. Also, the area was close to the India–Nepal border. Constable Pasi was from Bihar. Since there were no cars around, he suggested that we travel in a newspaper van. At dawn, near Lucknow bus station, we found a private van carrying newspapers. We persuaded the driver to take us along and paid him Rs 3000.

We got off on the highway near Kansi Simli. There was no vehicle available. We had been awake for almost two to three days and were exhausted. We walked all the way to the village which consisted of just eighteen to twenty huts. They had thatch roofs plastered with mud. Rasul pointed to Ramu's house.

It was 9.30 a.m. We knocked at Ramu's door, and his father opened it. He asked, 'What do you want?'

'Is Hridayram at home?'

'You want Nanku?'

We gathered that Hridayram, alias Ramu, was also called Nanku. When we told him who we were, his father insisted that Ramu would never commit such a crime. I understood that he was trying to protect his son and warned him of dire consequences. He then told us that Ramu had gone to his father-in-law's house.

I forced him to accompany us and show us Ramu's in-laws' village. In an attempt to mislead us, he said that his brother (Ramu's uncle) lived in Barabanki. When Constable Pasi told me that Barabanki was around 25 km on the road back to Lucknow, I decided to take a chance. We managed to hire the same newspaper van to head back. In Barabanki, Ramu's father was left with no option but to show us his brother's house. Following his instructions, we left the main village and arrived in a sparsely inhabited area. Pointing to a small hut, the father told us where

Ramu's father-in-law lived. I stopped the van and handed him over to Constable Pawar. Constables Pasi, Rasul and I walked towards the huts. To avoid identification, we made Rasul wear a burqa. We stopped under a tree. Just as we were planning our next move, a door opened and a young man carrying a bag came out. On seeing him, Rasul whispered, 'Sir! That is Nanku!'

To avoid suspicion, we pretended to talk amongst ourselves and began observing Nanku. He walked down the path leading towards us. We had our backs to him. Every moment was crucial. Nanku crossed us. That was when I grabbed him. We took him to the van. I noticed his father's ashen face. Since we had caught Ramu, we let his father go. He began to plead, 'Where are you taking my son?'

I gave him vague answers. After travelling for a few hours, we reached Lucknow. We made our way towards a hotel and noticed a few rickshaws trying to block our van. A smile came on to Ramu's face. He belonged to a community that plied rickshaws, and now his brethren had picked up on his trail. We reached the hotel and entered without much trouble. People had gathered outside the hotel, meanwhile, and were keeping a close watch. When they saw us, they began to yell.

'Where are you taking our child?'

'You cannot take our child!'

I wondered how they knew about the police coming to Lucknow. I realized that when we went looking for Ramu, his father got information about our destination from the driver of the newspaper van. After we let him go, he had contacted his relatives in Lucknow and told them that we were on the way. The situation was tense here. I called the local police for assistance, and they sent two constables. The mob demanded to meet Ramu. I faced them. 'We cannot allow you to meet Nanku here.'

'Then where will you allow us to meet him, Inspector Sahib?'

'At Lucknow railway station.'

'Why there?'

'We are heading to Bombay by train. In the presence of the railway police, we will allow you to meet Nanku.'

The firm stance had the desired effect. In a few minutes they agreed. I called for an Ambassador car and proceeded towards Lucknow railway station, followed by Ramu's supporters in rickshaws. I asked the driver to speed up. Soon, we left the rickshaws far behind. Once they were out of sight, I told the driver, 'Bhaisahab, not the railway station, drive to Lucknow airport!'

My words left the local policemen and the driver confused. I explained that this was the only way to get Ramu out of the city. At the airport, I paid the driver, thanked the constables and checked in. I took Ramu to the security area and explained the matter to the authorities. They agreed to assist us and we succeeded in bringing Ramu, alias Nanku, to Bombay.

Upon interrogation, Ramu narrated the sequence of events from the day of the murder. Mr Agarwal had left for work as usual. The children had gone to school while the other domestic help too had left. Ramu and Sarla were alone in the house. Ramu made advances towards her but she pushed him away. Her resistance frustrated him and he proceeded to stab her in the stomach sixteen times before slitting her throat.

Ramu had a suitcase with him when we arrested him at Gandara. We found gold ornaments inside it and a very vital piece of evidence—Sarla's mangalsutra. We also found currency notes with dried bloodstains. All the evidence proved that Ramu had murdered Sarla. The next step was to recover the murder weapon. After sustained interrogation, Ramu told us that he had thrown the knife into the building's basement parking. We recovered the knife covered in blood. This was important evidence. The case was presented before Justice Thube who sentenced Ramu to life imprisonment.

57

A ROBBERY IN A POSH AREA

One night, the Crime Branch received information about a robbery in an apartment in the posh area of Bhulabhai Desai Road (Warden Road). SI Shankar Desai, constables Pasi, Pawar, Wagmare, Naik and I immediately left for the crime scene.

Manju Kapoor lived with her aged mother on the ground floor of the building. I noticed that the door to the apartment opened in such a way that it cut them off from the rest of the residents. She told us that someone had rung the doorbell around midnight. She opened the door to find four young men with handkerchiefs covering their faces. One of them slashed her hand with a knife. They then proceeded to take away the gold jewellery her mother and three other women in the house were wearing. They also took away the cash from their wallets. I asked the watchman about the incident. He said, 'Sir, I was on night duty when four young men came to the gate. They told me that they wanted to go to Manju Madam's flat. I made an entry in the register and let them in.'

'Who were they? Why had they come? Why didn't you ask any questions?'

The watchman was a little puzzled. When I persisted, he said, 'Sir, what do I tell you? Every day new men come to Manju Madam's house. When I know why these people come, why would I ask questions?'

He explained to me that Manju Kapoor ran a clandestine brothel from her flat. Visitors would frequent her apartment every day. Now, she had been robbed by men posing as customers.

The watchman also said, 'Sir, they had been inside for about ten minutes. When they came out, they got into a taxi that was waiting. I remember the number.'

I asked the watchman, 'Did they come and leave in the same taxi?'

'Yes, Sir, they must have come and left in the same taxi.'

'Why do you say that?'

'Sir, when those men went in, the driver of the taxi waited outside and was constantly looking at Manju Madam's flat. This means they must have come in the same taxi.'

'What did the taxi driver look like? Was he tall, short, dark, fair? What clothes was he wearing? What was his hair like? Did he resemble any actor? Was he wearing any specific style of clothes?'

Those days, many criminals were influenced by Bollywood and tried to copy their favourite actors and villains. I was aware of this, and I was proved right. No sooner had I asked this question, than the watchman replied, 'Sir, the driver looked like actor Amjad Khan.'

Something clicked in my mind. Around midnight, I took a team of policemen and reached the slums of Pratiksha Nagar in Matunga. I knocked on the door of one of the chawls there and called out, 'Raees, I am Bagwan. Open the door.' After a few moments, a woman answered, 'Sahib, my husband is not feeling well. He will come to the CID office later and meet you.' I, however, did not give up and kept asking for Raees. This went on for a while. By now, the neighbours had started peeping through the windows. I was beginning to lose my cool. I gave him a final warning. Raees knew my temper and came out buttoning his shirt. I dragged him to the jeep and took him to the crime scene.

When the watchman saw him, he exclaimed, 'Yes, Sahib, this is the same taxi driver, the Amjad Khan duplicate.'

Once the watchman had identified Raees, it did not take long to solve the case. Raees named his partners—Kumar, a member of the Kaliya Anthony gang, and Raja Nerurkar. We picked both of them up. They revealed the names of two more partners. We caught them as well. I asked Raees who had given him information about Manju Kapoor? He said that he had gone to her apartment with a pimp and observed that there was not a single man there. He also knew that since she ran a brothel she would not be in a position to report the robbery. He then planned to rob her without getting his own hands dirty by getting his partners to do it while he waited outside in his taxi.

We recovered all the cash and jewellery. My seniors asked how I had managed to solve this case so quickly. How did I know that it was Raees who had committed the robbery? I told them that Raees was an informer of a respected officer of the Crime Branch, Lalit Godbole. Raees often visited the Crime Branch to give information. That is how I recognized him. It was easy to identify him, given his resemblance to Amjad Khan.

I had also received information that he had created an atmosphere of terror in Pratiksha Nagar and bullied people there saying he was close to the police. In reality, no informer reveals his identity. I had exposed him, and he was banned from coming to the Crime Branch.

58

MADHYA PRADESH DACOIT NABBED TWICE

On the night of 16 August 1981, around 8 p.m., the Howrah–Bombay Express left from Howrah railway station. It was a long journey. Some travellers were chatting, some were playing cards while some were lying down. The train had left Piparia station and was about to reach Itarsi. Suddenly someone shouted, 'Thief!'

The sound came from the women's compartment. A few passengers from the adjoining compartments ran towards it. A woman whose chain had been snatched had grabbed the thief. She was calling out to her fellow passengers for help. Seeing that he was almost trapped, the thief pulled out a Rampuri, a kind of knife, and stabbed her several times. As the woman collapsed, the passengers froze. Three passengers managed to gather courage and moved towards him. In a bid to escape, he started waving the knife at them. He injured a man grievously. By now, the train was pulling into Itarsi station. Taking advantage of the train's slow speed and the darkness, the thief jumped off. The train entered Itarsi station. The GRP took the wounded persons to the hospital. Unfortunately, they succumbed to their injuries. A case was registered at Jabalpur police station.

Investigation revealed that the crime was committed by notorious dacoit Kailas Chhotelal Thakur of Madhya Pradesh.

The Jabalpur Police began hunting for Chhotelal. A month later, they got information that he had recently run away to Bombay. On 14 October 1981, the Jabalpur Police arrived in Bombay. They explained the details of the entire case to ACP (Crime Branch) D. Ramachandran and ACP Ranbir Leekha. The case was handed over to our branch which was headed by Sr PI Vinayak Dange. The same day, I received information that two strangers had recently come to reside at Shakur Gafur's opium den in Nagpada. I decided to crack down on them immediately. On 15 October 1981, we raided Shakur Gafur's den. We arrested Chhotelal and Illiyas Taj Mahammad Pathan and confiscated nine swords, six types of knives, a revolver, thirty-four live bullets and thirteen live hand grenades.

Having recovered live grenades, I immediately contacted Sr PI Dange. In those days, we did not have a bomb disposal squad. Sr PI Dange contacted a bomb expert who advised us to immerse them in large drums of water. The gunpowder inside the grenades would get wet, rendering them useless. The thirteen bombs were then tied with coir ropes and immersed in water. The Jabalpur Police took custody of Chhotelal. Newspapers in Jabalpur ran a full-page article praising the Bombay Police.

Later, the Jabalpur Police completed the investigation in the case and filed a chargesheet against the offenders in a court. The case was to be heard on 18 January 1982 at the Hoshangabad Sessions Court.

On 17 January 1982, the Jabalpur Police left for Hoshangabad with Chhotelal by the 11 p.m. train. Around 4 a.m., when all the passengers were sleeping, Chhotelal complained of a stomach ache and asked to go to the bathroom. Bound by handcuffs and chains, he was taken to a bathroom at the next station. The police released his left arm to let him go into the bathroom. As a precaution, one hawaldar stood outside the door holding on to the other chain. Chhotelal emerged from the bathroom a few minutes later and attacked the hawaldar. He managed to free himself. When the other hawaldar moved towards Chhotelal, he pushed him aside and fled. A case of 'runaway from police custody' was lodged at Itarsi railway police station. Two months passed by.

The Jabalpur and Itarsi police had failed to trace Chhotelal. In March 1982, they informed ACP Ramachandran that he had fled. Sr PI Dange, PI Kolekar and I started searching for him. An informer told us that on 10 February 1982, Agripada police station had arrested Sheikh Salim Sheikh Abdul for possessing a knife. A case had been registered under sections 37 and 134 of the Bombay Police Act. We reached Agripada police station where I immediately identified the criminal as Chhotelal. We completed all formalities and handed him over to the Jabalpur Police. ACP Ramachandran told them, 'You are lucky that our Crime Branch helped arrest Chhotelal for the second time. Be careful with him now.'

I received an award on two occasions for this case. This truly was a rare moment.

59

DIAMOND PICKPOCKETING CASE

On 29 June 1984, a diamond merchant boarded BEST bus no. 122 from Nepean Sea Road. The bus was crowded due to the morning rush hour. He bought a ticket to Opera House and looked around for a vacant seat. Since he could not find one, he travelled standing. He got off at Opera House bus stop. He had just started walking towards Panchratna building, well known for housing offices of diamond merchants, when he noticed that the briefcase he was holding was open. He was shocked as he realized that a small pouch was missing from it. It contained forty-six packets of white diamonds, valued at nearly Rs 2 lakh.

The merchant rushed to file a complaint at Dr Dadasaheb Bhadkamkar Marg police station. The local police began investigating. A week had passed since the incident, but the thief had not gone to any market in Bombay to sell the diamonds. Given the seriousness of the crime, the Diamond Merchants Association approached Commissioner J.F. Ribeiro. He ordered the Crime Branch to investigate. Just the word 'pickpocketing' was enough for PI Zende. He asked me to call our team of Hawaldars Surve, Sarfare and Parshya Kadam.

This team knew exactly which pickpocket operated in which area. We began collecting information about pickpockets at work, particularly those operating on bus route no. 122. We were sure that the stolen diamonds would come to the market for sale.

On the morning of 8 July 1984, Hawaldar Kadam informed PI Zende that the diamonds were going to be brought for sale to Zaveri Bazaar on Sheikh Memon Street. We laid a trap under PI Zende's guidance. We arrested expert pickpocket Ramesh Mahadeo Kamble and recovered all the diamonds.

60

SUGAR TURNS BITTER

One morning, a sugar merchant from Baramati, Chandarmal Juvarmal Oswal, came to visit me at the Crime Branch. Since I hailed from Baramati, I was happy to see him. But when I saw the stress on his face, I gathered that the matter was serious.

A merchant in Bharuch needed 100 sacks of sugar. Accordingly, Oswal bought these from Malegaon Sugar factory and sent them to Gujarat by truck. However, the truck didn't reach Gujarat even two to three days later. The merchant in Bharuch complained to Oswal.

Oswal was worried because his prestige was at stake. He contacted Baramati taluka police and filed a report. The police began investigating. Meanwhile, Oswal came to visit me in Bombay. I asked him for the registration number of the truck, the colour and a description of the driver. He described the thirty-two-year-old driver, Nanamal Ram Narayan Shah. At the octroi toll, where all goods carriers were required to pay octroi duty and charged an entry fee, I found no trace of an entry in the register. I was sure that the truck had never left Maharashtra. I tracked down Shah's connections in Bombay, the places he frequented and the dhabas he visited. I received information that he had sold the goods within Maharashtra and would come to Kanhaiyya Stores in Ghatkopar to collect cash for the goods he had sold. We nabbed him there. He confessed to having sold fifty sacks of sugar to Jagan Kuber Singh Yadav of Chunabhatti and fifty bags to Kanhaiyya Stores. Based on his confession, we recovered the stolen goods. However, in that short period of time, the store keepers had sold small quantities of the sugar.

Even at this stage, we had strong evidence to help us recover the goods. This was the sugar factory's stamp on the sacks. We seized empty gunny bags from the shops and presented this as evidence before the court. We recovered cash equivalent to the value of the sugar along with the empty sacks and handed it over to Oswal following a court order.

61

INFORMERS

I had a successful tenure at the Crime Branch. While senior officers, colleagues and the constabulary of course had a big role to play in this, I can honestly say that my informers, too, played a part. While I was in service, and even after retirement, I have been asked, 'Bagwan, what do you mean by informers exactly? Who are they?'

'What makes the informers come to you?'

'How do you identify informers?'

'How do you determine if the information given is accurate?'

'Do you give them money? If yes, how much?'

It is time to answer all these questions.

An informer can be defined as a person who remains anonymous and gives the police information about criminals, crime scenes, or anything related to a crime. Every officer who joins the police service is fascinated by the thought of solving cases. To crack cases, the police need background information. A successful police officer is one who has a great network of informers. When you are in the police, you happen to interact with a variety of people. Criminals involved in big or small cases, pimps, drug addicts, pickpockets, car washers, hawkers selling pani-puri on the beach, taxi drivers, and indeed a variety of people working in different sectors are scrutinized by the police. It is from among these people that an informer can be cultivated. Any officer can create a network of informers, but the most important thing is to understand and recognize an informer's psyche, behaviour and morals. I will explain this in some detail.

When a criminal is arrested, he is separated from his associates. This is to allow him or her to provide information about them. At times, he or she does so out of enmity, and sometimes because he wants something from the police in return.

The first step is to ensure that the informer can trust the police officer. Therefore, it wouldn't be wrong to say that irrespective of caste, creed or clan, the officer must make all possible efforts to win an informer's trust. Once the informer trusts you, he or she risks his or her life to give you a tip-off. At such times, the informer must be able to believe that the officer will back him up strongly. The officer's behaviour should be assuring. In many cases, however, the informers try to take advantage of the officer's goodness. Thus, an officer must never take an informer at face value and should check for possibilities such as whether the informer is lying or telling the truth or providing information with an ulterior motive in mind.

My first posting was at Colaba police station. In those days, in the lanes behind Taj Mahal Hotel, there used to be opium dens at every corner. Hashish was sold openly. Morphine and 'brown sugar' were new in the market. The police would raid these stalls and catch the druggies. During one such raid, I met a strong, muscular young man. He was an addict who committed crimes to buy drugs. I understood his weakness and, using that as leverage, turned him into an informer. He would take foreign tourists who wanted drugs to Shakur Gafur's hang-outs at Nagpada and Colaba. Gafur was a notorious drug dealer. My informer would get free drugs from dealers in return for bringing new customers. He would give me information about the stock that would come and where it would be stored. Sometimes, foreign tourists would take narcotics to sell. My informer told me about one such tourist.

I seized 9 kg of narcotics from him during one raid. I came across another young man who was arrested for his involvement in a narcotics racket when I was posted at Colaba police station. He had been in jail and knew the criminals and their way of working well. I motivated him to give up drugs, and he got me useful information that helped to solve a few cases.

I knew of a taxi driver who was part of the narcotics net. He was also a rash driver who would often be caught by the traffic police. I identified his weakness and included him in my group of informers. He, in fact, helped me bust a gang involved in car thefts. Not only did he give me vital information about the car thieves, but also kept a watch on them and helped me during the operation with help from other informers. I could solve the murder case of the hockey player because of him. In a separate incident, my informers traced the girlfriend of an accused and brought her to me.

After Colaba, I was posted at Santacruz police station. I found three young men who would sell cinema tickets on the black market outside Milan theatre. Their rivalry often resulted in fights. I knew their weaknesses and made each of them understand the 'new job' that would help them earn money. I convinced them to help the police by keeping their eyes and ears open. They liked their new job and agreed to become my informers. I was at Santacruz for just about a year, but they helped me a lot during that period. They knew everything that was happening in Bombay—who belonged to which gang, which gang had committed which crime, they knew it all. When I was transferred to the Crime Branch, I was able to arrest dangerous criminals like Jaffar and Munna with their help. These informers not only gave me tips, but also helped in police operations by offering undercover assistance. Hardened criminals would be able to identify the policemen but not the informers. Eventually, most of my informers found decent jobs but we still keep in touch.

One drug addict gave me information about Iqbal Charoli, alias Pistawala, who was involved in a narcotics racket. While I was posted with the Crime Branch, my informers risked their lives to help me. In one case, they kept watch for forty-eight hours at a stretch, extracted information, found names and addresses of the accused and even participated in raids. Pushkin Marlbrose and his sister Sabrina played an important role in the Shaikh Munir operation.

One of my informers lived on Shuklaji Street. He owned a small factory that manufactured cheap aerated water that was used in illicit liquor bars and would often be inebriated himself. He would often drink with members of Bombay's underworld and thus knew about their whereabouts. One day, there was a robbery at a jeweller's shop on Princess Street. In those days, I held a non-executive post at the Local Arms Division. Sr PI Sahasrabuddhe, who was in charge of Crime Branch (Administration), asked me to investigate. I contacted my informer and told him about the case. He instantly said, 'Sahib, this was done by a UP gang. I will get you the exact information soon.'

Two days later, he called me in the night. The gang involved in the robbery was staying with Gulya Kashmiri in a small chawl close to Navjeevan Society in Bombay Central.

I immediately called PI Sahasrabuddhe. 'Sir, I request you to please give me my old staff from the Crime Branch for this operation.' He agreed. The same night, I raided the den and arrested Zuber and his three associates from UP. Further investigation led us to information about three to four large robberies, which the police were able to solve. Zuber, the 'supari killer' hitman, also confessed to murdering Rusi Mehta, the municipal corporator. Thus, multiple cases were solved based on one tip-off.

Since my informer was part of the same circle as the criminals, he acquainted himself with Zuber and his partners before getting them drunk to an extent where they lost consciousness.

My informer risked his life to lead me to them. My network widened when I was at the Crime Branch because of PI Zende's encouragement. At the Crime Branch, I was able to solve many cases thanks to my informers. Among these were the Belgian diamond robbery and the Sarla Agarwal murder case.

There were also some instances where my informers had a close shave.

When I was posted at Dr D.B. Marg police station, one of my informers gave me a tip-off about a gang that dealt in drugs. I conducted a raid and seized several weapons and a large consignment of drugs. My informer was attacked and stabbed in the back and chest. Thankfully, someone informed me and I was able to save him. An informer risks his life only when he feels assured that he will be taken care of in times of need.

My informers had immense faith in me. One of them gave me information about a big crime lord whom I arrested. His associates came to know who had given me the information but were scared of attacking him because they knew I would not spare them. However, after I was transferred from the Crime Branch, the gang attacked my informer. When I came to know that he had lost his fingers in this attack, I was filled with regret. I did everything in my capacity, right from admitting him to a hospital to providing monetary help. I also gave information about his attackers to Pydhonie police station and ensured that they were put behind bars.

When I was with the Crime Branch, one of my informers tipped me off about a large drug deal being done by a foreigner in Bombay Central. I laid a trap as per the tip-off and seized 19 kg of contraband. These drugs were worth several lakhs in the international market.

The raid had caused a great loss to Ijaz from Murgi Mohalla. He began to wonder how I had got information about this deal. He managed to find out the name of my informer and began following him. One day, he caught hold of him near the

J.J. Hospital junction. His associates were ready to attack with choppers. Having been cornered, my informer threatened them, 'If you kill me, Bagwan Sahib will not spare you. Your days will be numbered. You know that, don't you? But if I survive, I will put in a word with him and help your business in Murgi Mohalla to flourish.'

A frustrated and angry Ijaz hesitated. Then he withdrew his men and left. God alone knows how my informer thought of speaking those words. Later, a similar incident happened with another of my informers. One morning, his father-in-law came to the Crime Branch. 'Sir, there is a problem.'

'What happened?'

'Sir, my son-in-law hasn't stepped out of the house for two days. He is scared of something. Please help him.'

I knew my informer well. I had never seen him gloomy or depressed and was convinced that something was wrong. I immediately went to his house. He had locked himself inside. As soon as he saw me, he broke down. 'Sir, they are going to kill me. They have given me three days. Two days are up. Today I will not be spared.'

My informer was trembling as he spoke. I heard him out patiently. He calmed down after venting. I asked him, 'Now, tell me, which gang is going to kill you? Tell me the name.'

The phone rang before he could answer my question. He was petrified after seeing the number on the caller ID. 'Sir, look, those people are calling again.'

I saw the number. It belonged to a dangerous criminal. I wasn't aware of what had transpired between them. My informer hadn't given me any details either. The phone kept ringing. With every ring, the tension was mounting. I picked up the phone. 'This is CID officer Isaque Bagwan. The man you want to kill is my man. If anything happens to him, I will not spare you. If anything has happened between the two of you, sit across a table and resolve it.

If my man is at fault, I will punish him appropriately, but do not dare to think of harming him in any way.'

The call was disconnected from the other end. My informer's father-in-law fell at my feet. He had never dreamt of a policeman doing something like this. My informer, too, was shocked. The next day, I received a call from the gangster. He said, 'Sir, forgive me. I made a mistake. Your man is free now.'

Such incidents are not uncommon. A similar thing happened with another informer.

Ranjit ran a brothel on the ground floor of Naju Mansion on Wodehouse Road. One day, my informer went to him. While the two were talking, Chintya Dada, a dangerous criminal, came with a sword to loot the brothel. When he saw my informer, Dada was enraged. He charged towards him. Everyone told Dada, 'He is Bagwan Sahib's informer. If you touch him, Bagwan Sahib will not spare you.' This was enough for Dada. He left quietly. My terrified informer realized that he had been saved because of me and returned the favour by tipping me off in other important cases.

All I want to say here is that tip-offs from informers can help solve many crimes. A policeman gets awards, rewards and fame. For the informers, their life is at stake as they have to face the criminal world every day. I also had several women informers. They, too, were involved in the crime world. Some were gang lords, some were prostitutes while some were involved in the drug trade.

In those days, there were no mobile phones. My informers would call me at the Crime Branch office. If I was not available, they would leave a coded message. For example, 'Tell sir that Raju mechanic had called. Sir's car is ready.'

The person receiving the call would never know Raju's real identity. Only I knew what that meant. I would always meet my informers outside police station limits. But where did I meet them? Read on to find out.

62

THE AWE OF THE BOMBAY CID

It was 7 p.m. on 7 February 1983. All my colleagues had left. I was about to leave too when a taxi driver came to meet me with a foreigner. They looked troubled. I asked the taxi driver, 'What has happened?'

'Sir, I took this foreigner from Ritz Hotel in Churchgate to Byculla. Something terrible happened there. I do not know English. Please ask him for details.'

The foreigner introduced himself as S.A. Dawre from South Africa. He had come to India as a tourist and was staying at Ritz Hotel. He spent four days sightseeing. His friend in South Africa, who was of Indian origin, had given him some items to be handed over to his relatives in the city. He hired a taxi outside the hotel and asked the driver to take him to an address written in Hindi on a piece of paper. In Byculla, Dawre started asking passers-by for directions. A young man offered to help. He led Dawre into a small bylane where he was surrounded by five persons armed with choppers, swords and revolvers.

They robbed him of 1700 rands, his gold cigarette lighter, gold watch, four diamond-studded rings and two gold rings. Dawre had not imagined such a thing even in his worst nightmares. He had been looted in a foreign country in broad daylight.

Passers-by were wondering why this foreigner was screaming. That was when Dawre saw the same taxi which had brought him to Byculla. Somehow, he managed to explain to the taxi driver that he wanted to go to a police station. The taxi driver realized that something was wrong and drove him to the Crime Branch.

The Crime Branch had nothing to do with this incident. The crime spot came under the jurisdiction of Agripada police station. However, since a foreigner had been robbed, this was a blot on our country's image. I had prepared an album of photographs of criminals operating in the area. I showed it to Dawre. He identified one of them. Babu Reshim was a known criminal in Byculla. However, there was one problem. As per police procedure, the case had to be registered in Agripada. I explained the procedure to Dawre, but he was not inclined to register a complaint. He only wanted his property back. Finally, I convinced him to go to the police station. I gave him my visiting card and, on the reverse, wrote a note requesting the duty officer to help Dawre. He left with my visiting card, and I carried on with my work.

The next day, when I reached the office, I was told that I had been urgently summoned by the ACP (Detection Crime Branch) D.P. Shringarpure. He was the Sr PI, while Mr Zende was the API, when I was attached to Colaba police station. This was the time when I had probed the Arab national's death at Taj Mahal Hotel.

I went to his cabin, not knowing what was in store for me. When I entered, he came down on me heavily. I was stunned when he said, 'Where is the foreign currency, gold and diamond jewellery recovered from the Byculla gang, Bagwan? There is no record of the recovery in the office!'

I could not believe the allegation being levelled against me—the charge that I had looted Dawre. I refuted the accusations, but my pleas fell on deaf ears. I returned to my office on the ground floor. PI Zende, who had been asked to look into this allegation, questioned me. I told him the facts of the case. He was convinced of the truth of my statement and asked me to accompany him to the ACP's cabin.

PI Zende told ACP Shringarpure, 'Sir, you have levelled serious charges against an officer working under me and demoralized him. If you have to take any action, please take it against me and then Bagwan. But I would like to know who has made these allegations.'

The ACP said, 'A gang leader from Byculla approached chief minister Vasantdada Patil with the help of a political leader. The allegation is that Bagwan took Rs 25,000 from Dawre to beat up a gang leader and then took away all his belongings.'

PI Zende understood the gravity of the situation and quickly sent two constables to Ritz Hotel to get Dawre. I was extremely tense and clueless. I breathed a sigh of relief when I saw Dawre entering the Crime Branch with the constables. He met Addl Commissioner (Crime) D. Ramachandran and ACP Shringarpure. When told about what had transpired, Dawre was shocked. 'Sir, I really don't know who told you this. The fact is that I got all my stolen property back because of this visiting card.'

He held out the visiting card I had given him and took us through the entire incident. He had left my office and was on his way to Agripada when he spotted the same gang on the street. He stopped the cab and showed them my visiting card. The gang had heard of me. They whispered for a while and decided not to cross swords with me. Without any arguments, they returned Dawre's property to him. He could hardly believe that he had recovered his valuables merely on the basis of a Bombay CID officer's visiting card. He was overjoyed and had come back to the Crime Branch to meet me. Since I was not in the office, I did not know what had happened.

My seniors calmed down after hearing this and congratulated me instead.

I realized that this was the work of Babu Reshim who had used his contacts to influence the chief minister and get me punished. Dawre wrote to PI Zende from South Africa. It read: 'I am going to preserve Bagwan's visiting card as a memento of my visit to Bombay. I am going to tell my countrymen that merely by showing the visiting card of a Bombay CID officer, all my stolen property was returned. The mere mention of the Bombay CID strikes terror in the hearts of criminals.'

This certificate from a foreign tourist had done the Bombay CID proud. PI Zende showed the letter to DCP Arvind Patwardhan, who was stationed at Maharashtra State Police Headquarters. DCP Patwardhan had been an ace detective of the Bombay CID with a track record of solving baffling cases of bank fraud and cheque forgery. DCP Patwardhan was pleased to know that the flag of the Bombay CID was flying high. Later, Sanjay Raut, a well-known journalist who covered the crime beat for *Loksatta*, happened to meet DCP Patwardhan. While discussing the police and crime in the city, Raut said that there were no longer any officers of Suresh Pendse and Vinayak Vakatkar's calibre in the Bombay CID.

DCP Patwardhan replied, 'You are wrong, Raut, when you say that there are no officers like Pendse and Vakatkar. Here is proof!' A seasoned journalist, Raut understood the value of the letter written by a foreigner. The next day, *Loksatta* carried an article with the headline 'Awe of the Bombay CID' on its front page in praise of the Bombay Police.

When I had joined the Crime Branch, the Assistant Commissioner of the Detection Crime Branch was Madhav T. Gupte. He was a cool, even-tempered, good-natured and soft-spoken gentleman. It was difficult to find such a competent and dedicated officer in the police department. He was truly a stalwart and had thorough knowledge about the intricacies of the department. He understood the working of criminal minds like no other. He commanded the respect of all the officers and men working at the Crime Branch and provided them with excellent advice when needed.

He kept track of my work and made the following remark in my confidential report: 'Excellent officer. This outstanding officer is "The Pillar of the Crime Branch".'

63

HOTEL BERRY'S

One day, I was having tea with my wife when the doorbell rang. I opened the door to find taxi driver Vinod Kunder standing outside with a stout, well-dressed young man. Vinod was my informer, but he had never come to my house before. 'Vinod, what is the matter?'

'Sir, this is Nasir Bhai, the owner of Berry's Hotel. I have come here about a matter that concerns him.'

I was furious and shouted at Vinod because I did not entertain anyone at home, irrespective of the case. Vinod knew why I was angry. He replied politely, 'Sir, I know you do not like to meet anyone at home, but I have brought Nasir Bhai to you with great hope. Please hear him just once.' I calmed down a little and spoke to Nasir.

'Tell me. What happened?'

Nasir broke down and fell at my feet. He spoke between sobs. Two years ago, Nasir Amlani had bought a restaurant called 'Berry's' in the posh area of Churchgate. Nasir introduced an orchestra there. In those days, many hotels served food and drinks, but none of them had an orchestra. The novelty clicked. Hotel Berry's became popular. Every evening, the hotel would be frequented by music lovers. Nasir's business began to flourish. It was not long before Hamid, the son of Dongri's gambling den conductor and illicit liquor dealer, Aziz Dilip, heard of the hotel's fame.

Hamid and his gang marched into the hotel. They showed Nasir a revolver. Nasir, who was sitting at the cash counter, was petrified. Hamid's associate noticed this and said, 'Seth, this is Hamid Bhai. From today, our boss will sit here every day.'

Hamid had recently committed a murder and had many other cases registered against him. Everyone knew about it and feared him. Nasir, too, was scared. From that day, Hamid came to the hotel every evening. Nasir was left with no choice but to serve him. He would sit in the hotel, drink to his heart's content and never pay the bill. Not only that, he did not allow anyone else to sit on the tables adjacent to his. Nasir watched this happen every day. Soon, Hamid began to take money from Nasir's counter and throw it at the orchestra singers. To avoid an argument, Nasir started locking the cash counter and leaving the hotel before Hamid came. Hamid noticed this and caught hold of Nasir one day. He put his revolver on the counter and demanded money. Nasir refused. Hamid, under the influence of drugs, lost his temper and threatened Nasir, 'Within two days, I will pick your son up. Even your father will be forced to give me money!'

Nasir was filled with fear at the thought of any harm coming to his eight-year-old son, Riyaz. He decided not to send Riyaz to school. He even booked a room in Hotel President and kept him there. This sparked tension at home, and there were arguments between the husband and wife. His wife wanted Nasir to approach the police. Nasir was afraid to go against Hamid. Finally, Nasir met Commissioner Ribeiro, who asked him to file a written complaint and sent him to DCP (Zone 1) Ranjit Singh Sharma. Nasir met Kunder outside Berry's Hotel. He knew Kunder and told him of the problem he was facing.

'Nasir Bhai, don't be afraid. There is a Crime Branch officer who has given Hamid a tough time. Come with me.'

Kunder had brought Nasir to my house because he was afraid of meeting me at the Crime Branch office. I told Nasir to meet me there the next day. I sent a constable to Dongri to summon Hamid. I made Nasir sit behind a glass partition in an adjoining room.

Hamid came to my office. 'Salam, Sahib. You called me?'

I ignored his greeting. 'Hamid, the matter about Hotel Berry's has reached me. Tell me, what should I do about it?'

His face lost colour. He literally fell off his chair. 'Sir, I was drunk that day. I swear on Allah that I will not do anything to Nasir.'

'Hamid, the day you are seen near Churchgate will be your last.'

Hamid knew my temper. I called Nasir in. He came out shivering. Hamid apologized to him. Today, Riyaz Amlani is the owner of a famous chain of restaurants.

The next day, Nasir came to my office. I asked, 'What happened? Did Hamid once again . . .?'

Interrupting me, he said, 'No, Sir. Hamid did not do anything. I came to meet you. Actually, my doctor's clinic is near your office. I visit him every day to get my blood pressure checked. So I dropped in.'

I asked him if he would like a cup of tea. He refused and asked me to visit his hotel instead.

One day, I went to the hotel. I was not fond of alcohol or meat, neither did I enjoy the orchestra nor the atmosphere. Nasir made it a habit to come to my office every day on the pretext of visiting the doctor and inviting me to his hotel. Once I realized this pattern, I started making excuses and began avoiding him. Despite this, Nasir would wait for me outside my office. He would take me to his hotel and chat with me in the verandah outside. Having my constables and my police vehicle parked outside his hotel, Nasir felt safe. With Hamid out of the way, his business increased. I, meanwhile, found a place to meet informers. It was not possible to call them to the Crime Branch, so I would meet them there.

Every night after dinner, I would go to Hotel Berry's with my team—Pawar and Pasi. Whenever we received a tip-off from my informers, we would immediately leave from there. This went on for a couple of years until one of my colleagues informed the ACB about me holding stakes in Hotel Berry's. When my ACP heard this, he asked me, 'Bagwan, why do you go to that place?'

'Sir, where else can I meet my informers. They cannot come to the office.' The ACP laughed at this. He was aware of the truth. The same was the case with PI Zende who supported me at every step. Whenever I had to go to meet an informer, I would seek his permission. He was a witness to all the incidents that concerned me. If anyone spoke against me, he would say, 'I know where Bagwan is. Don't try to instigate me.'

My success grew in the Crime Branch, and so did the number of well-wishers—in those days, 'well-wishers' meant enemies. Eventually, I stopped visiting Hotel Berry's. The chapter ended on a happy note but, at the Crime Branch, a new chapter—a sinister one—was about to begin.

64

THE HOTEL PALM GROVE INCIDENT

J.F. Ribeiro was the Commissioner of Police, Greater Bombay, from 1982–85. He was one of the most outstanding officers to have served as the commissioner. He introduced a sea of changes in the department and took strict action against corrupt officers. This did not go down well with two officers in particular: Rahu and Ketu (names changed). It was rumoured that they had joined hands with the then home secretary and tried their best to get him transferred. A journalist with *Navakal*, a Marathi newspaper, was a close acquaintance of the two officers.

It was April 1985 when the journalist came to me. 'Sir, I have some important work. Can you please come with me?' I knew him as he frequented the police press room. He took me to his house and, after some pleasantries, inserted a video cassette into the VCR. 'Bagwan Sahib. See this video.' It was of a glamorous party in full swing. There were many well-known government officials and police officers. They were inebriated and dancing. I froze in my seat. He said, 'Sir, excluding the police officers, please tell me the names of the other people you see in the video.' I understood his intention.

I politely refused and left his house. I was extremely uncomfortable after watching the video. I remembered that about four months ago, on 12 December 1984, Babbu, alias Kriparam Khera, had invited several important government and police officers to attend a party at Hotel Palm Grove on Juhu Tara Road.

A video recording from this party had landed into the hands of this journalist. I recollected that Babbu had come to invite me, but I had torn the invitation into pieces in front of him.

This was the time when the Subhash Tuli gang operated in Bombay. The gang would target foreign tourists outside hotels like the Taj and Oberoi. Once they selected their target, they would show him or her a bundle of Rs 100 notes and promise them an exchange rate higher than usual for the dollars. The bundles had real currency notes at the top and bottom, but blank notes in the middle. In case a foreign tourist agreed to the deal, they would take him or her to a corner. They would say that the police were moving around in the area and would proceed to quickly take away the dollars and hand over a bundle of fake notes wrapped in paper. Some police officers knew of this con game, which is why the Subhash Tuli gang continued to operate in the city.

Originally from Delhi, Tuli had inducted Hansraj and Rajkumar, con men from the capital's Connaught Place area, into his gang. Since they needed one more person to do odd jobs, Tuli also got Babbu to Bombay. Babbu formed close ties with people who had good connections with police officers. Gradually, he took over Tuli's gang, which the latter was unable to accept. He was frustrated, but he couldn't do anything at that point. Having earned a lot of money by conning tourists, Babbu invited all officers, irrespective of whether he knew them or not, to a five-star hotel, Hotel Palm Grove. He spent a fortune to ensure everyone had a good time. He also videotaped all the officers who were a part of the celebrations. He could now blackmail any officer who went against him in the future. But Babbu's ulterior motives were known to just one person present at the party—Subhash Tuli.

It was 1985. Three months had passed. Tuli managed to acquire the video cassette from the party through one of Babbu's gang members. He was thrilled for two reasons. First, he would now have an upper hand over Babbu and, second, he would be able to expose the police officers who had acted against him. He got a journalist on his side. Armed with the video cassette, the journalist was in possession of deadly evidence. He informed Rahu and Ketu about it. The trio then passed on this information to the home secretary. He was pleased with the idea of exposing these officers. The journalist had approached me with the hope of identifying all the police officers and criminals at the party. He was unhappy when I did not help.

I took my close friend, SI Raja Tambat, into confidence and told him about the Hotel Palm Grove party video cassette. He informed the officers who had attended this party. They immediately asked him, 'Raja, who gave you this news?' He told them it was me.

A day or two passed. News of this party was splashed on the front pages. The entire police department was shocked. Commissioner Ribeiro transferred all the officers involved in this party out of Bombay. He transferred me to the Local Arms Division. Surprised, I asked him, 'Sir, why have I been transferred? I did not go to that party.'

'Bagwan, it's a routine transfer.'

He had spoken to all the officers who had attended the party. 'Who did this?' The response had been unanimous, 'Bagwan!'

That did it. I was on the transfer list. I believe this happened because one officer from the department instigated all my colleagues against me and created a wall of distrust. When PI Zende heard about this, he was distressed. He had immense faith in me. He tried to stand by me and bluntly told the reporters, 'Had Bagwan done this, he would have handed over the cassette to the commissioner or the ACB. Why would he give the cassette to a reporter? Why would he bring shame to his own colleagues through the media?'

Over a period of time, everyone came to know that it was the journalist who was behind this drama. This cleared the misunderstandings that had crept in.

65

HARASSMENT IN SERVICE

My good work during my tenure at the Crime Branch caused some heartburn among my colleagues. I will give you some examples. On 13 March 1986, Charles Sobhraj, a criminal on Interpol's most wanted list, distributed sweets among the staff and prisoners at Tihar Jail to celebrate his birthday. Sobhraj, a French national, was a psychopath and serial killer who would bewitch women with his charm and then murder them. He was responsible for twelve murders and had taken refuge in India. The sweets he distributed were spiked. Once the other prisoners and the jail staff lost consciousness, Sobhraj escaped. Since Sr PI Zende had arrested him in 1971, Commissioner D.S. Soman handed over the responsibility of nabbing him again to Sr PI Zende.

He included me in his team for operation 'Mission Charles Sobhraj'. However, my name was crossed out by the commissioner and substituted by an officer of his choice, SI Emmanuel Amolik. The team arrested Sobhraj at Coquoiero Hotel in Goa. This operation required Sr PI Zende to use all his skills to restrain the trigger-happy Amolik.

Here is another instance. I was checking the papers of a car theft panchnama at the Crime Branch. I got up to take a phone call. I returned to my table to find the papers missing. I had been well-trained under Sr PI Zende, so I made a systematic note of the missing papers in the station diary. A few days later, I received a message that Addl CP (Administration) Sudhakar Dev wanted to see me urgently. He was a disciplinarian and did not hesitate to suspend anyone for the slightest of mistakes. I went to his chamber. He held the car theft panchnama papers in front of me and asked me sternly, 'Bagwan, what is all this?'

He was under the impression that I was involved in the thefts. I told him how the papers had gone missing and that I had immediately made a note of it. I showed him the evidence. He laughed and said, 'Bagwan, you have a "well-wisher" in the department. You are a hard-working man, which is why someone is plotting against you. I have understood this. Continue exercising precaution in the future.'

Another incident happened when I was about to receive the police medal for gallantry on Republic Day. The award had been announced after I arrested David Pardeshi, the man who had killed Amirzada in a sessions court.

Every day after 20 January 1985, I had been attending the parade rehearsal at Shivaji Park. On 24 January, the newspaper carried a report about how I had extorted money from a woman. A photograph of me receiving a medal had also been printed. Commissioner Ribeiro was annoyed when he saw this. He had announced the medal for me in the presence of the judge, right after the shootout in court. Given the serious allegations against me, he decided to withdraw it. ACP (Crime Branch) M. T. Gupte requested him to take a decision only after a thorough inquiry. Commissioner Ribeiro had great faith in ACP Gupte and agreed. Sr PI Zende was asked to get to the bottom of the matter.

Mustafa Dossa's brother-in-law, Jaffar, had been arrested. It had been alleged that I had tried to extort money from Jaffar's sister-in-law. Sr PI Zende produced Jaffar and his sister-in-law before ACP Gupte. Both of them told him that I had never made any such demand and that they had been forced to say so by some other officers in the department. The finger of suspicion pointed towards a journalist working with an English newspaper. This journalist had an axe to grind with Sr PI Zende too and was trying to kill two birds with one stone. ACP Gupte understood this and immediately went to Commissioner Ribeiro who was shocked. Later, I went on to receive my second medal for gallantry with honour. I am thankful to ACP Gupte and Sr PI Zende for standing by me like a rock.

66

A HISTORY OF PERPETUAL GANG
WAR IN BOMBAY

Gangs controlled by Haji Mastan, operating out of dens in Dongri, Pydhonie, Nagpada and Agripada, smuggled goods into Bombay through the sea and air routes. These gangs were also involved in settling land disputes. Mastan's gang comprised Dawood Ibrahim, Sabir, Khalid Pahelwan, Rajji, Chota Shakeel, Hanif Kutta, Taufique Takla, Mehmood Kaliya, Anjum Pahelwan and several others. Karim Lala's gang comprised Sayeed Batla, Ayub Lala, Amirzada, Alamzeb, Samad Khan, Iqbal Tempo and others.

The year was 1977. On 2 July, Iqbal Natik, the editor of an Urdu weekly, who was also a dear friend of Sabir and Dawood, was murdered by Sayeed Batla and Ayub Lala for writing against the Pathan gang. The Sabir–Dawood gang assisted the Dongri police in arresting these gangsters. From this point, the Dawood and Pathan gangs became bitter rivals. When Batla was out on bail, the Sabir–Dawood gang abducted him and took him to their den in Musafir Khana, where they cut off his fingers with swords. Later, differences cropped up between Pahelwan and Kaliya. The latter quit Dawood's gang and tried to kill Pahelwan by throwing a grenade at a funeral procession. The attempt failed and Kaliya switched loyalties to the Pathan gang.

In February 1981, Amirzada, Alamzeb, Jaffer and Abdul had killed Sabir at a petrol pump in Prabhadevi. The Pathan gang's next target was Dawood. They tried to kill him but failed thrice. Dawood joined hands with Rajan Nair, aka Bada Rajan, Rajendra Nikhalje, aka Chota Rajan, Rama Naik, Babu Reshim and Arun Gawli. On 6 September 1983, Amirzada was gunned down by David Pardeshi in a sessions court. It was Bada Rajan who had plotted his killing based on orders from Dawood. Chota Rajan took over the reins after Bada Rajan was murdered by Abdul Kunju's marksman, Chandrashekar Safaliga. Later, Chota Rajan killed Kunju in Tilak Nagar.

The two young Pathans, Samad Khan and Hamid Dilip, had turned into a menace while being at loggerheads with each other. Hamid had murdered a Bahraini football player in a case of mistaken identity, while Khan had shot down businessman S.K. Jain at Sea Rock Hotel when he was actually supposed to murder another businessman.

Karim Lala's nephew, Samad Khan, got Aziz Dilip, the matka king of Dongri, assassinated over a territorial spat. Dilip's sons, Hamid and Majid, then had Khan's father, Rahim Lala, murdered.

Later, he killed both Hamid and Majid, who were now part of Dawood's gang, in two separate incidents. Khan then challenged Dawood by looting his goods. On 4 October 1984, Dawood took help from Babu Reshim of Rama Naik's gang to kill Samad Khan in Girgaum's Sikka Nagar.

In 1985, Dawood fled to Dubai. He was followed by his gang members Chota Shakeel, Sharad Anna Shetty, Sunil Sawant, aka Sautya, and others. News reached Dawood about Mehmood Kaliya coming to Dubai for a holiday. He kept track of Kaliya's movements and even got to know when he would return to Mumbai. Dawood then informed SI Amolik about Kaliya's arrival from Dubai who encountered Kaliya at Mumbai airport itself.

He later had Kaliya's brother killed near Malabar Apartments on Nepean Sea Road.

SI Davkar killed Jaffer Jamal Siddique in an encounter at his residence in Thane. Dawood's gang informed the Gujarat Police about Alamzeb and Abdul Latif's hideout near Ahmedabad. The police killed both of them in separate encounters. Both of them were wanted by the Bombay Police in several cases. Rama Naik, who handled land disputes in Bombay for the gang, left for Dubai. During his meeting with Dawood, Sunil Sawant and Chota Rajan, a dispute over money matters enraged Naik. He returned to Bombay and decided to break all ties with Dawood. The Rama Naik gang then killed Arvind Dholakia, a real estate builder who was a member of Dawood's gang and the owner of a disco, Caesar's Palace, in Khar. The gang then killed Satish Raje, another of Dawood's associates. They blocked his car at Byculla Bridge and broke the bullet-proof glass with their hammers before shooting Raje dead. They later tracked down another of Dawood's gang members, Rajji, and killed him too.

In retaliation, Babu Reshim of Rama Naik's gang was attacked in the lock-up at Agripada police station. Vijay Utkar of the Kenjari gang, armed with grenades and guns, stormed in and killed Reshim. A constable on guard was also killed in the attack. Ashok Joshi of the Rama Naik gang and three of his associates were also gunned down in their car at Panvel by the Dawood and Chota Rajan gangs.

On 21 July 1988, Rama Naik was killed in an encounter in Chembur by PI Rajan Katdare of Nagpada police station. Arun Gawli then proceeded to establish a stronghold in Byculla's Dagdi chawl. His gang comprised Sada Pawle, aka Sadamama, Bandya Adivarekar, aka Bandyamama, Chota Babu, Tanya Koli—all sharpshooters—and forty to fifty other gangsters. The bomb blasts of 12 March 1993 resulted in a major split in Dawood's gang. Chota Rajan separated and moved to Malaysia. He used his resources to eliminate Sharad Anna Shetty and Sunil Sawant in Dubai, striking a major blow to Dawood.

Chota Shakeel attempted and failed to kill Chota Rajan in Malaysia. Hanif Kutta, a close associate of Dawood, died of kidney failure in Dubai. Dawood's younger brother, Noora, succumbed to a heart attack. Anjum Pahelwan, his henchman in Bombay, was killed in Santacruz. Amar Naik, who operated on his behalf in central Bombay, was involved in brown sugar smuggling. The late SI Vijay Salaskar killed Naik in an encounter. The relationship between Arun Gawli and Amar Naik's younger brother, Ashwin Naik, had become strained.

On 19 April 1994, Sada Pawle of Arun Gawli's gang sent Ravindra Sawant disguised as an advocate to kill Naik at the sessions court. The attempt failed and Sawant was arrested on the spot. His interrogation at Colaba police station revealed that he had been hired by Gawli and Pawle to kill Ashwin Naik. The case was handed over to the Detection Crime Branch, CID, for further investigation. While Gawli was in police custody, his sharpshooters—Sada Pawle and Bandya Adivarekar—were killed in encounters.

These are just a few of the many incidents. Many known and lesser known criminals have been killed in gang wars or police encounters. These gang wars have been going on in Mumbai for several years and will continue to do so.

67

DAWOOD FLEES BOMBAY AND INDIA

The year was 1985. The Bombay Police were under a lot of pressure to apprehend Dawood. He was no longer safe in Bombay, the city that had witnessed his rise to the pinnacle of the underworld. Worried that the law would crush him, he decided that this was the right time to flee with his close associates to Dubai. He had a well-established network in Bombay which could be remote-controlled from there. This allowed him to carry on with his clandestine activities in the city in a hush-hush manner.

The Babri Masjid demolition in December 1992 and the widespread riots that followed made him seethe with anger. Revenge possessed him. He planned the Bombay bomb blasts of 12 March 1993 which left more than 200 people dead. The city had never witnessed such loss of life and property, the wounds of which are etched in the mind and heart of every Mumbaikar.

Investigations revealed that Dawood and Tiger Memon were the masterminds of the tragedy. They had carried out the horrendous terror attacks with help and guidance from Pakistan's ISI. Ever since, Dawood and his associates have been on the most wanted list of India, Interpol and many other anti-crime and anti-terror agencies across the world.

68

MUSHTAQ MEMON, AKA TIGER MEMON

In 1985, PI Madhukar Zende was transferred from the Crime Branch to the Agripada police station as Sr PI. One afternoon I received a call from him.

'Bagwan, the Customs officers have arrested a person and brought him to the police station. While bringing him here in their car, he snatched a revolver from them and fled. They chased and nabbed him. He refuses to say a word except that his name is Mushtaq. Come and see if you can identify him.'

At the police station, the Customs officers told me that they had been monitoring the phone calls of a person of interest in the Manish Market area of Crawford Market, which had become a hub for smuggling operations. While intercepting one such call, they learnt that a person on a scooter was to deliver some gold biscuits to another individual in Bombay Central. They followed him from Manish Market to Saat Rasta in Agripada. They nabbed him just as he was about to hand over the gold. A search revealed twelve gold biscuits valued at about Rs 6 lakh. They pushed him into their car and made him sit between two officers. All of a sudden, he pushed one of them, snatched his revolver from the holster and, brandishing the weapon, fled with the officers in hot pursuit. He entered Almas, a four-storeyed building at Saat Rasta. While running up the stairs, he lost his balance and fell, hurting himself. The officers grabbed him but could not find the revolver. I entered the lock-up and looked at him.

'Sir! This is Mushtaq Memon, aka Tiger Memon! He is part of a big smuggling ring!'

Memon had started his career as an accountant with Memon Cooperative Bank in Imamwada, Dongri. He was intelligent, well-built and known to be daring. He had also worked as a bodyguard for Dawood's brother, Noora. He got involved in smuggling operations with Mohamed Dossa and Mustafa Majnu. When I questioned him about the revolver, he said he had no knowledge of it. I threatened to take him to the Crime Branch for interrogation. That got him talking.

'Sir, I got caught with the gold and wanted to escape, which is why I grabbed the revolver and fled. I threw it into one of the municipal garbage vans near Thackersey Mills.'

We took him to the spot and managed to recover the revolver. Since it was lunch time, the vans had not moved away. The Customs officers were relieved to have found it.

In another episode a couple of days later, the newspapers reported that the Customs had seized a Gypsy vehicle along the coastline of Raigad district. The vehicle was carrying gold worth crores. It had been smuggled in from an Arab country and was to be brought to Bombay. The Customs had arrested several of the accused, along with their informer Manju, to avoid arousing suspicion. They were locked up at Azad Maidan police station. The Customs offered a reward of 20 per cent of the seizure to tempt informers. Manju was one such informer and a partner of Chota Kasu, a member of Dawood's gang member who ran a matka gambling joint in Pydhonie. Memon was suspicious of Manju. He got into a stage-managed fight in order to be arrested and put in the Azad Maidan lock-up. There, Memon beat Manju savagely and burnt him with cigarette butts till the latter could bear it no longer and confessed to having tipped off the Customs authorities. The next day, the Customs got Manju released, but he was on Memon's hit list. Tiger Memon's gang killed him a couple of days later.

Memon, one of the masterminds of the 1993 Bombay blasts, fled to Dubai two days before the attack. He, too, is on India's list of most wanted terrorists.

69

GALLANTRY MEDALS MADE THE DIFFERENCE

In 1986, I was transferred to Lamington Road police station, now called Dr D.B. Marg police station, as an SI after a successful tenure at the Detection Crime Branch, CID. I was placed on station house duty. For a month, I continued with this. When DCP (Zone 2) S.M. Mushrif came for a night round, he noticed the ribbons on my uniform. He said, 'You have a bar on your shoulders which means you have been awarded the police medal for gallantry twice. Besides, you have served at the Crime Branch. Why are you on station duty?'

I was at a loss for words. A bar on the uniform signifies an extraordinary act of bravery and indicates that the officer is a two-time awardee of the prestigious medal.

'Bagwan, give me the order book.'

I handed it over to him. He wrote a remark in it, 'In the jurisdiction of this police station, there has been an increase in crime. In such circumstances, it is wrong to place an officer of high calibre on minor duty. He has worked in the Crime Branch and been awarded the President's gallantry medal twice. Therefore, immediately appoint him as the detection officer.'

My seniors knew about me as I had dealt with many gangsters and criminals. Now, I was being made to do station house duty which is usually offered to a newcomer. The police station already had Subhash Chutke as the detection officer. He was my batchmate. The next day, DCP Mushrif sent a memo to ACP Gajanan Takne, who called me immediately. 'Bagwan, you have been with the Crime Branch. Pick up quality cases that will do Lamington Road police station proud. I will support you.'

I went about my work with great enthusiasm after being encouraged by my seniors. In those days, an organized gang in south Bombay was involved in car thefts and robbing petrol pumps and shops by threatening the victims with weapons. The gang was headed by the Jathan brothers.

An army officer, Sriniwas Jathan, had three sons: Rajan, Harish and Satish. They took to crime because of negligence by their parents. The eldest son, Rajan, was arrested in connection with an airport robbery along with another notorious criminal, Mukhtar Lakdawala. Harish and Satish were part of the Shetty gang which was headed by the former. Their partners included Nasiruddin Liaquat Ali, alias Shakti, Nizamuddin Mohammad Basir, alias Bulldozer, Mohammad Hanif Akka, Salim, alias Shams, Mohammad Ali Zaveri, Ajmal Tajmal Khan and Pradeep Anant Mane. They splurged their ill-gotten wealth on liquor and women. This gang had also entered a video library in the vicinity of Bandra police station and threatened the shopkeeper and his help with weapons before fleeing with cash and a video player. On 22 January 1988, Shams stole a car from Colaba and went to Krishna Jewellers in Matunga to survey the place. The same evening, the gang entered the store around closing time and threatened the owner, Murti Seth, and the other staff. They took away jewellery and Rs 1.5 lakh cash. They then fled in the stolen car and abandoned it near Maratha Mandir.

Murti Seth filed a case at Matunga police station. PI Sakhare, who was investigating this case, advised him to install siren alarms at his store. The owner did so immediately. The gang, meanwhile, grew stronger each day. All police stations were on the lookout for them. Despite this, they managed to rob Sehgal Grocery Store in

Bandra and take away the shopkeeper's gold chain. Another case was registered at Mulund police station.

The gang targeted Krishna Jewellers once again. But this time Seth pressed a button to sound a siren. The gang was flustered for a moment but managed to run away with some jewellery. In the resulting commotion, some of it was dropped. Seth had to file a case once again. The police, however, accused him of deliberately getting his shop robbed to obtain insurance money. This was because there were no eye witnesses to the daylight robbery. The investigation in this case was poor. The police concluded that Seth had staged the robbery to claim insurance. This left Seth agitated.

One day, a car thief, Yunus, called me. I met him at an undisclosed place. Yunus and his wife gave me information that the Jathan brothers were hiding in Mumbra's Kothari chawl. I raided the place with my team, arrested Harish and Satish and recovered the jewellery stolen from Krishna Jewellers, along with revolvers and choppers. Upon interrogation, they told us that their partners—Nasiruddin and Nizamuddin—were in Ghatkopar. We then arrested them too. A few days later, we arrested Mohammad and Shams from Pydhonie while Ajmal Tajmal was arrested from Mulund. We took them into custody and they confessed to their involvement in fourteen car thefts, looting nine petrol pumps, robberies at twelve jewellery stores and other large stores. They also confessed to having robbed Krishna Jewellers twice. The next day, I asked for the papers of the case from Matunga police station.

Rakesh Maria (DCP, Zone 4) came to know about this. Matunga police station came under him. He came to our police station asking for details about the case. He asked me to step out of the cabin while he personally questioned all the accused in the case. After hearing them out, he asked Seth to identify the jewellery. Once this was done, the DCP was convinced that Seth had been wrongly accused of staging the second robbery. He took all the officers from Matunga police station to task and praised me for having solved the Krishna Jewellers double robbery case. The accused in this case were kept in our custody.

One day, SI Davkar's staff from the Crime Branch (Thane) came to me. They showed me a memo and asked me to hand over Pradeep Mane, a member of the Jathan gang, to them in connection with another crime. I requested them to get permission from the court. We handed Mane over after receiving a court order. A month later, we received a copy of his death certificate. It said that SI Davkar had killed Mane in an encounter.

70

TEARS TURN INTO SMILES

One day, a forty-two-year-old Gujarati woman came to Dr D.B. Marg police station. She looked shaken.

'Sahib, Sahib . . .' Saying this, she fainted. The women constables made her lie down on a bench and sprinkled water on her face. I called for tea and biscuits. I had been taught by my seniors that every complainant should be made to feel at ease.

After regaining her composure, the woman told us her story. Her husband had died four years ago of a heart attack. To take care of her sons and daughter, who was of marriageable age, she worked hard all through the night to make papads. She would sell them door to door during the day. She wore a seven-*tola* (carat) gold mangalsutra. Since it was risky to keep it at home, she would wear it when she would go about her daily work. That day, her mangalsutra had been snatched in broad daylight. I decided to spare no effort to get it back. Which area did the snatching incident take place? What time was it? What was the description of the offenders? I began collecting information.

I gathered information about women who went for morning walks, to temples, to the market on D.B. Marg, Princess Street and Gamdevi, who had been victims of chain-snatching. I decided to concentrate on railway thieves who were mentioned in the Crime Branch records. I put the operation into action and arrested five such thieves: Raju Nadar, Jaya Shetty, Mahadev and two others.

They confessed to about eighteen crimes on local railway trains, D.B. Marg, Princess Street and Gamdevi. They sold the stolen gold to goldsmiths who melted it. Criminal proceedings were initiated against these greedy and corrupt receivers of stolen property. All the gold was recovered and returned to the women who had registered complaints of chain-snatching at various police stations.

One of these women was the Gujarati lady. She had tears of joy in her eyes. The next day, she returned to the police station. I was surprised to see her again. She said, 'I wish to perform an aarti for the person who returned my life savings. This is all a poor sister can do for her brother.' I was overwhelmed by her gesture. I felt like I had done my duty, and that I had done justice to the uniform I wore. After solving several cases of chain-snatching, I decided to concentrate on matters of pickpocketing which were being reported on BEST buses. After all, the hard-earned money of the salaried classes was being robbed.

What was the route of these buses? At which stops were the wallets picked? Which pickpocket operated in that area? I managed to arrest several offenders.

Seeing my effort, Sr PI R.V. Lele said, 'You have worked at the Crime Branch and are aware of all the tactics that can be used to get to these criminals.' When the then Commissioner Vasant Saraf was reviewing cases, he found that Dr D.B. Marg police station had solved the maximum cases and received the 'Best Police Station' award. I received a special award from him.

71

SO CLOSE, YET SO FAR

I was racing my motorcycle towards Colaba, but I had to halt at the Cadbury junction when the signal turned red. It was almost 3.30 p.m. and I was extremely hungry. Lunch had been delayed because I was wrapping up urgent paperwork. I was then posted with Traffic Control (A Division). Despite being a traffic policeman, I really felt the urge to speed away, but I waited.

Just then a car zoomed past, jumping the signal. The traffic constable on duty waved for the driver to stop, but he sped away. An empty stomach and, to top it, a man who had no regard for a traffic policeman infuriated me. I raced after the car. I overtook him and made him stop a little ahead of the junction. A dark-complexioned young man wearing a stylish suit with a tie got out and started giving me an explanation in fluent English. He appeared to be a south Indian. His tone alternated between one that sought forgiveness and one that tried to threaten me.

I looked into his eyes and sensed something odd. I took him to the nearest police station and handed him over to the duty officer, SI Lolankar of Gamdevi police station. I told him this man's speech and appearance were deceptive and that he may be an impostor. I asked him to hold this man in custody until I came back to question him. I had thought of having lunch and then taking him to the Crime Branch. When I came back, I was shocked to see that SI Lolankar had let the man off with a petty fine. The man had told him that he had a flight to catch and was ready to pay a fine. I knew this was a lie. I was angry that I couldn't question him.

A couple of days later we received a description of the man who had plotted the Tribhovandas Bhimji Zaveri and Sons jewellery store robbery on 19 March 1987—young with short hair, dark complexion, always dressed in a suit with a tie, of south Indian origin and a few other details.

Mon Singh, or Mohan Singh, the person I had apprehended at the junction, had placed a classified advertisement asking for 'Dynamic Graduates for Intelligence Officers' Posts and Security Officers' Posts' in the 17 March 1987 issue of the *Times of India*. Applicants were told to reach the Taj Mahal Hotel between 10 a.m. and 5 p.m. the next day. Mon Singh had rented an office in Mittal Towers at Nariman Point to interview candidates. After selecting twenty-six candidates, he had asked them to report to the hotel the following day. He had also briefed them about a mock raid.

They arrived at the Opera House branch of Tribhovandas Bhimji Zaveri and Sons Jewellers around 2.15 p.m. in a bus. Singh introduced himself to the owner, Pratap Zaveri, and produced a search warrant. He ordered the CCTV cameras to be turned off and for the licenced revolver on the premises to be surrendered. Singh and the fake contingent of officers did not allow the staff to make any phone calls. They took samples of ornaments to assess the quality of the gold. Singh picked the samples and had them sealed in polybags. The fake officers also collected cash. After forty-five minutes, Singh asked two men to put the briefcases containing the samples in the bus. He asked the others to keep a watch on the shop while he left in the bus to supervise another raid. The owners called the police after an hour.

My jaw dropped when I realized that the man I had caught at the Cadbury junction fit this description perfectly. I couldn't express my disbelief at having let this master conman slip away.

THE CRIME BRANCH: DRUG CONTROL

72

NARCOTICS

Wealth, wine, lust and intoxication often cause people to commit heinous crimes. However, there is another deadly addiction that can put one on the path to crime. Narcotics had affected not just Bombay but the entire nation. It was the youth who primarily came under its influence. Many college students, from rich and poor families alike, were easy prey.

I tried to understand how narcotics worked. I noticed that the addiction usually started at a young age. Most children are watched over by their parents while they are in school. But once they graduate to college, the addiction starts to take over, especially through the use of cigarettes. In those days, drugs were most commonly used in cigarettes. They were mixed with tobacco and consumed as ordinary cigarettes by unsuspecting adolescents. These young men and women were highly influenced by films and movie stars who were often seen smoking on screen.

Holding a cigarette made them feel like celebrities. Initially, the college students would be dependent on their parents for money to purchase drugs, but once they started earning they would easily be able to buy them. Let me give you an example.

A respected and famous man, who was the owner of a showroom for men's western clothing in Colaba, came to me one day. He had come to report the theft of jewellery from his wife's cupboard. In such cases, the suspicion usually fell on the domestic helps. I spoke to them and verified all the places that they frequented. I was convinced that they were not involved in the theft. Often, people working for rich families try and win the trust of the owners. Once the family starts trusting them, they rob the house and flee to their native place. But that was not the case in this incident. I asked the showroom owner, 'How did your wife come to know that the jewellery had been stolen from her cupboard?'

The wife said, 'I have several jewellery sets, and I use them as the occasion demands. That is when I realized that one particular pendant was missing. I looked in all the jewellery boxes and noticed that one item from each set was missing.'

I went to the showroom owner's house posing as his friend. I was introduced to his son. One look at his blank eyes and I understood what was wrong. He was a drug addict. To establish the truth, I spoke to him about his college life, his daily activities and his friends. That is when I realized the shocking truth. The man would always be out for parties with his wife. His son would be alone at home. Without his parents to guide him, the boy came across some others who were involved in car thefts. In their company, he was introduced to drugs and eventually and inevitably got addicted to them. His desires overcame his morals. To satisfy his need of going to parties and discos, he got a duplicate set of keys made to his mother's cupboard. He stole her jewellery at will. When the time came for me to act according to the law, the man withdrew his complaint as he did not want his status to be affected. The result was that the son continued to be an addict. If only the man had cared about his son's future! The intention here is to highlight how parents and children are equally responsible in such situations.

Here are some other narcotic cases I handled:

The Ajay Sharma Drugs Case

In 1977, when I was stationed at Colaba police station, I was given charge of beat no. 2, which included the Air India building. When patrolling outside it, I noticed a fair-skinned young man, who resembled a foreigner, selling something. I called out to him, but he started running away. I gave chase. I caught up with him and found small packets of morphine in his possession. Brown sugar had not been introduced in Bombay then, but the morphine business was flourishing. The man I had arrested was Ajay Sharma, a resident of Delhi who had hired a room in the Metropole Hotel in Dhobi Talao. We raided his room and found about 7–8 kg of morphine. We interrogated Sharma. He confessed that the morphine was supplied from Delhi, and that he would sell it to people on Mereweather Road, an area frequented by hippies. We learnt that Ranjit, alias Kala Pahad, had got the Babbu gang from Delhi to Bombay. We arrested the gang members. In those days, they were arrested under section 66 (1B) of the Prohibition Act as the Drug Act had not been introduced. Anyone possessing drugs could get bail immediately. The same thing happened with this gang as well.

The Hotel Delamar Drugs Case

When I was posted at Dr D.B. Marg police station, my informer Jumbo, who acted as a guide for foreigners and took them to places in Bombay where drugs were sold, told me that some Nigerians staying in Hotel Delamar on the corner of Marine Drive were dealing in drugs and exporting brown sugar to foreign countries. Jumbo was an addict himself and I could rely on his information. I told ACP (Girgaum Division) D.A. Kurne about this. He said, 'Bagwan, you have worked at the Crime Branch. You must pick up such quality cases. It will bring credit to our station.'

'Sir, I agree with you. However, this case falls under the jurisdiction of Azad Maidan police station. What if the seniors object?'

'You need not worry about that. You have my permission. If you want, I will participate in the operation.' Once ACP Kurne gave me the green signal, I asked my informer to be on the alert. On 11 December 1987, the informer called me. 'Sahib, this evening a big deal is going to take place at Hotel Delamar.'

I raided the hotel with ACP Kurne. We seized brown sugar from one of the rooms occupied by the Nigerian nationals. The total value of the narcotics was estimated to be around Rs 30–35 lakh. We also found a large quantity of cocaine which was worth Rs 1 crore per kg at that time.

We arrested five Nigerian nationals including the leader, Michael Uka Chukva. During interrogation, he revealed that a coconut vendor had hidden more drugs in a wooden box at the entrance to the hotel. Who had supplied such a large quantity of drugs to these foreigners?

We questioned Chukva who was strong both physically and mentally. He refused to open his mouth. We were left with no choice but to use harsher tactics. It was after this that he told us that the drugs were supplied to him by an Indian citizen who was around fifty years old. Who was this man? Where did he live? How did he meet Michael? We began to look for answers to these questions and found out that a suspended police officer was behind this racket. He lived at the Tardeo police quarters. We raided his house but could not find anything there. When he heard that the Nigerian had been arrested, he immediately destroyed all evidence. However, he knew that the arrested Nigerian would identify him, and that he would be taken into custody. He fell at ACP Kurne's feet and began to cry.

'Sahib, please forgive me. I am no longer in service. I have no means of surviving. How will I feed my family? I did this under stress.' We pitied him. Also, we knew the Bombay Police would lose face if news of his involvement became public. We had to release him after an inquiry because we didn't have strong evidence against him. Also, since this officer was close to the Pathans who sold brown sugar, our seniors reprimanded him and warned him to stay away from such dealings. Since the Nigerians had been nabbed red-handed, we launched criminal proceedings against them.

From 1988–91, I was posted at the Crime Branch (Drugs Control). This branch was then headed by Addl CP (Essential Commodities) A.K. Ankola. A special team was allotted to this branch. It consisted of PI Shanker Desai, SIs Kaiser Ahmed, Shantaram Birge, Dundappa Jodgudri and me. In those days, the use of drugs had begun to spread in Bombay. We launched a full-scale operation against the drug mafia. Meanwhile, a complaint was filed against me at the Crime Branch. I was accused of selling the cocaine I had seized from Hotel Delamar. ACP Y. Bodhe asked me, 'Bagwan, where are the drugs you confiscated in the Nigerian case?'

'Sir, I raided Hotel Delamar and seized the drugs under the guidance of ACP Kurne. After the raid, I brought the criminals and the drugs to Dr D.B. Marg police station. After taking permission from Sr PI R.V. Lele, I sealed the drugs and placed them in his cupboard. I made a note of this in the seized goods register. I suspected that the drugs might be stolen from the police station, so I took due precautions.' ACP Bodhe listened to me carefully. The keys to the Sr PI's cupboard were either with the officer himself or with his orderly. ACP Bodhe knew this. After listening to me, he contacted Sr PI Lele who confirmed, 'Those drugs are still sealed in my cupboard.'

My diligence came to my rescue and I got out of the situation without a problem. Later, I came to know that the brain behind this allegation was the suspended police officer.

73

MY ACCIDENT

It was April 1992. I was in Baramati when I received a call from the DCP (Crime Branch) Hassan Gafoor, informing me that Special Executive Magistrate Dilip Naik had been murdered. Since I had worked at Dr D.B. Marg police station, they needed my help in identifying the killer. I had to leave at once. I cut my leave short and was on my way back when the van I was in overturned and rammed a stationary roller. My face was smashed. I was rushed to Sion Hospital and later shifted to Hinduja Hospital, even as PI Zende and many others from the department rallied around. I was there for over a month. My jaw had to be reconstructed with wire, including my teeth. The morning I was being discharged, I was told that my bills had been paid. I was stunned and wondered who had done this. It turned out that some shopkeepers from Colaba had pooled the money. They simply refused to accept money from me, no matter how much I requested them. It was after a lot of persuasion that they agreed to do so.

I knew I had been given a second shot at life. Even though my seniors requested me to join the Crime Branch again, I never ventured back, knowing that I should respect the chance I had been given.

I was lucky to have received a lot of support, love and respect at this time. These are the moments you cherish, the ones you take with you to the grave. Knowing you have made a difference to someone's life, being able to appreciate the tiny hint of nobility the profession offers—it's somewhere amidst all the haze and noise of petty politics and bandobast duty and the awful hours and sacrifices. The pride and nobility far outweigh the fear, ego and power that come with the job.

74

AGA KHAN: THE NARCOTICS KING

When I was posted with the Crime Branch (Drugs Control), I received information about drugs being brought into Bombay from Pakistan via Rajasthan. I began to study the narcotics market, which led to each layer unfolding one at a time. Between Afghanistan and Pakistan was a 500–700 km stretch of desert land. The underworld called this no man's land. Opium grew here in abundance. The opium buds were processed to make brown sugar which was then sold openly. The Pathan gangs, which had collaborated with Pakistani gangs, would buy this brown sugar and smuggle it into India.

In Barmer and Jaisalmer on the India–Pakistan border, camels were the main mode of transport. Virk Singh, the head of the drug mafia on the Pakistani side, would force the villagers who had herds of camels to transport brown sugar into India using female camels. Their modus operandi was ingenious. During the day, in order to get through the strict surveillance on the border, the villagers would take the female camels and their calves to a shed in a village on the Indian side. They would then tie up the calves in a shed and take the female camels back to Pakistan. Brown sugar packets, concealed under jute covers, would be hidden under the stomachs and on the back of these camels. They would later be released by the Pakistani villagers and would enter India in search of their calves without being checked or suspected by the border forces. The camels always found their way to the shed where the calves were tied up. There, their counterparts would unload the consignment. This illegal activity was conducted on full moon nights with the drugs buried at safe locations.

Once in India, the drugs would be brought to Bombay for sale. The tradition of bringing goats from Rajasthan via Ahmedabad for butchering is old. A truck transporting the goats would also carry brown sugar packets hidden under a tarpaulin sheet. The urine and excreta of the goats would overpower the smell of brown sugar. This way, the truck would not be stopped at either toll booths or nakas. The drivers bringing the goats would even bribe the staff stationed at the toll booths. When the truck approached Vashi checkpoint at the entry to Bombay, where it would have to be checked by the police, the entire consignment of brown sugar would be off-loaded into the trunk of an Ambassador car and brought into the city without any hassle. Similarly, when the truck came to Dahisar from a different route, the consignment would be offloaded and stored in *baithi* chawls near the Dahisar checkpoint. In Bombay, the consignment was kept with a gang member called a 'storer'. The men involved in this operation would then sell the brown sugar to dealers across the city.

Assuming that brown sugar was valued at Rs 10,000 per kg in Pakistan, the price in India was worth Rs 1 lakh per kg. The profit was manifold. Addl CP (Essential Commodities) A.K. Ankola, who was the head of Crime Branch (Controls), motivated us to take up big cases. One of my informers gave me a tip-off about Pakistani Pathans smuggling drugs into Bombay on a large scale and told me that the drug dealers lived in the city's posh areas. I was wondering where and how these dealers managed to get accommodation. An informer told me that the Pakistani Pathans would pose as Afghan refugees who had come to Bombay to set up dry fruit businesses and would contact brokers for flats.

They earned a lot of money from the dry fruits business and had no problem paying Rs 50,000 as monthly rent for a luxurious apartment. Brokers would blindly charge commissions and get them apartments on rent without doing a background check. The flat owners who received hefty rents, too, did not bother to check their antecedents. My informer also told me about the modus operandi of these Pathan drug dealers. To avoid suspicion, they made phone calls to Rajasthan from a STD booth located far away from their house and used code language. The informer gave me the lead but did not know where the Pathans lived.

Slowly but steadily, I managed to gather more information about the Pathan drug racket from dealers who sold drugs in the lanes of Bombay. That is when I came across Aminabai.

Aminabai and her son-in-law were involved in drug dealing. Not only that, she herself was a drug addict. I kept an eye on her. She came to know of this and was scared. I took advantage of her fear and pressurized her.

Finally, one day she asked me, 'Sir, why are you after me?'

'Look, Aminabai, you take drugs yourself and I can arrest you, but if you want to be spared, give me information about the Pathans who bring drugs into India.'

After some hesitation, Aminabai relented. 'Sir, his name is Aga Khan. If you have the guts, try and arrest him.'

Sayyed Kutubuddin Imamuddin Pathan, alias Aga Khan, was a big drug dealer in Bombay. He had contacts in the police and the Customs. I took Aminabai into confidence. She told me about a Gujarati girl, Pushpa, who was in touch with Aga Khan.

'Aminabai, where can I find Pushpa?'

Laughing heartily, she said, 'Sahib, that girl is my contact. She is Aga Khan's mistress.'

Aga Khan ran an estate agency business in Bombay as a front for his drug trade. Pushpa worked as a receptionist in his office. Since there was no other earning member in her family, she had no choice but to become Khan's mistress. Khan's family lived in Karachi, and he had a son and daughter older than Pushpa. However, to satisfy his lust, he kept her as his mistress. Desperate for money, Pushpa had given in to his demands.

It was important that I cultivate Pushpa as a source to reach Aga Khan. The only thing that could get Pushpa to help me was money. I met Addl CP Ankola and told him about my plan. 'Bagwan, go ahead. I trust you.'

Operation Aga Khan was underway. I immediately contacted Aminabai. She arranged for a meeting with Pushpa at her house. Aminabai had told me about Pushpa with great trust. Therefore, I spoke to her in a manner that would allow me to win her confidence. I assured her that I would protect both Pushpa and her. When I met Pushpa, she exclaimed, 'Sahib, Aga Khan himself has told me about you. He said, "There is an officer called Bagwan in the Crime Branch. He has been involved in shootouts. He is a daring officer. Be careful of him."' I realized that just like the police maintained a dossier of criminals, the criminals also kept track of police officers. After a few more meetings, Pushpa started trusting me. She told me that she would give me a tip-off about Aga Khan, but only for money. She stayed in touch with me and one evening in November 1988, she called me.

'Sahib, meet me near Hotel Pravin in Panvel.'

I immediately left for Panvel. Pushpa met me some distance away from the hotel. She said, 'I have come to Panvel with Aga Khan in his Ambassador car. He has left the car here and gone to the Gujarat border to get a new consignment. Look, this is his car.' She pointed towards a blue Ambassador car in the hotel's parking lot. I made a mental note of the colour and number plate. Pushpa told me about Khan's plan. I knew the modus operandi— the drugs would be brought in a truck transporting goats. They would be off-loaded into his car near Talasari. To avoid suspicion, he would make Pushpa wear a burqa, making them look like a couple. He would then be able to cross Vashi Bridge with the drugs and enter Bombay without any hassle.

Acting on the tip-off provided by Pushpa, I posted SI Jodgodri, Constables Madhu Khutwad, Sheikh and others at the octroi naka before the Vashi checkpoint. We did not know when and from which direction Khan would come. He had not told Pushpa that. We began preparing. We hammered some nails into a plywood board and tied it to a handcart. In case Aga Khan tried to speed away, we would throw the handcart on to the road and bust his car's tyres.

Two days passed, but there was no sign of Aga Khan. The team was tired. There was no canteen or tea stall at the checkpoint. We had to send the jeep to get snacks and bottles of water. The cars that passed us released a lot of smoke. Our faces had turned black, and we looked as if we had come out of a coal pit. Soon, my team began to lose patience. 'Sahib, let it be. Our information appears to have failed.'

'No. I am 100 per cent sure. The blue Ambassador will come any time. The registration number is MMG 5864. There will be a girl in a burqa in that car along with a Pathan.' I had never seen Aga Khan. I only had his description.

On 13 November 1988, around 6.30–6.45 a.m., we noticed a blue Ambassador approaching. We took positions. As the car came towards us, we pushed the handcart towards it. Seeing it appear out of nowhere, the Ambassador came to a grinding halt. Aga Khan, dressed in Pathani attire, stepped out. We were in civilian clothes. I took out my revolver and identified myself before firing a round in the air. He was shaken by the sound. Before he could move, my team had arrested him. Pushpa was watching from inside the car. We knew Aga Khan had a revolver, so we searched the car. He was not armed that day, but for the first time he had been caught red-handed with drugs. We found 56 kg of brown sugar packed in tin boxes in the trunk. It was valued at approximately Rs 56 crore in the international market. When he realized that the game was up, he told us the names of the truck drivers who got the drugs from Rajasthan to Bombay.

Hussain Pandhi Sindhi and Rafiq Salim Sindhi were to meet Aga Khan the next day at an Irani hotel near K.E.M. Hospital in Parel to collect the payment for the delivery. Based on this information, we arrested them and registered a case against Aga Khan, Hussain Pandhi Sindhi and Rafiq Salim Sindhi. The news of Aga Khan's arrest spread like wildfire. All officers from the Customs and DRI departments were shocked. Addl CP Ankola called a press conference and praised my team's efforts in nabbing the 'drug kingpin'. He patted me on the back and said, 'Bagwan, by arresting a criminal like Aga Khan, your team and you have solved a "quality case".'

Khan suspected Pushpa since no one else knew about the drugs consignment. Pushpa was scared for her life. I gave her the money I had promised and also provided protection. There was no Drugs Act then, and Aga Khan was released on bail a few days later. His passport was confiscated. Yet, he vanished from India and still hasn't been found. Aminabai passed away recently.

75

NIRANJAN BHULLAR

After the Aga Khan case, I dealt with other narcotics matters too. One day, I received an anonymous phone call. The caller told me, 'Bagwan Sahib, I am a friend. You have been solving many drug cases, which is why I want to give you some information.' With this, he hung up.

Several days later, the same person called again. 'Sir, Niranjan Singh Dalip Singh Bhullar is fifty-five years old, six feet tall and lean. He lives with his family in an old bungalow at Kalachowki. Raid his bungalow now and you will find a large quantity of Mandrax tablets.'

Only God knew what the enmity between this person and Bhullar was. What if I raided the bungalow and found nothing? I would have to face the music. Since I was solving one case after the other, the number of my 'well-wishers' in the police department was increasing. I decided to keep an eye on Bhullar's bungalow. My constables and informers kept up the surveillance for about a month. I got reports that Bhullar's movements were indeed suspicious. On 29 March 1988, around 3.30 p.m., we raided Bhullar's bungalow. He started arguing with us. We searched the bungalow and the area around it. We found some boxes in a small room in the bungalow's pump house. They contained sealed plastic bags of Mandrax pills. Bhullar, who was caught red-handed, was a sight. His face had lost colour. In those days, the cost of manufacturing a Mandrax pill was less than Rs 3. They were sold to African nationals for as much as Rs 300. The value of the goods seized from the bungalow was estimated to be at least Rs 20 lakh. We also found 7 kg of charas in the raid. Bhullar had got these pills from Madhya Pradesh. We registered a case against him, but he was released on bail. It wasn't long before he was arrested again in a similar case and sentenced.

I had a faint idea that these pills were also being manufactured in Bombay. Accordingly, I put my informers on the job. I got information that Shaikh Abdulla Akhtar, who lived with his family in a bungalow in Kurla, put up a front of manufacturing medicinal pills in Sakinaka, B.N. D'Souza Road, Khairani Road, but was instead producing Mandrax pills in large quantities. He would secretly show a sample of these pills in the market and receive orders. Nevertheless, it was important to confirm this information. I sent a bogus customer to get me a sample of the Mandrax pills from Shaikh's factory. I got these tested by addicts who confirmed that they were of good quality.

On the morning of 2 December 1989, Akhtar left his bungalow with my team following him. Once he reached his factory, we raided it and seized 10,000 Mandrax tablets that were valued at about Rs 50 lakh. We sealed all the machinery. Akhtar confessed that these tablets were made from methaqualone powder. He also told us that Satish Doshi, a well-known trader in Bombay's Dawa Bazaar, supplied him with this powder. Based on this information, we arrested Doshi too.

76

THE SET-UP

An informer told me that an African national staying in room no. 4 of the Gateway Inn guest house on the ground floor of the building next to the Taj Mahal Hotel possessed brown sugar. The informer gave me a description of a man too. Since I had such detailed information, I believed it to be true. Another reason was that some foreigners who came to India as tourists were secretly involved in the drug business. I immediately went to the guest house with my staff and the informer. We saw a man in his thirties, fitting the description given by the informer, watching television in the reception. I asked the manager about the occupant of room no. 4. He pointed towards the man watching TV. I showed him my identity card and told him that I wanted to search his room. He seemed taken aback and asked us for the reason behind this. When I told him that we had information about some drugs in his room, the man became serious.

'I am a student. I am not a drug addict. Go ahead and search my room.'

First, I checked his passport and then searched the room but did not find anything. My informer, who was with me, said, 'Sir, check in the bathroom.'

I went into the bathroom. On the water tank above the commode, I found two plastic bags containing 1 kg of brown sugar each. When he saw the packets, the young man was shocked. He said, 'I don't do drugs. I don't sell drugs. I don't know who kept these in my room.' He repeatedly told us that he had nothing to do with drugs. We did a proper panchnama of the contraband seized and arrested the man. We interrogated him, but he denied having anything to do with narcotics. I cross-questioned the informer.

'How did you get the tip-off?'

'Sahib, let's forget about that. I helped you find the drugs.'

'You are right. But who gave you this tip-off?'

'Sahib, the end justifies the means. Don't worry about who gave me the tip-off.'

The way he spoke made me suspect that he was hiding something. I took him to task. 'Tell me the truth or I will trap you in this case.'

'Arey, no, Sahib! Don't do that.'

'Who gave you the tip-off?'

'Mehmood Bhai.'

'Where will I find this Mehmood Bhai?'

'In Dongri.'

I went to Dongri with the informer. We brought Mehmood back and questioned him. He was not forthcoming with his answers. My suspicions grew stronger. I brought the African before him. 'Do you know him?'

The African answered in the negative. I asked Mehmood the same question. He, too, denied knowing the African. I told a constable, 'He won't speak like this. Take him to the inquiry room.'

As soon as Mehmood heard this, he panicked. 'Sahib, don't beat me. I will tell you the truth.'

A South African national had contacted Mehmood and told him that he would reward him if he planted drugs in room no. 4 of Gateway Inn guest house. I asked Mehmood to describe this man. On hearing the description the arrested African shouted, 'That is my brother-in-law. He is in India too. My wife and he do not get along and don't even stay together. He is plotting against me even here.'

When I heard this, I was convinced that the African in custody was the victim of a conspiracy. We had arrested an innocent man and that made me very uneasy. However, according to the circumstantial evidence, the drugs had been found in room no. 4. I became restless. The same night I drove to Worli Sea Face and met Addl CP Ankola at his apartment in Sagar Tarang building.

I woke him up and explained the story to him. He said, 'Bagwan, you never hesitate before arresting a criminal, and you constantly strive to ensure that an innocent man is not punished. You have to decide what is to be done. I am confident that you will not take a wrong decision.'

'Sir, we have found the drugs in this case but not the culprit. Till we find him and show that the drugs were found on Ramchandani Marg, a street near the guest house, we can avoid injustice being done to an innocent man.'

'Bagwan, I trust you completely. Go ahead.'

That night, I released the African. Unfortunately, despite our best efforts, we could not find the real culprit. This bothers me even today.

77

BERNARD UGO CHUKO

One day, one of my informers, Gullu, told me that a trader from Bombay was going to deliver brown sugar to a Nigerian after receiving it from Pakistani Pathans. The deal was to take place at Bombay Central station. As soon as the Nigerian would get the drugs, he would board a train to Delhi. There were two reasons why this was being done at the railway station. One was that it was convenient to leave the city immediately. The other reason was that there were no metal detectors on the railway stations in those days. The railway police only searched bags randomly. Also, they did not stop foreign tourists. The brown sugar tip-off was accurate because my informer had seen the Nigerian discussing the deal with some Pathans. On the morning of 6 April 1981, police officers in civil clothes were posted around Bombay Central station. In the evening, we saw a Nigerian walking towards a train about to leave for Delhi. He matched the description given by the informer. When I signalled, my men surrounded him. He tried to escape but could not succeed. We searched his bag and found 18 kg of brown sugar. The drugs were valued at Rs 20 lakh in the Bombay market and around Rs 18–20 crore in the international market. The Nigerian, Bernard Ugo Chuko, was sentenced to ten years' imprisonment in this case.

78

TAKI AHMED SHAKIL MARUF

The Bernard Ugo Chuko episode taught me that between the Pakistani Pathans who imported the drugs and the foreigners who bought them, the middleman or the broker was the key to cracking these cases. The intermediary, who undertook the dangerous job of making the drugs available to customers, was an important cog in the machinery. I decided to target the brokers and started collecting information about them.

I managed to understand their modus operandi. I got to know that, first, the foreigners who indulged in smuggling caught hold of small-time addicts. They gave them money to take care of their drug needs and won their trust. Then, the foreigners would show them large bundles of currency notes and ask for information about the top drug dealers. The addicts, happy at the prospect of receiving more money, put the foreigners in contact with the brokers. If one deal was successful, the brokers agreed to more deals.

It was time to take action. I caught hold of one such addict. With his help, I got a sample of brown sugar from one broker. I got the sample checked. Once I was convinced about its authenticity, I sent a bogus customer to the broker. This fake customer was carrying Rs 18,00,000 and was accompanied by the addict. The money was arranged in bundles. Only the top and bottom of the bundles had real Rs 100 notes. The others were blank pieces of paper. The broker, who saw the bundles only from the top, was convinced.

On 22 May 1989, a broker called the bogus customer and asked him to meet near Andheri railway station. My decoy met the broker and showed him the bag of money. I was watching from a car. At one point, the broker vanished into the crowd for a while. He then told my decoy to engage a rickshaw and follow his scooter. We followed the rickshaw and reached Cooper Hospital in Juhu-Vile Parle. Within minutes, we were at Mithibai College. From there, the broker led us to Space restaurant on Gulmohar Cross Road. He got off his scooter, leant towards another parked scooter and started removing neatly packed drug packets from its storage compartment. I moved swiftly towards the broker. I caught him red-handed just as he was about to hand over the brown sugar to my decoy. We seized about 12 kg of brown sugar from him. His name was Taki Ahmed Shakil Maruf. We registered a case against him. Thirty-year-old Maruf lived in Oshiwara. He had turned to this dangerous business because he was unemployed. He confessed to having received the brown sugar from a Pakistani Pathan.

We searched for the man Maruf spoke about but couldn't trace him. The court sentenced Maruf to life imprisonment. This case made me realize that the Pakistani Pathans were the chief culprits when it came to bringing brown sugar into Bombay. I decided to monitor their activities closely.

79

PAKISTANI DRUG LORD AT
A POLITICAL BIGWIG'S RESIDENCE

After arresting the king of narcotics, Aga Khan, I knew how brown sugar was brought into Bombay from Rajasthan. My team began to monitor the Dahisar checkpoint on the outskirts of the city. Meanwhile, my informer told me that some Pakistani Pathans had unloaded their goods in Dahisar's Rawalpada. I asked him to keep a close watch on the area. A couple of days later he called me. 'Salaam, Sahib! I have found your man. His name is Jamal. He came to live in room no. 3 of Tiwari chawl in Rawalpada about six months ago. Pick him up. Your work will be done.'

I immediately informed Addl CP A.K. Ankola. He said, 'Bagwan, narcotics have spread across the country. Your efforts to eradicate this menace have been successful since you joined the Crime Branch. I wish you the best of luck.' His words gave me confidence.

After confirming that the tip-off about Jamal was genuine, on 8 June 1989, around 10.30 p.m., I reached Tiwari chawl with PI Shankar Desai and other policemen. I knocked on the door of room no. 3. A man opened it. We entered and arrested Jamal and two other accomplices. During our search, we found two aluminium trunks under the quilts. They contained 38 kg of the finest quality of brown sugar.

Thirty-year-old Jamal Pandi Mangolia was originally a resident of Barmer in Rajasthan. He told us more about the drug racket. The Pathans from Pakistan would load the drugs at the border into trucks carrying goats. These trucks would come into Bombay. In the city, these drugs would be unloaded in slums like Dahisar's Rawalpada. Jamal was the chief storer. The Pathan residing in Bombay instructed Jamal over the phone about the location where the drugs were to be delivered. He never showed up himself. I understood that Jamal was simply a puppet in the hands of the Pathans. I told him, 'Jamal, you are the brown sugar storer and have been caught red-handed. You are going to be punished severely. If you want a reduced sentence, help the police. Tell me who is behind this drug racket.'

Jamal thought for a moment before replying. 'Okay, Sahib. I will lead you to my boss. He lives in Worli.' We had caught Jamal at 10.30 p.m. It was past midnight by the time we interrogated him, confiscated the drugs and performed a proper panchnama in the presence of two *pancha*s. We then went to nab Jamal's boss. I was driving as per his directions. Around 2 a.m., we reached a posh building near Worli Sea Face. Jamal said, 'Sahib, wait. My Pathan boss lives on the tenth floor of this building.'

'What! In this building? Have you gone mad?'

But Jamal was sure. 'Sahib, I can't forget this building even in my sleep.' The entire team was shocked. It was Vainganga building. It housed the residences of ministers and MLAs. I asked Jamal again, 'Are you sure it is this building?'

'Yes, Sir.'

We explained the matter clearly to the two panchas who had accompanied us. We gave them details about the operation we were about to undertake. With Jamal in the front, we reached the porch of the building. The watchman was dozing. I ignored him and instructed my men to block the exit. The security guard woke up on hearing my voice.

'Whom do you want to meet?' Since we were in civilian clothes, he was terrified at the sight of the revolvers in our hands. We told him, 'We are police officers. Back off!'

We hurried with Jamal into a lift and reached the tenth floor. Jamal pointed towards a door, 'Sahib, that is the flat. My boss lives there.'

We were shocked to see the name plate on the door—Kokilabai Gavande. What were we going to find in this flat? Curiosity and fear took us over. We latched the servant's room next to the flat. I made Jamal stand in front of the peephole and asked him to ring the doorbell. Its ring echoed in the eerie silence. I crouched before the door. A few seconds had passed before a rough voice asked, 'Who is it?'

'Jamal.'

Once Jamal identified himself, the person inside opened the door slightly, with the safety chain still on. Convinced that it was Jamal, he opened the door. That was it. Before anyone could bat an eyelid, I pushed Jamal on to that person. The man, who was half asleep, stumbled. Taking advantage of this, I entered the flat with my team.

'Don't try to act smart or I will shoot you on the spot.'

The two revolvers in my hand, my authoritative voice and my angry demeanour were enough to make the Pathans freeze with fear. 'My name is Isaque Bagwan.'

The Pathans trembled on hearing this. They probably knew about me. They fell begging at our feet and begged for mercy.

'Sahib, my name is Mohammad Mirza Hajilal,' said one.

'Sahib, I am Jaan Mohammad Abdul Wahab. I am better known as Khushrang in this business,' said the other.

We recorded their statements in the presence of the two panchas. It was dawn by then. The doorbell rang. We took positions again, expecting this to be another member of the gang. My fellow officer looked through the peephole. We held on to our weapons tightly, prepared for the worst. The officer then calmly opened the door. We saw ACP Kurne at the door. We were confused. He said to me, 'Bagwan, I saw the Crime Branch control van under the building. What is the matter?'

'Sir, this is Jamal from Rawalpada. We raided his house and found 38 kg of brown sugar. After he was questioned, Jamal led us to this location. He said this is where his boss operated from. We found these two criminals here. They have confessed to the crime.'

'Bagwan, you have done good work.'

I hesitatingly asked him, 'Sir, how did you come here suddenly?'

'Look out of the window.' I did so and saw the entire building surrounded by the police. I was stunned. 'What is the matter?'

ACP Kurne narrated what had happened. Our weapons had scared the security guard. He rang the doorbell of BJP MLA Vinod Gupta's flat on the first floor. 'Sahib, some gangsters have entered our building with weapons.'

Gupta looked at the clock. It was around 5.30 a.m. He called up the then chief minister, Sharad Pawar, at his residence—Varsha Bungalow. Gupta was one of the few people who knew of Pawar's habit of beginning work early in the morning. He told Pawar, 'Sir, some armed gangsters have entered Vainganga building after threatening the guard.'

The next moment, a call had been made to Commissioner Vasant Saraf. He called the control room and ordered: 'ACP (Worli division) should immediately leave for Vainganga building.'

ACP Kurne then called Sr PI Uday Shinde, asking him to come along. They cordoned off the building and were prepared to take down the gangsters. It was 6 a.m. We had completed all formalities. ACP Kurne said, 'Bagwan, because of the direct call from Varsha Bungalow, the commissioner's sleep was disturbed. I am not going to call him. You do that and give him an explanation.'

I was weary of disturbing the commissioner again so early in the morning. Still, I called him. 'Good morning, Sir. I am SI Isaque Bagwan from the Crime Branch.' I told him the sequence of events. Commissioner Saraf knew about the cases I had handled earlier.

He said, 'Bagwan, you have caught the criminals and seized a large quantity of brown sugar. This is a great feat. Please call up the chief minister and convey to him what you just told me. It is important that he is made aware of the actual story. You will be able to explain it better than me.'

The day was turning out to be really unusual. I had never called up the chief minister directly. I took a long breath and called Varsha Bungalow. 'SI Isaque Bagwan from the Crime Branch here. I want to give the chief minister an important report. Please connect me to him.'

'One minute, Sir. The chief minister is on another line. Please wait.' Moments later, I heard the chief minister, 'What happened at Vainganga?'

I told him the details in one breath. The chief minister asked me just one question, 'Have the criminals been arrested?'

'Yes, Sir.'

'Okay.'

The chief minister hung up. As far as I was concerned, this topic ended that day. The next day, my wife woke me up. 'Please get up. Look at the paper.' The headlines read, 'Pakistani criminals arrested along with brown sugar in Vainganga.' The Maharashtra Assembly was in session at that time. The news caused a sensation.

Since the drug dealers had been arrested from a government cooperative housing society, the cooperative minister, Abhay Singh Raje Bhosle, had to face the fury of the Opposition. The atmosphere at the Vidhan Sabha was heated. The only topic discussed during the question–answer hour was this news report. To clarify the situation, and to convince the Opposition of the truth, the Speaker asked for me. I presented the entire story and evidence before the Assembly. That is when the storm subsided. The question on their minds was: How did the Pathan come to live in Kokilabai Gavande's flat?

Gavande's nephew had approached a real estate broker and told him that he wanted to let the flat out on rent. The Pathans approached that broker and told him that they were in the dry fruit business. They agreed to pay a handsome amount as rent and managed to seal the deal. This was proved during further investigation.

In another episode, an informer told me that a man called Vazir Mohammad Sheikh, who was originally from Indore, was secretly trading in brown sugar. He was staying with his girlfriend who was the daughter of a Delhi Police officer. I again sent a bogus customer to Vazir to confirm the information. I laid a trap for him in front of Lalit Bar near Metro Cinema in Dhobi Talao and called him there on the pretext of doing business with him. During interrogation, Vazir said that a person named Shivnarayan, who stayed in Santacruz and was a big real estate dealer in Goregaon, was the main culprit behind the brown sugar business. I arrested Shivnarayan and his brother-in-law from Thakur Complex. We seized 13 kg of brown sugar from them and registered a case against them.

My fellow officers and I received a lot of praise from all sections of society. With this, I had solved as many as forty to fifty 'quality cases', as Addl CP Ankola would say.

80

EVERY POLICE OFFICER CAN CONFISCATE NARCOTICS AND ARREST CRIMINALS

One day at the Crime Branch, I received a call from DCP Raja Sood (name changed).

'Good morning, Bagwan.'

'Good morning, Sir.'

'Bagwan, the charge of the Anti-Narcotics Cell has been handed over to me. From now on, you will work under it.'

'Yes, Sir.'

The same day, I told Addl CP A.K. Ankola about it. He was furious. 'You dare not go to the Anti-Narcotics Cell. You will stay at the Crime Branch. Whoever has been given that department should handle it on his own.'

'Sir, I will do as you say.'

Incidentally, Addl CP Ankola was DCP Sood's senior. Yet, the DCP insisted that I join his department. I decided to sit quietly for the next two months because I did not want to get involved in a tussle between two senior IPS officers. I did not want to add fuel to the fire. Two to three months later, Addl CP Ankola called me. 'Bagwan, why have you stopped taking up narcotics cases?'

'Sir, forgive me, but I stopped taking up narcotic cases to avoid any further arguments between you and DCP Sood.' Addl CP Ankola was a seasoned officer. He thought for a few moments before saying, 'Bagwan, no matter which branch you are posted with, every junior or senior police officer has the authority to investigate crimes. Go ahead, Bagwan. I want you to solve more cases.'

I reactivated my network of informers. Within a week, I got information that a taxi driver, Riyaz, supplied charas in Dongri. The leaders behind this racket were the Pathans. I sent out bogus customers to confirm if Riyaz actually sold charas. Once the information was confirmed, we trapped Riyaz and arrested him. He knew of my reputation with drug cases and was terrified. He fell at my feet. Taking advantage of this, I took him into confidence. 'Look Riyaz, if you tell me the truth, I will try and find a solution to your problems. But if you lie, this will be a dead end for you.' This had the desired effect on him.

'Sahib, Anilbhai provided me with the charas.'

'Give me his address.'

'Maharashtra Industrial Development Corporation, Sher-e-Punjab colony, Sunrise building.'

'Now describe Anil.'

Riyaz described the man. We kept a watch on that address for eight days. On the evening of 11 April 1990, Anil Sabarwal stepped out of Sunrise building. He stopped a taxi and spoke to the driver. The driver dropped the meter. Anil went back into the building. Minutes later, he came out with two big bags. The driver opened the trunk of the taxi for Anil to keep the bags there. That was when we caught him. We found neatly packed plastic bags containing 80 kg charas.

Originally from Jammu, Anil lived in Bombay with his family. He told us that vehicles carrying apples from Jammu brought the contraband to the city. I returned to the Crime Branch with Anil and the seized charas. DCP Sood came to know of this operation. He was upset at me stepping into his domain after refusing to work with him. His ego was hurt. He immediately sent an officer over and asked me to hand over the seized drugs and Anil's case papers. My team was a little unnerved. Not only that, he also sent a report to Commissioner Bhave saying that the Anti-Narcotics Cell had the right to take up narcotics cases and not the Crime Branch. The report also made defamatory remarks against me, stating that I had a nexus with the underworld and should be transferred out of Bombay immediately.

Commissioner Bhave signed my transfer papers without consulting Addl CP Ankola or making any inquiry. As per procedure, my file from the commissioner's office was sent to the Director General of Police (Maharashtra) Vasant Saraf. Even he signed the orders despite knowing my work.

I got to work the moment I caught a hint about DCP Sood's plan. There was no point in losing time. Sharad Pawar was the chief minister of Maharashtra then.

The next day, I went to the Vidhan Bhavan. The Assembly was in session. I met chief minister Pawar and explained the matter to him. He understood that I was being transferred only to soothe the ego of an IPS officer who held a grudge against me. He called for my file. That very day, JCP (Administration) P.S. Pasricha visited the chief minister's office with my file. The latter read my file and calmly pointed out, 'According to the law, every police officer has the right to confiscate narcotics and arrest criminals.'

Mr Pawar had spoken sternly against all the officers who had played a role in getting me transferred. My transfer orders were cancelled. Instead, I was promoted to the rank of a PI and posted to Colaba police station. I had returned to where I started from.

I would like to thank former chief minister Sharad Pawar for showing faith in me and supporting me. I owe him respect and gratitude.

POSTED TO COLABA
POLICE STATION AGAIN

81

ULHAS SEA FOOD ROBBERY

At Colaba police station, Sr PI U.B.R. Singh handed me the charge of PI (Crime). One day, a man came to the police station.

'Sir, my name is Laxman Yashwant Chavan. I own a fishery business called Ulhas Sea Food at Sassoon Dock. Every day, I buy fish from the Koli fishermen at wholesale rates and then export it. The entire business is conducted in cash, so I have to store large amounts of money in my godown. This morning, I saw that the cupboard was open and Rs 20 lakh was missing from it.'

This was a serious crime. I visited his godown. When I saw the cupboard, I realized that it was not the work of experienced robbers. It was the job of an insider. I made inquiries about Chavan's servants and people associated with his business. A check revealed that none of them were involved in any theft cases. That was when I noticed that a twenty-year-old tea vendor, Rammurti Vyankatswami Nadar, had been missing for a few days.

I contacted people from Nadar's community through my informers and got his Andhra Pradesh address. I took my team there and nabbed him. We found only a small amount of the stolen cash with him. In Bombay, we produced him in court and got remand custody. He confessed to robbing Ulhas Sea Food with the help of Sundar Munnaswami Nadar and Sindh Raj, alias Raju R. Nagan.

263

Upon further interrogation, Nadar told us that his partners had taken away half of the stolen cash. After the robbery, he went to VT station, now called Chhatrapati Shivaji Station, to board a train to his village. He was carrying a bag full of money. The railway police had stopped him and asked him to open the bag. He told them that the key was with his brother and that he would come back for the bag. He then had left the bag with them and fled to his village. I took Nadar to VT railway police station and asked the officers there about the bag. The officer in-charge said, 'Bagwan, no such bag containing money has been found. How could you question us like this? Your suspect is lying. Why are you relying on a criminal's statement?'

I took Nadar back to Colaba police station. Despite intense interrogation, he stuck to his original statement. The next day, I took him back to the station and showed him the places where the police usually conduct checks. Nadar pointed to an officer in plain clothes. 'Sir, he is the railway policeman who had stopped me and taken the bag from me.'

I met the officer incharge of the railway police station again. I was greeted in a rough tone. 'Bagwan, what has happened now?'

'My suspect has identified the policeman, and he is attached to your police station. So please try and help me recover the stolen cash.'

The officer was livid. 'You believe the word of a criminal and suspect my men. Such things do not happen in my police station. Leave immediately. I am warning you.'

Disappointed, I stepped out of the police station. Two days later, we arrested Sundar Munnaswami and Sindh Raj and recovered a large amount of money from them. However, the cash from Nadar's bag was not to be found. I tried to meet the officer incharge of VT railway police station again, but each time I would be told that 'he is busy' or 'he is out on his rounds'. My suspicion grew. I began to make secret inquiries. I met a constable of the railway police who had once worked with me. I asked him about the matter. He said, 'Sir, since you started inquiring about these constables, they have either called in sick or gone on leave.'

I was now convinced that Nadar wasn't lying. I immediately went to meet senior railway police officers. I directly accused their officers of taking the money. They were furious and drove me away, but I was not going to let them get away so easily. I met DIG (Railways), Maharashtra, Sudhakar Ambedkar. I showed him all the evidence regarding this case. He heard me out and agreed with me.

'Bagwan, I have received a lot of complaints about the senior officers and the policemen in civil clothes. Go on with your proceedings and take strict action against them.'

Nadar, meanwhile, was still in custody at Colaba police station. However, the custody period was to end in fourteen days after which he would be granted bail. The officers from VT railway police station were planning to pick him up as soon as he was released. I re-arrested Nadar by claiming that I suspected his involvement in another robbery, thus extending his custody for another fourteen days. This ploy worked.

Finally, two constables from the railway police came to me with half of the stolen money, which they had taken from Nadar's bag, and pleaded with me to close the case. I questioned them about the other half. They tried to cut a deal with me and said that the other half was with the Sr PI of VT railway police station. I remained adamant and threatened to arrest them and the Sr PI. They hurriedly left and came back the next day with the entire amount. I then completed my investigation and filed a chargesheet. I also informed DIG Ambedkar about this, who already had information about the Sr PI's involvement in this matter. He was glad that I had recovered the money.

He again asked me to take action against them, but I hesitated. I could not do anything that would bring shame to the uniform. We registered a case against Nadar and his associates and filed a chargesheet in the court. They were sentenced to eighteen months' imprisonment.

82

THE OYSTER APARTMENTS MURDER: COLABA TO TEZPUR

One morning, the telephone rang at Colaba police station. The duty officer received the call. 'We will come immediately,' he said.

He hung up and rushed into Sr PI U.B.R. Singh's cabin. I had just reported for duty, so I was also in the cabin. 'Sir, there has been a murder and robbery at Oyster Apartments on Pilot Bunder Road in the Colaba Army area.'

A team comprising ACP Vasant Gosavi, Sr PI Singh, Naik Madhu Khutwad, the detection officer, me and other staff reached the crime scene. Oyster Apartments was a nine-storey building overlooking the harbour. We reached the fifth floor apartment that belonged to Vardekar, a businessman from Pune. His nephew, Chetan Joglekar, and their manager, Anil Zaliyal, told us what had happened.

Joglekar and Zaliyal stayed in the apartment owned by Vardekar who owned a firm called Jahanvi Investments. Both Joglekar and Zaliyal worked in this firm. Their supervisor was Birju Bihari, who handled all the cash transactions. Satyavan was the cook and Gopal would do odd jobs around the house. Gopal had been working there for one and a half years. Every night, Joglekar and Zaliyal would bring cash from their office to the flat. Bihari would deposit it in the bank the next day. Every Saturday, Joglekar and Zaliyal would go to Pune. They would return on Monday.

The incident in question had happened on Saturday. The previous evening, Joglekar and Zaliyal had come home with Rs 25 lakh. They handed it over to Bihari and told him to deposit it in the bank on Monday. Bihari kept the bag in the safe of the cupboard and gave the keys to Satyavan. The next morning, Joglekar and Zaliyal left for Pune as usual.

Bihari returned to the flat the next morning. He rang the doorbell but did not receive a response. He opened the door with his key and was aghast at what he saw. Satyavan had been murdered. His body lay in a pool of blood with a grinding stone next to it. Gopal was missing and so was the Rs 25 lakh.

We asked everyone present about Gopal. All of them said the same thing, 'We do not know Gopal's full name or address. We called him Nepali. We have no other information about him.'

I asked them, 'Where did he keep his luggage? Where did he sleep?'

Anil showed me the room where Gopal slept. I found an inland letter from his sister. The address was Tezpur in Assam. The people in the flat said they called Gopal 'Nepali', which suggested that he was from the north-east. This address offered a clue. I brought it to the notice of my seniors. They gave me the signal to go ahead. Gopal was not likely to take a flight with so much cash. It was important to reach Tezpur before he got there by train. We took Anil with us so he could identify Gopal. We took a flight till Calcutta.

Hoping to nab Gopal before he left for Tezpur, we monitored Calcutta railway station for two days but saw no sign of him. We then travelled to Guwahati and, with help from the Guwahati Crime Branch, got Gopal's brother's address. His brother was a cook in the army. The address directed us to the Tezpur military camp. We hired a tourist car to get to his brother's house. While searching it, we found an old bank deposit slip showing that Rs 10,000 had been deposited in a savings account at the Colaba Navy Nagar branch of the SBI. The name on it said 'Gopal Bhattaraya'. I kept the slip carefully. For the next two to three days, we kept watch outside his brother's house, but Gopal did not turn up there. Exhausted, we returned to Bombay empty-handed.

The other officers felt that we would never catch Gopal. However, I had still not given up hope. I went to the SBI branch in Navy Nagar. I spoke to the staff there and got a reference for the Dena Bank branch in the Fort. The manager there looked at the account and said, 'Sir, this account is Gopal's. The photograph fits his description too. The account has Rs 10,500 balance but has not been operated for four or five months.'

I decided to post two men in plain clothes at the bank. The manager agreed and told his staff to monitor this account. Two weeks passed. My constables at the bank were bored and my seniors were beginning to get annoyed.

'Bagwan, have you gone mad? After robbing Rs 25 lakh, who will come back for Rs 10,000? As it is we face a staff crunch. Drop the obsession with Gopal. Call the constables back.' However, I did not relent.

One morning, the SBI manager called me. 'Sir, that man has come to the bank. We have given him a withdrawal token to make him wait. He is wearing a cap.' I immediately rushed to the bank. As soon as I reached there, I ensured that all doors were blocked. I entered the bank and saw Gopal sitting on a bench with his head lowered. He was toying with the token. I went up to him and called out his name.

He looked up in surprise. I grabbed him. We brought Gopal, alias Nepali, to Colaba police station and questioned him. However, he refused to utter a word. After sustained interrogation, he confessed. 'I killed Satyavan since he had the key to the cupboard.' I asked him where the money was.

'In Kalyan.'

We went to Kalyan with him. In a small guest house outside Kalyan station, he had booked a room for Rs 300 per day. When we searched his belongings, we found Rs 2.5 lakh in a bag. We even found newspapers carrying reports about the murder and robbery. Since we had only recovered a part of the stolen property, we interrogated Gopal again. He told us that he had kept the remaining amount at his sister's house in Nagao, a small village 10–12 km away from Tezpur. After placing the money there, he had returned to Bombay to withdraw the Rs 10,000 in his account. My plan had succeeded.

I took Sr PI Singh's permission to go to Guwahati to recover the rest of the money. Zaliyal accompanied me to identify the bag and the cash. We took a flight to Calcutta and then proceeded to Guwahati by road. From there we drove to Nagao. Our journey continued through the night. Some CRPF personnel stopped our car at one point. I identified myself, after which they told us that ULFA terrorists had killed twelve people and that is why they were keeping watch there. The moment Zaliyal heard this, he began to cry. 'I am a family man. The terrorists will kill us too. I don't want to go any farther. I am going back to Bombay. If anything happens, I will not get my life back.'

I managed to make him understand the importance of our mission. He decided to call his wife and spoke to her for a long time. He then agreed to come with us. It made me smile. Finally, we reached Gopal's sister's house. It was at the top of a hill. Gopal had buried the bag in a barn next to a dilapidated house. The bag contained Rs 17.5 lakh. Zaliyal was relieved to see the money. But what about the rest? It was a dangerous area, and we had recovered most of it. I decided it was safer to leave for Bombay.

We reached Calcutta airport and faced another problem. When I placed the bag into the screening machine, the security personnel stopped me. They asked me to open the bag. I told them that I was from the Bombay Police and explained that this was a case of murder, and that the money had been recovered from the accused. I said, 'I will not break the seal. If you want to open the bag, then let me perform a proper panchnama.'

The Calcutta Police did not pay heed. I remained adamant. I was frustrated because they did not understand my position. 'If you want to open the bag, please go ahead. However, if you break the seal, I will make a panchnama here. Then I will send you a summons from the court. Every time there is a hearing, you will have to come to Bombay.' The airport security officers succumbed to the pressure of my reasoning and did not open the bag, but they called me a mad man for threatening them.

The flight was being delayed because of this argument. Our names were being announced repeatedly. The passengers were getting impatient. One security official triggered another argument by saying that I could not take Gopal on the flight with handcuffs.

I replied, 'I will remove the handcuffs. However, if the accused escapes, you will be responsible. I will remove his handcuffs, but I will tie a towel around his hands.' The security personnel finally permitted us to board the aircraft after keeping a copy of the panchnama. In Bombay, Gopal told us that the rest of the money was at his uncle's, Khemprasad Upadhyay, house in Nalbari village near the Nepal border. We went to Guwahati for the third time. In Nalbari, we asked for Khemprasad Upadhyay. The people there looked at us with anger. Upadhyay was standing as a candidate in the upcoming Lok Sabha elections. The people were distressed to know that the Bombay Police had come to arrest him. But despite that, we arrested him. The moment Upadhyay was released on bail he filed a case of assault against me in Calcutta. An inquiry was ordered, but it did not lead to anything.

Later, Gopal Bhattaraya was sentenced to life imprisonment.

CUFFE PARADE POLICE STATION

83

SENA SUPREMO'S INSTANT JUSTICE

In 2005, when I was posted at Cuffe Parade police station, the Shiv Sena–BJP government was in power in Maharashtra. Manohar Joshi was the chief minister. The legislative assembly was in session. It was at this time that some miscreants desecrated a statue of B.R. Ambedkar. Riots erupted in Mata Ramabai Ambedkar Nagar in Ghatkopar. Some people were killed and there was tension in Bombay. Such was the situation that a tanker was burnt on the Mumbai–Thane highway.

At this point, Chhagan Bhujbal, a former Shiv Sena member, criticized the party over its stand on the issue. The party retaliated by plotting an attack on his government residence—B-10, Nariman Point. Bhujbal called the police control room in the night, 'There is a possibility of an attack against me. I need protection.'

ACP Suresh Kandle, who was incharge of the Colaba division, received the message and posted a police van at the bungalow. He visited the spot and instructed Sr PI Vasant Aagawane of Cuffe Parade police station to arrange for further bandobast before leaving. The next morning, the Shiv Sena had called for a Bombay bandh to protest Bhujbal's statement. Everything was quiet at the Mantralaya. In view of the bandh, I was present for bandobast duty from 6 a.m. I was in charge of Hotel Samrat chowki. A few constables, including some women, accompanied me. Despite it being a holiday, I saw a large number of people coming out of Churchgate station and walking towards the Mantralaya. Looking at them, I realized that they were Shiv Sainiks. Just then, Sr PI Aagawane came to the chowki. I told him, 'Sir, Shiv Sainiks have been arriving since morning in large numbers. Before anything untoward happens, should we look into the security arrangements at Bhujbal's bungalow? We should . . .'

Sr PI Aagawane struck his baton on the dashboard of the car. 'Send five male constables and five women constables to his bungalow. I am on patrol. Don't worry.'

Back then, we didn't answer back when our seniors spoke. Therefore, I kept quiet. Soon, the Shiv Sainiks began to increase in number. I rushed to Bhujbal's bungalow and told his bodyguard, Sanjay Paradkar, to alert him.

I went inside and met Bhujbal. I explained the situation to him in detail and maintained vigil at the bungalow along with my staff. I messaged the control room from the security cabin. 'Hello, this is Bagwan. Who is speaking?'

'Sir, this is API Prakash Landge.'

'Landge, send additional forces to B-10 immediately. There are chances of the situation turning violent.'

'Okay, Sir. For further orders, I will inform the seniors.' As soon as Landge hung up, I heard a commotion. A crowd shouting slogans was walking towards the bungalow. The situation was tense. I had already closed the main gate in anticipation. The bungalow had been surrounded by the mob. I felt like I was trapped in a gas chamber that would blow up any minute. It did not take too long for the agitated crowd to attack. They began to climb over the gate. I had barely a handful of men with me and instructed them to take positions. Meanwhile, around seventy people who were hiding in the next bungalow that belonged to Gulabrao Gavande also came out to support the crowd.

This was an ambush! The mob entered the bungalow and ransacked it. My team and I tried to push them away. Just then, chief minister Manohar Joshi sent a wireless message to the bungalow's security cabin. 'Do not attack the crowd. Try to get them out of the bungalow peacefully. No one should be harmed.' The next instant, home minister Gopinath Munde sent a message asking us to lathi-charge the mob. We were confused as we had received two contradictory orders. I decided to take advice from my seniors. Unfortunately, DCP A.K. Dhamija was summoned by the chief minister to watch the video cassette of the Ghatkopar riots. We were unable to contact him. The mob took advantage of our lack of number and threw flowerpots at us from the neighbouring bungalows. One of them hit my leg. It started bleeding profusely.

The mob that had entered the bungalow removed the carpet from the reception area and set it on fire outside. They demolished the telephone operator's cabin. They got all the chairs and tables out of the cabin and burnt them. Despite all this, they were not satisfied. They uprooted the carved wooden railing along the compound and burnt that too. The leaders of the mob kept instigating the crowd by shouting slogans. Even though I was injured, my team and I prevented the mob from entering the room where Bhujbal had taken refuge. I gathered my men and lathi-charged the angry crowd out. We managed to save Bhujbal that day.

The SRPF platoon and additional police force arrived after half an hour. The fire brigade vans arrived as well. With orders to peacefully disperse a rioting crowd, our senior officers stood with their arms crossed. We, too, could not make any move without their orders. Despite being capable, we had no choice but to accept the government orders. The crowd was in no mood to leave. The agitation went on for another hour or so. It was a sad day for our department. I do not have the slightest doubt that all my fellow

officers would agree with me. A live telecast of this incident and
news updates reached Delhi and created a commotion. Politicians
took advantage of the situation for their own gain.

The next day, PIs Puntambekar, Aagawane and I received
suspension orders. Overnight, there was a revolt in the department
over the 'government against police' policy. Each police officer
who had taken part, directly or indirectly, in this operation was
worried about his livelihood. Despite all my toil, I was staring at
an uncertain future. This incident made me furious. I went to
Matoshri, the Shiv Sena headquarters, with a very close friend
and was able to meet the party supremo, Shri Bal Thackeray, and
tell him about my ordeal. In his typical way, he told his secretary,
'Raje, *pantanna phone lava*! (Raje, call the chief minister!)'

Shri Balasaheb spoke to chief minister Joshi in detail. Not
satisfied with his explanation, he told him, 'Let the government
go to hell! What is these boys' mistake? Why should they be
suspended? Whatever has happened is enough. Everything must
stop this instant!'

Our suspension orders were withdrawn. I will always remain
indebted to and be grateful to Balasaheb Thackeray.

MARINE DRIVE POLICE STATION

84

THE QUEEN'S NECKLACE

In 2003, the Marine Drive police station came up in the barracks behind Yashodhan building on Sir Dinshaw Vacha Road opposite the Cricket Club of India. S.L. Patil was the first Sr PI posted to the station, but he worked there for barely six months. Commissioner R.S. Sharma then handed over charge to me. The jurisdiction had been carved out of areas that previously came under Azad Maidan, Cuffe Parade and Colaba police stations. It was a challenging job because my station was located in the political and business hub of Mumbai.

Opposition parties would often hold rallies and march towards the Vidhan Bhavan and Mantralaya. Self-immolation or burning of effigies was often attempted. The police had to stay vigilant about people barging into ministers' cabins to express displeasure over various issues. A massive bandobast was required during the summer and monsoon Assembly sessions. Most officers dreaded the thought of being posted here. Prakash Agarwal was the PI (Administration) in those days. The moment he would hear that I was going on leave, he too would call in sick. This was because he would have to shoulder my responsibilities. Marine Drive was not just a sensitive area but also remained under the constant scrutiny of the top brass. The other PI assigned to the station was Vivek Hemmady.

The Telgi 'stamp paper' scandal was in the news. Former deputy chief minister Chhagan Bhujbal was under the scanner.

When the Assembly was in session, as many as eight to ten morchas were held against the ruling party every day. The crowd would try to enter Mantralaya by hook or by crook. If they broke barriers and disrupted peace, we risked receiving suspension orders. On the other hand, if we engaged with them, tried to hold them off, they could blame the police for manhandling them. We were always in a dilemma. Under such circumstances, I had to handle every situation very tactfully.

I faced another problem. Out of the sixteen officers in my team, eleven were promoted to the rank of SIs from constables and had been posted to Mumbai from other districts of Maharashtra. They did not know much about the city. The appointment of direct entry SIs had been temporarily put on hold. I was working with inexperienced staff. At this point, I received a lot of guidance from DCP (Zone 1) Himanshu Roy. He supported all those who worked under him by standing behind them. DCP Roy also made sure that the senior officers were aware of the stress the policemen worked under. To top it all, officers at Marine Drive police station were under greater pressure as they had to contend with JCP (Law and Order) Javed Ahmed. He resided on the fourth floor of Yashodhan building behind the police station. He would call the police station at the slightest of disturbances like firecrackers being burst in the vicinity. He would say, 'Is the senior inspector sleeping? Where is he? Ask him to call me at once!'

We would try to explain. 'Sir, the sound of firecrackers is coming from the Cooperage Maidan area, which is not under our jurisdiction. It comes under Cuffe Parade police.'

He would invariably call me on weekends. 'Bagwan, horse carts are causing a traffic jam at Nariman Point. Please go and take action. Report to me about how many carts you charged.' The JCP's order could not be ignored.

Often, a day would begin at this police station with news of some rally or the other. Let me describe the most eventful ones.

Medha Patkar's Narmada Bachao Andolan

The Assembly was in session. A constable covering the Mantralaya beat called me at night.

'Sir, Medha Patkar, a social worker of Narmada Bachao Andolan Samiti, has taken over the Mantralaya garden gate with about 125 people.'

No one is allowed to conduct a rally within 200 metres of Mantralaya. Despite being aware of this, Patkar had approached it at night. We had to take action against her and the crowd that had gathered. If the ministers saw them there in the morning, the police would have to face the music. I went there immediately and posted officers and men on bandobast duty. I stayed there the whole night.

The rally blocked the gate to Mantralaya. JCP Ahmed issued an order: 'Pick up all the people from the rally and take action against them at once.'

I was aware of Patkar's political clout. When Rebecca Mark had visited India in connection with the Enron deal, Patkar had led a rally to oppose it. I was then a SI. PI Manekshaw had stopped that rally and an argument had ensued between the police and the protesters. The atmosphere grew tense and a lathi charge was ordered. The police officers involved were transferred. I had not forgotten that incident.

I was extremely tense because of JCP Ahmed's orders. The protesters were adamant and not willing to budge. With each passing moment, the tension was building up. The JCP called me, 'What happened, Bagwan? Did you pick up those people or not?'

I said, 'Sir, 70 per cent of the people in the rally are women. I do not have women police officers.'

'Call for a women police team then.'

Just then, I received a call from DCP Roy. 'Bagwan, why are you not taking any action against the crowd?'

'Sir, if I take action it may backfire.'

'But the JCP is getting angry. What about that?'

'Sir, I will think of something. Till then, we are blocking them off.'

Meanwhile, IAS officer Khot, who was a secretary with the Forest department, came to meet Patkar. A message came from Mantralaya that chief minister Sushil Kumar Shinde himself would meet her. I instructed my team to hold on to the barricades.

JCP Ahmed was getting agitated. 'Has the crowd been dispersed yet? Suspend Bagwan for not taking action!'

On hearing this, DCP Roy said, 'Bagwan, take some action now or suspension orders await you.'

'Sir, please look at the scenario. If I take any action, we will be victimized. In five minutes, the chief minister is coming to meet Ms Patkar. Let's wait for the outcome of that meeting.' DCP Roy looked at me for a moment and said, 'Okay, I am giving you five minutes.'

Soon, the chief minister arrived and, ignoring the crowd, walked up to Patkar. After greeting her with folded hands, he sat down to speak to her.

The crowd soon dispersed. I had handled the situation without using any force. DCP Roy praised me. However, what if I had executed the JCP's orders and resorted to force? I would have become a scapegoat yet again.

N.D. Patil: Shetkari Kamgar Paksha (Peasant and Workers' Party)

This was when the Assembly was in session. N.D. Patil, an old and respected politician, along with 150 people including farmers and women, marched down to Mantralaya. They reached early in the morning and occupied the garden around Jawaharlal Nehru's statue. As soon as JCP Ahmed heard about this, he gave orders: 'Arrest all of them!'

DCP Roy also reached the spot. 'Bagwan, why are you not arresting them?'

'Sir, the situation is the same as in the Patkar incident.'

'What is the reason?'

'Sir, N.D. Patil does not hold a good opinion of the police, and he is aged. If we take action and something happens to him, we will be in trouble.'

'But if you don't do anything, the JCP will take action against you!'

I stayed calm. 'Sir, nothing is going to happen here.'

'Are you predicting the future?'

'Sir, I may not know the future, but I am aware of relationships.'

'What relationships?'

'Sir, Patil is Sharad Pawar's brother-in-law.' DCP Roy understood the significance. However, the JCP insisted that we arrest them. Just then, a call came from Vidhan Bhavan that home minister R.R. Patil was on his way to meet N.D. Patil. He came and touched N.D. Patil's feet and had a word with him. Soon, Ajit Pawar, the then minister of rural development, also arrived. He, too, showed his respect for N.D. Patil. They assured him that they would find a solution to his demands. N.D. Patil and some select committee members then entered Vidhan Bhavan for discussion. The rally began to disperse. Within a few minutes, the area was clear. DCP Roy patted me on the back and said, 'Once again, you have saved us a lot of unnecessary trouble. Your experience and understanding of the political scenario have been of great help.'

Whistle Rally

One morning, the police were allowing people to enter Mantralaya after a mandatory check. It was work as usual. Suddenly, the shrill sound of whistles was heard from the sixth floor. We reached the chief minister's office on that floor. Several women were incessantly blowing whistles there. We took them into custody. After questioning them, we came to know that they were from the 'Save the Slums' committee. In those days, huts were being demolished at a fast pace. The women had entered with whistles during the time allotted for hearing complaints and issues of the public. They came up with this idea to ensure that all the ministers heard them loud and clear. The women had assembled outside the chief minister's office and sat down in the lobby outside with their hands locked together. The staff at Mantralaya was unable to move them because of this. All work came to a halt. DCP Naval Bajaj and I, with the assistance of some women police officers, arrested them and initiated legal action.

Dalit Panther Morcha

One morning, Constable Jagtap 'Mill Special' came into my cabin.
    'Sir.'
    'What's the matter?'
    'Namdeo Dhasal, the Dalit Panther, and his men are planning to enter Mantralaya to protest the injustice done to the community. They are going to tonsure their heads and throw the hair at the ministers.' This was a serious situation.
    'Jagtap, keep a close watch on their movements and call me on my mobile when they start moving towards Mantralaya.' Jagtap left my cabin. Extremely diligent, I was confident that he would do what was required.
    The textile mills had dominated central Mumbai before and after Independence. Mill workers came from the Konkan, Marathwada and Vidarbha areas to earn a living. Their meagre salaries became the cause of protests against the mill owners. As a result, rallies and demonstrations were common. The police often had to intervene to maintain law and order. One or two constables

from each police station were selected to mix around within such circles in civilian clothing and obtain information about possible agitations. Ever since, a post called 'Mill Special' had been created at all police stations.

However, after the mills were shut down, the Mill Specials were entrusted with keeping track of possible/future law and order problems that could be caused by crowds, morchas, protests, etc. In the case of the Marine Drive police station, a Mill Special was required to keep track of news of self-immolation or suicide attempts, attacks, or a crowd gathering at Mantralaya, Vidhan Bhavan and ministers' residences at Malabar Hill.

I conveyed this information to DCP Naval Bajaj. He encouraged us to work fearlessly. He said, 'Bagwan, see that no untoward incident happens.'

'Yes, Sir.'

A while later, Jagtap called me, 'Sir, about eighty people have gathered at Manora building and shaved their hair and filled it in plastic bags.'

'What's next?'

'Sir, they have planned to go in small groups, congregate at the Mantralaya gate and then force their way in.'

'Jagtap, as soon as these people leave Manora, call me.'

'Yes, Sir.'

I immediately arranged for three empty vans and got them stationed in the administration building opposite Mantralaya. I instructed the drivers to wait for my call. I ordered for thick ropes which are usually used for barricading during the Mumbai marathon. With the help of SIs Shivalkar and Patankar, I tied these ropes around the electric poles and tall trees to form a barricade outside Mantralaya. Everyone was confused. I explained my plan to them. I got the main gate locked and stood at the entrance. The media had begun gathering near the gates in the hope of some breaking news. Any minute now, the rally would be there. I alerted my team but did not inform DCP Bajaj as I was confident that I could handle the situation. Also, I did not want him to worry about this.

It is usual practice in the department to circulate a list of the next day's likely events to all police stations. We had received information about this rally the previous night. I had a tentative plan in mind. The clock was ticking. The media personnel adjusted their cameras and were ready to report a tussle between an agitating crowd and the Mumbai Police. Suddenly, a group of forty to fifty people charged towards the main gate of Mantralaya. I yelled, '*Ghyatyanna*! (Take them!)'

This was the signal my team was waiting for. They rushed forward from all corners of Mantralaya and encircled the crowd with the ropes. They closed in and pushed the crowd into the police vans that had appeared on the street. The crowd had been removed within ten minutes. Their plan had been foiled as they had been taken by surprise. A wireless message, meanwhile, had been sent to the control room that a rally had entered Mantralaya. Hearing this message, DCP Bajaj arrived at the spot. However, he found the area clear. He asked one of the officers on duty, 'Where is Bagwan? Where is our bandobast? A rally is about to come here.'

The officer replied, 'Sir, Bagwan has taken the whole crowd to the police station.' As soon as DCP Bajaj heard this, he called me and asked, 'How did you manage this miracle?'

I was happy that nobody was hurt. It had ended before it could even start.

85

INDIA VS AUSTRALIA: FAKE TICKET RACKET CASE

Nainmal Jain, a trader who lived in Colaba's Nafizabai building, left home at 9 a.m. Seeing him leave earlier than his usual time of 11 a.m., his neighbours asked him, 'Nain Bhai, you are leaving early today. What's the matter?'

Jain happily showed them a ticket and said, 'Today is the final one-day match of the India vs Australia triangular cricket series. I am going to see it live at Wankhede.'

A large crowd had been pouring into Churchgate since early morning. The police had been stationed at Wankhede Stadium and nearby areas to maintain law and order. An SRPF platoon had also been deployed for assistance. The doorkeepers were checking tickets of all those standing in the queue and letting them in one by one. The stands were filling up quickly. The atmosphere was electric and emotions were running high. It was Jain's turn to enter the north stand. He enthusiastically showed his ticket to the doorkeeper who examined it and frowned. He got a little suspicious and showed the ticket to a colleague.

'What is the matter?'

The doorkeeper replied, 'Sir, your ticket is bogus.'

Jain was taken aback.

A similar scene played out at the other gates too. All the gatekeepers had encountered bogus tickets. The gates were closed. People who had genuine tickets were not allowed to enter either. There was chaos everywhere. The fans were livid at being made to wait under the scorching sun for hours. Meanwhile, the match started. Sharad Pawar, a cricket buff and BCCI chief, was also present in the stadium. The Wankhede could accommodate 35,000–40,000 people, but that day there were about 60,000. He questioned the secretary of Mumbai Cricket Association, Ratnakar Shetty, and manager Chandrakant Naik about the overcrowding. By then, Pawar was informed about the bogus tickets. He called Commissioner R.S. Sharma, expressed his anger, and ordered him to look into the matter immediately. Shetty and Naik came to Marine Drive police station to file a complaint. We registered a case of cheating and began investigating.

Since the first lead in this case was the bogus tickets, we tried to understand the difference between the fake and genuine tickets. We noticed that there was a particular watermark on the original tickets. We then looked at the way the tickets were distributed. We were told that BCCI reserved some tickets for VIPs and private clubs and gymkhanas. Once this quota was taken care of, the remaining tickets were sold to the public. The demand for tickets had far exceeded the actual number available. A short while after the sale commenced, BCCI had to declare a full house.

Jain, one of the victims of the bogus ticket racket, registered a complaint of cheating. He told us that he had purchased the Rs 700 north stand ticket for Rs 10,000 from Dinesh Kumar Joshi of Agarwal House at Churchgate.

An informer told me that the boys who sold cinema tickets in black at Sterling, Metro, Minerva and Naaz theatres had stood in queues days before the sale began. We arrested them. One of them was Ismail, who informed us that the bogus tickets were being printed at Ghatkopar. We raided a printing press there, seized the machines and arrested the culprits. During interrogation, we learnt that the tickets were also being printed in Delhi and

Hyderabad. Shetty and Naik promptly arranged for our flight tickets. We arrested the entire gang and seized printing machines from Hyderabad and Delhi as well.

Sharad Pawar and the BCCI commended SI Sambhaji Patankar and me for solving this case in such a short time. The BCCI, in fact, has preserved the photographs of the accused in this case. Every time there is a match at Wankhede, their photos are displayed at ticket counters with the caption: 'Beware of these bogus ticket sellers!'

86

THE BEAUTY AND THE BEAST

This case dates back to 2004. One morning, I received a call from DCP (Zone 1) Himanshu Roy. 'Bagwan, I am sending an important industrialist to you. The chief secretary of Maharashtra, Nalinakshan, referred him to me. Register a case after hearing him out.'

Half an hour later, my orderly brought me a visiting card bearing the name Hanumant Rao Varat (name changed). I asked my orderly to bring him in. A gentleman around forty-eight years old, dressed in a suit, entered my cabin.

'Hello, Mr Bagwan. How are you?'

'I am fine. Please have a seat and be comfortable. Tell me what the matter is.'

'Yesterday I went to Chintamani Jewellers in Dadar. I bought gold bangles and a necklace worth Rs 7–8 lakh for my wife. A model named Poonam Singh (name changed) stole this jewellery.'

'Who is this model and how do you know her?'

Smiling at my question, the industrialist replied, 'I am a movie buff and had planned to produce a big budget film. I had signed Poonam Singh for a role. She visited my office at Nariman Point several times to discuss the script. Sometimes, I would give her a lift till her residence in Oshiwara. Yesterday, too, I dropped her home. When I reached home, I realized that the jewellery box I had kept on the back seat was missing.'

I asked SI Patankar to file an FIR. Thanking us, the industrialist left. The next day SIs Patankar and Hodekar, accompanied by a woman constable, arrested Poonam from her residence and brought her to the police station. She was a tall, slim and good-looking young woman. Distress was evident on her face. Before I could say anything to her, she burst into tears.

'Sir, you may take whatever action you wish, but please hear me out first. I have been falsely accused. I am being portrayed as a robber when the actual culprit is someone else. You have got it all wrong.' I had a feeling that there was more to this than met the eye. I asked her to sit. Offering her a glass of water, I spoke to her gently, 'Okay, Madam, what has gone wrong? Please tell me the truth.'

She gulped the water down without pausing for a second. She told me that she was staying as a paying guest in a housing society in Oshiwara. She had come to Mumbai to make a career in Bollywood. Though she took up modelling assignments, she dreamt of becoming a big Bollywood actor. She had been getting photo shoots done in the hope of bagging a film. That is when she received a call from the industrialist's Nariman Point office. It came in response to her photographs in a magazine. The industrialist called Poonam for a meeting and told her that he had selected her as the actress for his movie opposite a big actor. Poonam was ecstatic at hearing that she would work with a superstar. She readily agreed. Her dreams were about to come true.

Poonam was given some money as signing amount. While giving her this money, the industrialist placed a condition. 'My dear, you are about to become a star. You must not be seen in small advertisements. It is imperative that you stop appearing in those at once.' Poonam nodded in submission. But since she had to earn a living, she asked hesitatingly, 'Sir, ads are my bread and butter. If I don't earn . . .'

Cutting her off, the industrialist replied, 'My dear, you need not worry about anything. I will take care of all your problems.'

Poonam kept receiving money from him for some months, but soon the payments stopped. After her patience and money ran out, she visited him. 'Sir, it has been a few months since I signed your film. When will we begin?'

'Very soon. I am finalizing some technical details, after which we will start shooting. I know you are very eager as it is your first film. A little more patience, my dear, and you will become a big star.'

Months went by and there was no word from the industrialist. Poonam again went to his office. With a big smile, he waved two flight tickets before her. 'Poonam, a very good friend of mine has invited me to his daughter's wedding in Lucknow. Will you accompany me? Not as an actor but as my girlfriend.'

Poonam was shocked. She did not know what to say. She had thought of this man as an elderly gentleman, but the veil had slipped off. The industrialist tried to comfort her. 'Poonam, these things are normal in the film industry. Haven't you heard about the casting couch? Not that I want to force you, but I only want everyone to see the new face I am about to launch. It will be like a PR activity for you, my darling. You will accompany me, right?'

Poonam nodded for fear of losing her role. However, at the last minute, she excused herself under the garb of an illness. Days passed. Her financial resources had dwindled as the industrialist had stopped giving her money. She decided to ask him about the movie one last time. She reached his office. As soon as he saw her, the industrialist said, 'Welcome, my darling, I was just talking about you. Ask our panditji if you don't believe me. I want him to make your horoscope before starting with the film.' He introduced her to the pandit.

The pandit said, 'Child, my predictions are never wrong. I have made the lives of many actors and businessmen. Everything happens at the right time. Work done before its time is never successful. Therefore, before starting work on the film, I want to make your horoscope. Please tell me your date of birth.'

Poonam played along. She gave him her date of birth and some other details. The industrialist told her that he would get back after the pandit made his predictions about her and the movie.

Two days later, the pandit met Poonam at her home. He told her, 'This man's wife is very ill and may pass away soon. He is a loving and caring man. According to your horoscope, an industrialist is going to come into your life. Once you marry him, your life will be prosperous. You will be a very successful actor then.'

Poonam fumed at hearing this. The industrialist had proposed to her through the pandit, by stating that his wife was very ill. Despite having children her age, he had stooped to such an extent. Since Poonam had invested so much time in him, she tried to outsmart him. She told him that she would first complete the movie and then give marriage a thought. The industrialist kept making fake promises about the film and kept pursuing her. She began to avoid him. In the meanwhile, the industrialist's staff caught a whiff of what was happening as Poonam had met him at his office several times. He could no longer contain his obsession for her. He took her to Chintamani Jewellers opposite Siddhivinayak temple and bought her some gold jewellery. Giving her the box, he dropped her home saying, 'We will get our marriage registered in court after two days. Wear this jewellery when you come, my darling. I promise you that I will leave no stone unturned to make you my heroine once we are married.'

Puzzled, Poonam stood motionless after being dropped off. Having been dependent on him to make her dream come true, she was being forced into marrying him. He had forbidden her from modelling, and there was no sign of the movie. He had even stopped giving her money. Poonam's debts were mounting. She was heartbroken. To ease her burdens, she went to a goldsmith, sold off the jewellery the industrialist had given her and cleared her debts. The next day, he called her. She firmly rejected his proposal.

Faced with rejection, the industrialist plotted against her by framing her in a case of theft. I was sure that Poonam was innocent, but it was important to verify her story. I sent SI Abdul Gani Hodekar to her house. There, she handed over birthday cards, love letters, a horoscope and a receipt for the jewellery that she had been accused of stealing. Hodekar then took her to Chintamani Jewellers. The sales clerk confirmed that the man she had come with had bought the jewellery as per her choice. The bangles were evidence too as every woman's wrist size is different. The bangles had been custom-made to fit her wrists. Our next stop was the industrialist's office. His own staff, too, gave statements against him. In addition, we took the pandit who had made Poonam's horoscope to the police station. He confessed that the industrialist had forced him to make a false horoscope. I had this man cornered now. All the evidence went against him.

The same evening, I took Poonam to DCP Roy and explained what had happened. I showed him the evidence against the industrialist. DCP Roy understood that the industrialist was the culprit. We registered a case against him for filing a false complaint.

Given his connections in the department, he was not easy to arrest. He tried to implicate me by complaining to JCP Javed Ahmed that I was making false allegations against him. I explained the case to him and showed him the case papers and evidence. He acknowledged my investigation.

Since the industrialist knew he was in trouble, he also filed a complaint against me with Addl DGP (Anti-Corruption Bureau) Anil Dhere. Again, I explained the story and presented the evidence before him. He, too, was convinced. Having realized that he had failed to trap me again, he tried approaching more people. He complained to chief secretary Nalinakshan. Yet again, I presented the case papers and evidence.

The chief secretary said, 'He [the industrialist] had given me a completely different version. However, all the evidence is against him. Good work, Bagwan.' The industrialist had tried all sorts of tactics and failed.

Later, this case was filed as 'B' summary, which means that it is neither true nor false. In this case, Poonam Singh had been wrongly accused. This disturbed me a lot, but I was content that I had prevented any injustice from being done.

87

CONSTABLE SUNIL MORE RAPE CASE

This incident occurred when I was posted as Sr PI at Marine Drive police station during 2004–05.

Having worked for more than two years at this police station, and possessing the licence to ride a motorcycle, Constable Sunil More had been posted as the beat marshal. He would often be absent and was also known to consume alcohol on duty. He was often at the receiving end from me for his lapses and opprobrious conduct. One day, around midnight, a tiff broke out near Churchgate railway station between a pav bhaji stall vendor and a person hailing from Marathwada who was temporarily staying at the MLA hostel nearby.

The vendor, who shared a good rapport with Constable More, called for him. More reached the spot and beat up the hostel resident. He even took off his shoes and snatched his mobile phone so that the man could not contact anyone. The next morning, when I reached the police station, I saw a bruised man waiting outside my cabin. I took him inside and was shocked to hear about his ordeal at the hands of one of our constables.

I shouted, 'Where is More? Get him to me at once!'

After being on the night shift, Constable More had not reported that morning. I asked my orderly to call him right away. 'It's urgent!'

More reached the office in an hour. I made the hostel resident narrate the events of the previous night. I also asked More for an explanation but was not convinced. I reprimanded him for his misconduct and made him return the mobile phone and shoes he had taken away. I presented a report to DCP Roy, stating clearly that More was an embarrassment. I also asked for strict action against him and an immediate transfer.

More had a relative in the police department. As it turned out, this shielded him from harsh punishments. He would get away with mere reprimands and a stop on increments. Unaffected and unperturbed, he was free to do what he wanted as the beat marshal at Marine Drive police station.

In those days, the scene at Nariman Point and Marine Drive would change once it was dark. One could see cars parked haphazardly, vans serving Chinese food, illegal sale of alcohol, prostitutes carrying on with their business unfazed and innumerable horse carts blocking traffic. It was easy to gauge the vulnerability in the atmosphere. The local residents and managements of the nearby five-star hotels were exasperated with the chaos. Two beggars had been murdered in quick succession on the tetrapods along the shoreline.

I called for a joint meeting with the residents' associations and the managements of the hotels. I proposed that along with the police marshals who patrolled Marine Drive, there should be private guards too. The cost for this would have to be borne by the five-star hotels. Everyone agreed to my suggestion and arrangements were made accordingly. An old traffic police chowki under the Marine Drive flyover was used for controlling traffic during the day. I suggested that a beat marshal be posted there so that the area could be monitored continuously. The plan was put into action.

On 21 April 2005, I was at the Mantralaya gate at 10 a.m., supervising the arrangements to control approaching morchas. It was mid-noon when I got a wireless message, 'Sir, Sunil More has done something. A crowd has gathered at the chowki under the flyover.'

I set out along with my team towards the chowki. We saw a large crowd at the spot. Many media vans were parked around. We realized that something grave had happened.

That afternoon a security guard who was patrolling the shoreline below the Marine Drive flyover saw a young couple sitting in a compromising position on the tetrapods. He scolded them. The couple claimed to be students at a college nearby. He took them to the chowki under the flyover. Constable More opened the door. He was alone and held a bottle of mineral water mixed with alcohol. He was inebriated when he reprimanded the couple and took the girl, who was a minor at the time of the incident, inside the chowki. He told the guard to go back to patrolling and made the boy stand outside. He locked the door from inside. Soon, the boy heard the girl's cries from inside. He forced his way in and was shocked to see Constable More outraging her modesty. The boy called for help. Passers-by noticed him and gathered. The news of a drunk policeman raping a minor girl spread like fire. Within minutes, the place was swarming with protesters. The media, too, had descended.

We caught hold of Constable More, put him into our wireless van and took the girl with us to Marine Drive police station. Commissioner A.N. Roy came there with other senior officers. We filed charges against Constable More and initiated proceedings against him. The media, meanwhile, started a live telecast. The Mumbai Police was being ripped apart. Political parties and protesters flocked under the Marine Drive flyover and blocked traffic. They shouted slogans against the police and staged a *raasta roko* (blocking of roads). It was a moment of disgrace for us. I watched helplessly with DCP Naval Bajaj, Addl CP S.P. Yadav and other officers.

At 3 a.m., based on orders from senior officials, we uprooted the police chowki from under the flyover. The locals supported us. They offered assistance and showed us that they still had faith in the police. The local residents included Mr Anil Bhatia, Mrs Sunaina, Mr Parmanand Parikh, Mr Banker, Mr Verma, Mr Shivdasani, and Mr and Mrs Amit Patel who are the parents of actor Amisha Patel.

The next morning, I got to know that I had been transferred to the Protection Branch. I immediately went to the police station, made an entry in the station diary and went home. I had been made a scapegoat and was being held responsible for the debacle. Yet, I decided to follow orders. The next day, the *Times of India* carried an article about my transfer.

About a 1000 residents of Marine Drive took to the streets. My service and devotion to their security had led them to protest against my sudden transfer. When a few of them suggested lodging a public interest litigation in the high court, I stopped them from doing so. My DCP and ACP were unaware of my transfer. As soon as DCP Bajaj heard of it, he sent a police vehicle to pick me up and get me to Marine Drive police station. I took charge of the police station again. Addl. CP Yadav and DCP Bajaj supported me given my exemplary track record at Marine Drive. They promised to cancel my transfer, which they did. But just six days later, JCP Javed Ahmed transferred me to the Side Branch.

This case was later transferred to the Detection Crime Branch which further investigated the matter and filed a case in the judicial court. Sunil More was convicted and sentenced to twelve years' rigorous imprisonment. The judge further ordered that a compensation of Rs 26,500 be paid to the victim. Justice was delivered on 3 April 2006, within a year of the crime. This ugly incident could have been avoided had timely disciplinary action been taken against More.

MALABAR HILL POLICE STATION

88

TRICKS UP MY SLEEVE

I have always believed in giving my best to whatever I do. This applied to my work as a policeman too. I have discharged my duty with passion and strived to apprehend every accused, no matter how difficult it seemed or how time-consuming it turned out to be. My role as a policeman gave me the opportunity to interact with a variety of people.

I never left out any details. I dug deep into a criminal's activities and identified if they had past records. This helped me understand the way they thought. Chain-snatching, burglaries and forced robberies were some of the special cases in which I put additional pressure on the culprits to reveal more information so that I could recover the loot and return it to the victims. I was mostly successful in doing so. I also investigated cases of attempt to murder, murder, rape, assault and extortion. I used to be very strict with the criminals while they were under arrest or being interrogated. Sometimes I even had to beat them up to get them to confess. I tried to know what their motive was. But after I got what I wanted—confession of the truth—I did not hold a grudge against them. I even offered them medical assistance and food.

I have been posted to areas where I had to look after the law and order situation in colleges like Elphinstone, Kishinchand Chellaram College (K.C.), Jai Hind, Hassaram Rijhumal College of Commerce and Economics (H.R.), Government Law College and Sydenham. I handled cases of ragging, duplicate college IDs, harassment of girls, admission rackets and indecent behaviour on campus. While dealing with a student, I always kept in mind that his or her future and career was at stake. I made it a point to discuss these matters with their guardians. I also took on record their photos and an undertaking that they would not indulge in any illegal or indecent activity again. The ones who were stubborn and likely to repeat such activities were ordered to come to the police station every day for *haaziri* (attendance). Many students changed thanks to these methods. The administrations of these colleges are a testimony to this.

While at Malabar Hill and Marine Drive police stations, when I was a Sr PI, I realized that some constables were consuming alcohol on duty. I questioned this behaviour and tried to understand their side of the story. A few of them were reeling under stress due to the situations at their homes. To address such situations, I would call their family members and discuss the matter to find a solution. I would take the others to temples and make them pledge that they would change.

At Malabar Hill police station, I saw that people had to suffer a great deal at the hands of the police and face difficulties in getting passports verified. There were cases and complaints filed against the arrogant behaviour and non-cooperation of the police. As soon as I learnt about this, I vowed to bring about a change. I called a meeting of the people who had filed complaints, heard their grievances and discussed with them how we could help ease out the verification process. I urged them to let go of the past and reassured them that in case they faced any trouble in the future they could approach me directly.

I introduced a one-window system as part of which the constables would collect verification documents from the applicants' residences. The process became simpler. It even brought about an improvement in the way my staff approached citizens. Seeing this change, many people withdrew their complaints.

Days went by. DCP (Zone 2) Pratap Dighavkar was on a routine visit to our police station. After completing his check, he asked me, 'What magic have you done, Bagwan?'

'Sir, I didn't get you. What do you mean?'

'The citizens of this area had many complaints about the police officers here. After you took charge, I haven't heard any complaints. I am relaxed and assured that you have things under control. Even during my morning walks at Hanging Gardens, people speak well of you. What spell have you weaved, Bagwan?'

'Sir, the police is meant to listen to public grievances and help out.'

I feel that my success can be attributed to my mentor and role model, Madhukar Zende, who guided and inspired me to follow in his footsteps. I am what I am because of him. I feel humbled and will always remain indebted to him.

89

THE RED LANCER

On 11 January 2007, around 7.30 p.m., a middle-aged woman accompanied by an eleven-year-old boy entered Malabar Hill police station. She spoke to the officer on duty, SI Arun Dalvi. 'Sir, my name is Annul Srivastava and this is my son, Vicki, alias Ravi. We live in F. Ramnath Compound, Walkeshwar. Some criminals tried to kidnap my son today.'

SI Dalvi understood the seriousness of the case and brought it to my attention. Vicki and his friend, Prasad Shinde, who was twelve years old, were students of Manav Mandir School. In the afternoon, they went home for lunch, after which they had to attend a private tuition class conducted by Ms Shakuntala at her residence in Navyug Sagar building on Jamnadas Mehta Road. The boys were on their way to the class when a red-coloured Lancer stopped near them. A person stepped out and said, 'Your father has sent this car to take you to your class.'

Both the boys refused to accompany the stranger, but he forced them into the car and drove away. There were five other boys in the car, all of them blindfolded and their hands tied. Vicki and Prasad were also tied up and blindfolded. There were three people in the car with weapons. The car reached Grant Road railway station. The boys were taken to platform no. 2. Vicki's maternal uncle, Babloo Pardeshi, who was standing on platform no. 1, spotted him and called out. The kidnappers panicked. They took the boys to Grant Road Bridge, pushed them into the car again and drove to Dadar bridge where they released them. Once freed, Vicki and Prasad boarded a Churchgate-bound train. At Churchgate, they boarded bus no. 122 to get home.

This was the story the boys had told their parents and us. We started our investigation with general questions like 'Do you remember the number of the car?'

They showed us a piece of paper on which they had scribbled the number. We informed the control room and launched a search for the car. We also requested the RTO to verify the number and trace the owner of the car. We were wondering what had happened to the other five boys? Also, why hadn't any of them reported the incident at any other police station? The news of the kidnapping attempt had reached the media.

'Seven children kidnapped in broad daylight', screamed the headlines. Fear gripped schools all over the city and parents and guardians were panic-stricken. The RTO informed us that no such number was to be found in the records. We felt that there might be some error in the number. We tried a different number—MH 01 CA 7762—from the one we were given initially. This number was registered in the name of a prominent woman doctor, and the car was a red-coloured Lancer. We contacted her. She told us that her car was parked in the compound of her building on the day of the incident.

Her alibi was perfect. However, we showed the car to the boys and they identified that it was the one used in the kidnapping. I asked them, 'Can you tell me anything special about the car?'

'The car had movable rear seats. There was a mirror, and the kidnappers had kept the weapons behind it.' We examined the car and noticed that the rear seats were fixed. No incident of kidnapping had been registered at any other police station in the city. We knew that the boys were lying. They had told their story with conviction and were smart. I called Vicki to the police station alone. With a grim face, I told him, 'Your friend Prasad has told us everything. Why don't you tell me the truth now?'

I looked straight into his Vicki's eyes. He started shivering and broke down. 'Uncle, I lied. I have made a big mistake.'

Vicki had not completed his homework and knew that he would be scolded by the teacher. His mother had ordered a gas cylinder and kept Rs 300 on the table. Vicki took Rs 100 from that, went to Prasad's house, took him to the terrace of the building and showed him the money. Both of them decided to skip class and go to Dadar and have a good time. To their misfortune, Vicki's uncle spotted them at Grant Road railway station. In the meantime, a train arrived and they jumped into it and reached Dadar. They roamed around and spent the money on snacks. Then they boarded a train to Churchgate, got into bus no. 122 and reached their residence in Malabar Hill.

To avoid being scolded by their parents and teacher, they had decided to concoct a web of lies. They spotted a red Lancer on the road and noted its number, giving it a slight variation to mislead the police. They also tore their books and clothes to make their story look authentic. However, the police had seen through their game. Under pressure to apprehend the kidnappers, we had wasted our time and effort in investigating lies. The parents pleaded that their children's careers were at stake. Therefore, after consulting my DCP, the case was closed without any chargesheet being filed.

ASSISTANT COMMISSIONER OF POLICE

90

AZAD MAIDAN DIVISION

In 2007, I was promoted as ACP, Azad Maidan Division. This comprised Azad Maidan police station and Mata Ramabai Ambedkar (MRA) Marg police station on Pilton Road. My office was located opposite CST railway station. On 1 August 2007, I was doing some routine work when I received a message that a case of a break-in at a house had been registered at MRA Marg police station. A robbery of about Rs 10 lakh had been reported from General Post Office (GPO) opposite CST railway station. I immediately contacted Sr PI Sunil Babbar at the MRA Marg police station for details.

On 31 July 2007, around 6 p.m., Parab, the cashier at GPO, had handed over the collection for the day, which amounted to Rs 10 lakh, to his senior, Jadhav. They placed the cash in the safe, locked the office and went home. Next morning, when Parab reached the office, he found the lock broken. He looked at the office safe and saw that it was empty.

All government offices in Mumbai, at the end of the day, followed a safety protocol. All doors were locked after office hours. In this case, how did the robbery take place? Keeping this in mind, I began to investigate the case with the help of PI Ravindra Doiphode and SI Gangavane.

An employee was definitely involved. No one except an employee would know where the cash was kept in such a large office. After surveying the crime scene, it was obvious that it was not the job of a thief skilled in breaking locks. I began to collect information about the office. Two sets of the keys to the safe were with Parab and Jadhav. The chief cashier's office was frequented by numerous employees who came to collect their salaries. That is when I got to know that Machindra Chavan, who worked as a sepoy there, had not reported on duty since the day of the theft. I was suspicious and instructed my team to lay a trap. We were told that Chavan had left for his village. Later, we came to know that Chavan had been admitted to a hospital in Kalyan. My suspicion increased due to the contradictory nature of this information. I briefed my officers about the steps that needed to be taken to nab him. The officers then laid a trap at the hospital and caught him. He confessed to the crime and mentioned the name of his aide, Dilip Kadam. The police, with Chavan's help, retrieved the cash that had been hidden in a cyber café Dilip ran in Badlapur.

The court sentenced Chavan and Dilip to eight months' rigorous imprisonment and fined them Rs 1000.

91

26/11

It was 26 November 2008. I went to the office and performed all the routine duties like any other day. Until late afternoon, I supervised bandobast arrangements around Mantralaya. In the evening, I was back in the office, finishing routine paperwork. It was nearly 8.30 p.m. by the time I was done. I went to Nariman Point for my daily walk and reached home at 9.15 p.m.

I told my wife, 'I'll just freshen up. Let's have dinner.' Just then, my mobile phone rang. It was Commissioner Hasan Gafoor.

'Bagwan, bullets have been fired at Café Leopold. Go there immediately.' I put on a half-sleeved shirt and trousers. I took my revolver, called up the operator of my police vehicle and asked him to pick me up. He had dropped me off just minutes ago but I was restless. The clock was ticking. Since Café Leopold was just a stone's throw from my residence, I decided to walk. I rushed downstairs and saw the jeep with the driver, Tadvi, and operator Salunkhe.

Salunkhe said, 'Sir, after we dropped you, we were stuck in a massive traffic jam. When you called, we were not far away. We do not know what has happened, but people are talking of firing.'

I told them what the commissioner had said. We drove towards Café Leopold with the siren blaring. There was a huge crowd on the road. Police officers were running towards Taj Mahal Hotel. At the corner of Hotel Diplomat, we saw a police wireless van. Sr PI Sunil Deshmukh of Colaba police station came running. 'Sir, two terrorists fired randomly at Café Leopold and ran towards Taj Mahal Hotel from the direction of Northcote Hospital.'

'Come! Let us go to the Taj.'

'Sir, the terrorists have automatic weapons.' I was thinking of a plan of action when we heard bullets being fired. Some boys from the local Koli fishermen community had seen terrorists firing at Northcote Hospital and then entering Taj Mahal Hotel. The boys had fled under the cover of darkness. I received a wireless message that DCP (Zone 1) Vishwas Nangare Patil had just reached Taj hotel. I thought of going to help him. Just then, we heard an explosion. 'Bomb blast!'

The sound had come from the direction of Sassoon Dock. Within a minute of the explosion, my informer Salim called me.

'What is it, Salim?'

'Sir, there has been a bomb blast at the petrol pump next to Panch Payari. Please come immediately. The people are terrified and there is panic all around.'

I immediately took off in the direction of Panch Payari on Colaba Road, also called Shahid Bhagat Singh Marg. When I reached the junction of Indumati Sakhrikar Marg and Shahid Bhagat Singh Marg, a crowd surrounded our jeep.

'Bagwan Sir, terrorists have thrown a grenade. A man has been killed near the petrol pump.'

'One shop has been blown up.'

'Sir, in Colaba Chambers they have killed a Bohri family.'

'Sir, they have killed three more people.'

'They have gone into Panch Payari gully and entered Nariman House.'

A brief memory of Nariman House flashed through my mind.

I remembered that in 2004 there was a bungalow at the corner of Panch Payari gully. It was owned by a ninety-year-old

Parsi woman, Gulshan Khambata. She was a resident of Ravindra Mansion on Sir Dinshaw Vaccha Road next to Marine Drive police station. She was a widow whose daughter lived abroad. Her son lived with her and constantly harassed her for money to satisfy his drug addiction. Mrs Khambata had requested M.N. Singh, the then commissioner of police, to help her.

I was the Sr PI at Marine Drive police station at that time and had met Mrs Khambata. In order to check on her, I used to send a constable to her residence every day. She was very pleased with me. One day, she came to me and said, 'Sir, I need your help.' I asked her to explain.

Mr Verma, who also resided in Ravindra Mansion, had shown interest in purchasing the bungalow in Colaba. He was a bank manager who had just entered the construction business. Since Mr Verma was a neighbour and a bank manager, Mrs Khambata did not hesitate in drawing up the papers and handing the bungalow over to him. She received a couple of lakhs as initial payment. Mr Verma got the bungalow demolished and started redeveloping the plot, but he kept delaying the remaining payment. He also managed to convince Mrs Khambata's son to side with him. I managed to pressurize Mr Verma within the framework of the law, and he paid Mrs Khambata the pending Rs 6 lakh. Mr Verma then constructed a new building on the plot and named it Nariman House. He sold the building to a Jewish religious organization and made a handsome profit.

Nariman House, a six-storeyed building, was being used as a Chabad house (a community centre used for disseminating traditional Judaism) by Jewish residents and was, therefore, a possible terrorist target.

Every second was precious. The electricity to the building had been cut off. It was plunged in darkness. It was impossible to know how many terrorists were inside the building and how many people were trapped. The terrorists were firing at us continuously with automatic weapons. I called the control room, 'ACP Bagwan speaking. There has been a blast at Panch Payari in Colaba. Please send a wireless van immediately.'

The control room replied, 'We are sending MRA-I of Palton Road. Over!'

Before any assistance arrived, I called for a meeting of the local Koli fishing community, along with Ramesh Doshi, Puran Doshi and Navinmal Jain. They knew me well since I had served two tenures at Colaba police station. I also knew every street in that area. I appealed to them, 'Before the police arrives, we must evacuate all residents of nearby buildings.'

Each able-bodied citizen, young and old, came forward to help. The terrorists were constantly firing from Nariman House. The residents had faith in me and fearlessly joined in the operation to evacuate residents from the surrounding buildings. There was a blast at the gate of Nariman House. The compound wall was smashed. One person was killed.

I called JCP (Crime) Rakesh Maria at the control room to give him a situation report. 'Sir, I need reinforcements to take on the terrorists.'

'Don't move from there. I am sending in the SRPF to assist you.'

'Sir, I am not going to move an inch, but please send help immediately.'

As I put in all effort into this mind game, there was a distraction. A foreigner ran out of Nariman House. My team caught him. He claimed to be an Israeli Jew who had come to meet the rabbi. I immediately called up Commissioner Gafoor. He was engaged with the terrorists at Oberoi Hotel and said that the man could be a terrorist. We were asked to interrogate him thoroughly. The foreigner spoke to us in broken English. I sent him to Colaba police station for further interrogation. Later, I learnt that he had been let off after questioning.

I asked ASI P.M. Shinde of Palton Road's MRA-I wireless van, 'Shinde, how many men do you have?'

'Sir, I have three constables with SLRs.'

I decided to get into action before help came. I ordered the three constables to position themselves in separate buildings so that they could fire at the terrorists from different directions. Half an hour later, the SRPF consisting of nine young men, armed with .303 muskets and a tear-gas gun, arrived. I tried to boost their morale. 'Terrorists have attacked us. They want to destroy our city with their weapons and bombs. But you are all brave men. Do not lose confidence. This city needs you. Fight like warriors of Shivaji Maharaj. Show those terrorists what you are made of!'

'Yes, Sir!' they replied in unison.

This response inspired me to go ahead. I started positioning the SRPF jawans in surrounding buildings like Mehta House, Kasturi House, Prem Court, Pradip House, Rajiv Apartments, Ionic Park and Kolis Building. They occupied the rooftops too. I also ordered the front and rear of Nariman House to be blocked with gunny bags filled with sand. I then ordered the SRPF jawans to open fire one at a time. The terrorists on the second and third floor of Nariman House returned fire. I asked the tear-gas gunman to fire shells at the window from where we could see gunfire. The outraged and blinded terrorists replied with incessant firing.

We gave them a fitting response. A team of five commandos sent by the control room reached the spot. Seeing them, I was slightly relieved because we could now continue with our defensive plan as well as engage with the terrorists. ATS chief K.P. Raghuvanshi called me and asked, 'Bagwan, how many terrorists are there?'

'Sir, it is difficult to say in this darkness but there are definitely two or three. The exact figure will be known only in the morning. But what was the reason you called?'

'Bagwan, we have tapped the phones of these terrorists' Pakistani handlers.'

'Sir, what were they talking about?'

'They are saying that the police have surrounded them from all sides, that there is no way to escape. What exactly have you done at Nariman House?'

'I have positioned the forces in a way that they cannot escape.'

'Bagwan, you are doing an excellent job. Be careful.'

'Yes, Sir. I have already evacuated over 300 people.'

The ATS chief disconnected the call after praising my team. It was nearly 3 a.m. The intermittent firing continued. Just then, my mobile phone rang. It was Ajit Pawar, the minister. He said, 'I have been trying to call DCP Nangare Patil, but he is not reachable. I came to know that he is handling the operation at Taj Mahal Hotel.'

'Sir, I am at Nariman House.'

'Bagwan, I am aware of your situation, but please do something for me. My colleagues at Mantralaya, R.C. Shah and Tamboli, are trapped near the compound wall of Oberoi Hotel. Please try and rescue them.'

'Sir, but my operation at Nariman House is in progress.'

'Do what you want but rescue those two!'

I was in a fix. I knew I had to act fast. After giving instructions to my team, I drove to Oberoi Hotel with Constable Pawar. The hotel had been damaged by the terrorists. They had wreaked havoc and destroyed everything in their way. I decided to approach the hotel from behind. We parked the jeep on the pavement adjoining Sakhar Bhavan and the hotel's wall. We stood on top of the jeep and managed to rescue Shah and Tamboli. When we left, I asked them what had happened there.

They had finished their work at Mantralaya and gone to CST to board the train to Solapur that left at 10 p.m. They went to the railway canteen and had just placed their order when they heard bullets being fired and people screaming. They knew that something had gone wrong and quickly exited from the rear door. It was nearly midnight, and they decided to go to Oberoi Hotel for dinner. They got into a taxi. However, before they entered the hotel, they encountered heavy gunfire. They had landed from the frying pan into the fire. We managed to rescue them somehow.

I arranged for their accommodation at Garden Hotel in Colaba. I then returned to Nariman House. It was 3.30 a.m. and a horde of media persons had descended. Nariman House had been surrounded on all sides. The police and terrorists were engaged in sporadic firing. Just then, the terrorists reached the ground floor of Nariman House and tried to escape. We were extremely alert and spotted movement to the ground floor. We used heavy fire to force them to retreat to the upper floors. However, they still made two or three attempts to escape. Every time they tried, we sent them running back. B.D. More, JCP (Administration), and R.E. Pawar, Addl CP (Armed Police), paid a visit to assess the situation.

Around 6.30 a.m., a woman carrying a baby came out of Nariman House followed by a man. Initially, we thought that this was some sort of a ploy, but then we realized that the woman was an Indian nanny. She was followed by an Indian caretaker who had managed to escape with them. We carefully took them away. The woman was Sandra Samuel and the man was Qazi Zakir Hussain. While Zakir was a caretaker, Sandra was the nanny of the child, Moshe, the son of Rabbi Gavriel Holtzberg. Sandra told us that the parents of the child and six other Jews inside the house had been killed. Miraculously, Sandra, Zakir and Moshe had been spared and allowed to escape. We sent them to Colaba police station in an ambulance. I felt that the time had come to flush the terrorists out.

I called DCP Rakesh Maria, 'Sir, we have been successful in controlling the situation at Nariman House so far. We can enter the building by placing a wooden door between the roof of a neighbouring building and the third floor of Nariman House. Please give us permission.'

'Bagwan, have you gone mad? They have grenades.'

'Sir, then please give us some grenades.'

'Bagwan, we don't have access to army grenades and bombs and the police cannot lose any more men.'

'Sir, I don't understand.'

He then told me about the loss of officers like JCP Hemant Karkare, Addl CP Ashok Kamte and PI Vijay Salaskar. 'Bagwan, you will have to wait for the NSG commandos. They are on their way. Just hold on to your positions. Continue firing at the terrorists and don't let them escape.'

On 27 November 2008, around 4 p.m., six NSG commandos arrived. We showed them where the terrorists were. That night DIG (NSG) Gupta arrived with thirty more commandos. I showed him the area around Nariman House. He asked for fax machines and searchlights. We gave him both. We then shifted the Merchant family from the first floor of Merchant House to a safer place. Meanwhile, the terrorists continued firing. We kept retaliating. Their handlers, who had been following the events on TV, had told the boys to die proud. *'Shaheed ho jao, Allahu Akbar.'*

Lt General Thamburaj and Major General Hooda came to the spot along with senior police officers. They decided on a plan of action.

On 28 November, at 7.30 a.m., helicopters started hovering above Nariman House. According to the plan, this was the signal for us to fire tear-gas shells at Nariman House. The terrorists were confused by this sudden attack. At the same time, eighteen NSG commandos who were trained for such situations and equipped with superior weapons were lowered on to the terrace. However,

NSG Hawaldar Gajendra Singh Bisht lost his life during this operation after being hit by a bullet that pierced his head.

Our plan to distract the enemy finally succeeded. The commandos entered Nariman House from the top with their guns blazing. After a while, there was complete silence. There was anxiety on every face. Soon, the NSG commandos gave us the green signal.

'Mission successful!'

We heaved a sigh of relief. The sense of happiness and relief cannot be described. Sadly, we lost many men during this operation: Hawaldar Omble, who succumbed to his wounds while fighting Kasab and Khan at Chowpatty junction, Shashank Shinde at CST, and Hemant Karkare, Vijay Salaskar and Ashok Kamte, among others.

When we entered Nariman House, we found the bodies of the terrorists: Abu Akasha, alias Babar Imran, from Multan and Abu Umar, alias Nasir, from Faisalabad. One of them had a pin on his middle finger. He had pulled it out of a grenade, which was live. We were terrified on seeing this but our team managed to diffuse it.

We carried the bodies of Hawaldar Bisht along with those of the Jewish hostages, which included Rabbi Holtzberg, his wife Rivka, Yocheved Orpaz and others, out of Nariman House into ambulances for post-mortems. We recovered three AK-47 rifles, thirty-eight live cartridges, nine empty magazines, two Mausers with magazines, two pistols and fourteen live rounds, five Indian currency notes and mobile phones.

The operation, which began on the night of 26 November, ended on the evening of 28 November. The police were successful in minimizing loss of life and property with the support of locals. These residents played a great supporting role in evacuating as many as 300–350 people to safety. The mission would have failed had it not been for their help.

In what has come to be remembered as the 26/11 attack, ten LeT terrorists had held Mumbai hostage for four days. Their well-coordinated attack on Taj Mahal Hotel, Oberoi Hotel, CST railway station, Nariman House, Cama Hospital and Café Leopold resulted in a bloodbath that left over 166 people dead and more than 300 injured. A great many officers and constables also lost their lives. The media and the Opposition criticized the lapses in security and crisis management by the state government.

Chief Minister Ashok Chavan ordered a committee to be set up to conduct a high-level inquiry. It comprised Ram D. Pradhan, former Union home secretary and V. Balachandran, former special secretary (cabinet secretariat). The committee visited the sites where the terrorists had attacked and interviewed the residents. They examined all witnesses minutely to get a clear picture. They mainly looked at the lacunae and lapses in the police and administration's response to the attacks. They submitted their report to the government, relevant portions of which have been given in the appendix. The Inquiry Committee report came down heavily on many in the police department. However, it did praise a few, including me, for our role in containing the destruction and saving several lives. On 26 January 2010, I received another police medal for gallantry from Governor Shankaranarayan at Raj Bhavan for the operation at Nariman House. Even though I had already retired, the government gave me special permission to wear my uniform once again for the award ceremony. This was the third time I was awarded the gallantry medal.

I am grateful to have received an opportunity to serve my nation and beloved city, Mumbai, in its darkest hour by taking on terrorists, even if it was towards the end of my career. Like all Mumbaikars, I will never forget this episode.

APPENDIX A

Extracts from the Report of the High-Level Inquiry
Committee on 26/11

(Appointed by the Maharashtra Government vide GAD OR No:
Raasua.2008/C.R.34/29-A, 30th Dec 2008)

Option to storm into Cama from the rear side. Instead the three
senior officers opted to go towards the Rang Bhawan in one
vehicle to confront the terrorists from the front gate.

v) Nariman House:

3.41. Here the situation was handled almost single-handedly
by Shri. Isaque Ibrahim Bagwan, ACP Azad Maidan division,
who deserves high praise in containing the terrorists, keeping
them pinned down until NSG came on the 27th afternoon. He
originally was supposed to have gone to Leopold Café, but found
that the killing had already taken place there and police were
removing the injured to the hospital. Here he heard an explosion
in Colaba Market area. He initially faced a problem in not being
able to locate the target building since none in the locality knew
anything about the significance of Nariman House. It was only

after reaching the spot that he came to know that Jews were staying there. There were no policemen there from Colaba since they were busy elsewhere. After he reached there, MRA Mobile-1 came. (ASI Shri. Shinde with 2 PCs with SLRs). At 23:30 hrs SRP (striking mobile) arrived. With their help he cordoned off the area and moved out at least 300 people from the surrounding buildings. He deployed his policemen on the neighbouring buildings (Prem Court, Lalji Terrace, etc.) and started shooting at the terrorists. Although they could not see the terrorists (since the building inside was dark) they wanted to pin them down. On the 27th at about 08:00, an ayah (Sandra) ran outside with a baby followed by a servant. ACP Shri. Bagwan then ordered his men to fire tear-gas shells into the House. The terrorists closed the curtains. Continuous exchange of fire was going on between them and the terrorists till NSG came in at 16:00 hrs on the 28th and started their operations. NSG used the same nearby buildings which he had used. 'The Committee finds that ACP Shri. Bagwan had acted with great presence of mind in pinning down terrorists and saving lives almost single-handed.'